Théophile Gautier, M. M. Ripley

A Winter in Russia

A Winter in Russia

FROM THE FRENCH
OF
THÉOPHILE GAUTIER

BY
M. M. RIPLEY
Translator of Madame Craven's "Fleurange"

NEW YORK
HENRY HOLT AND COMPANY
1874

Entered according to Act of Congress, in the year 1874, by
HENRY HOLT,
In the Office of the Librarian of Congress, at Washington.

JOHN F. TROW & SON, PRINTERS,
205-213 EAST 12TH ST., NEW YORK.
Maclauchlan, Stereotyper,
145 & 147 Mulberry St., near Grand, N. Y.

TO

E. M. C.

CONTENTS.

CHAPTER	PAGE
I.—BERLIN	1
II.—HAMBURG	12
III.—SCHLESWIG	22
IV.—LUBECK	44
V.—CROSSING THE BALTIC	56
VI.—ST. PETERSBURG	66
VII.—WINTER.—THE NEVA	88
VIII.—WINTER	100
IX.—RACES ON THE NEVA	115
X.—DETAILS OF INTERIORS	125
XI.—A BALL AT THE WINTER PALACE	136
XII.—THE THEATRES	145
XIII.—THE TCHOUKINE-DVOR	154
XIV.—ZICHY	163
XV.—ST. ISAAC'S	187
XVI.—MOSCOW	236
XVII.—THE KREMLIN	261
XVIII.—TROÏTZA	279
XIX.—BYZANTINE ART	298
XX.—RETURN TO FRANCE	324

A WINTER IN RUSSIA.

I.

BERLIN.

WE seem scarcely to have started, and yet already France lies far behind us. Concerning the intermediate space traversed in his flight by the nocturnal hippogriff, I shall say nothing.

Imagine me at Deutz, across the Rhine, contemplating from the end of the bridge of boats that silhouette of Cologne, which the Jean-Marie Farina boxes have rendered so familiar, now outlined against the splendors of a sunset sky. The bell of the Rhenish railway strikes. We take our seats, and steam rushes off with the train at a gallop.

To-morrow at six, I shall be in Berlin; yesterday, when the street-lamps were lighted, I was in Paris. This surprises no one but myself, in our marvellous nineteenth century.

The train spins along across great plains gilded by the setting sun; soon night comes, and with it, sleep. At stations remote from one another, German voices shout German names; I do not recognize them by the sound, and look for them in vain upon the map. Magnificent great station-houses are shown up by gaslight in the midst of surrounding darkness, then disappear.

We pass Hanover and Minden; the train keeps on its way; and morning dawns.

On either side stretched a peat-moss, upon which the mist was producing a singular mirage. We seemed to be upon a causeway traversing an immense lake whose waves crept up gently, dying in transparent folds along the edge of the embankment. Here and there a group of trees or a cottage, emerging like an island, completed the illusion, for such it was. A sheet of bluish mist, floating a little above the ground and curling up all along its upper surface under the rays of the sun, caused this aqueous phantasmagoria, resembling the Fata Morgana of Sicily. In vain did my geographical knowledge protest, disconcerted, against this inland sea, which no map of Prussia indicates; my eyes would not give it up, and later in the day, when the sun, rising higher, had dried up this imaginary lake, they required the presence of a boat to make them admit that any body of water could be real.

Suddenly, upon the left were massed the trees of a great park; Tritons and Nereids appeared, dabbling in the basin of a fountain; there was a dome and a circle of columns rising above extensive buildings; and this was Potsdam.

Notwithstanding the rapidity of the train, I observed a couple, matutinally sentimental, pacing one of the deserted avenues. The lover had an excellent chance to liken his mistress to Aurora; doubtless he had recited to her all the sonnets that ever were made upon "*la belle matineuse.*"

A few moments later we were in Berlin, and a fiacre set me down at the Hotel de Russie.

One of the keenest pleasures of a traveller is that first drive through a hitherto unknown city, destroying or confirming his preconceived idea of it. All that is peculiar and characteristic seizes upon the yet virgin eye, whose perceptive power is never more clear.

My idea of Berlin had been drawn in great measure from Hoffman's fantastic stories. In spite of myself, a Berlin, strange and grotesque, peopled with Aulic councillors, sandmen, Kreislers, archivist Lindursts, and student Anselms, had reared itself within my brain, amid a fog of tobacco-smoke; and here before me was a city regularly built, stately, with wide streets, extensive public grounds, imposing edifices of a style half-English, half-German, and modern to the last degree.

As we drove along I glanced down into those cellars, with steps so polished, so slippery, so well-soaped, that one might slide in as into the den of an ant-lion,—to see if I might not discover Hoffman himself seated on a tun, his feet crossed upon the bowl of his gigantic pipe, and surrounded by a tangle of grotesque chimeras, as he is represented in the vignette of the French translation of his stories; and, to tell the truth, there was nothing of the kind in these subterranean shops whose proprietors were just opening their doors! The cats, of benignant aspect, rolled no phosphorescent eyeballs, like the cat Murr in the story, and they seemed quite incapable of writing their memoirs, or of deciphering a score of Richard Wagner's.

Nothing is more prosaic than Berlin, and it needed all the wild imagination of the story-teller to lodge phantoms in a city so full of daylight, so regular, so well-built, where the bats of hallucination could not find one dark corner in which to cling.

These handsome stately houses, which are like palaces, with their columns and pediments and architraves, are built of brick for the most part, for stone seems rare in Berlin; but the brick is covered with cement or tinted stucco, to simulate hewn stone; deceitful seams indicate imaginary layers, and the illusion would be complete, were it not that in spots the winter frosts have detached the cement, revealing the red shades of the baked clay. The necessity of painting the whole façade, in order to mask the nature of the material, gives the effect of enormous architectural decorations seen in open air. The salient parts, mouldings, cornices, entablatures, consoles, are of wood, bronze, or cast-iron, to which suitable forms have been given; when you do not look too closely the effect is satisfactory. Truth is the only thing lacking in all this splendor.

The palatial buildings which border Regent's Park in London present also these porticos, and these columns with brick cores and plaster-fluting, which, by aid of a coating of oil paint, are expected to pass for stone or marble. Why not build in brick frankly, since its warm coloring and capacity for ingeniously varied arrangement furnish so many resources? Even in Berlin I have seen charming houses of this kind which had the advantage of being truthful. A fictitious material always inspires a certain uneasiness.

The Hotel de Russie is very well located, and I propose to sketch the view seen from its steps. It will give a fair idea of the general character of the city.

The foreground is a quay bordering the Sprée. A few boats with slender masts are sleeping on the brown water. Vessels upon a canal or a river, in the heart of a city, have always a charming effect.

Along the opposite quay stretches a line of houses; a few of them are ancient, and bear the stamp thereof; the king's palace makes the corner. A cupola upon an octagonal tower rises proudly above the other roofs, the square sides of the tower adding grace to the curve of the dome.

A bridge spans the river, reminding me, with its white marble groups, of the Ponte San Angelo at Rome. These groups—eight in number, if my memory does not deceive me—are each composed of two figures; one allegorical, winged, representing the country, or Glory; the other, a young man, guided through many trials to victory or immortality. These groups, in purely classic taste, are not wanting in merit, and show in some parts good study of the nude; their pedestals are ornamented with medallions, whereon the Prussian eagle, half-real, half-heraldic, makes a fine appearance. Considered as a decoration, the whole is, in my opinion, somewhat too rich for the simplicity of the bridge, which opens midway to allow the passage of vessels.

Farther on, through the trees of a public garden of some kind, appears the old Museum, a great structure in the Greek style, with Doric columns relieved against a painted background. At the corners of the roof, bronze horses held by grooms are outlined upon the sky.

Behind this building, and looking sideways, you perceive the triangular pediment of the new Museum.

On crossing the bridge, the dark façade of the palace comes in view, with its balustraded terrace; the carvings around the main entrance are in that old, exaggerated German *rococo* which I have seen before and have admired in the palace in Dresden. This kind of barbaric taste has something charming about it, and entertains the eye, satiated with *chefs d'œuvre*. It has invention, fancy, originality; and though I may be censured for the opinion, I confess I prefer this exuberance to the coldness of the Greek style imitated with more erudition than success in our modern public buildings.

At each side stand great bronze horses pawing the ground, and held by naked grooms.

I visited the apartments of the palace; they are rich and elegant, but present nothing interesting to the artist save their ancient recessed ceilings filled with curious figures and arabesques. In the concert-hall there is a musicians' gallery in grotesque carving, silvered; its effect is really charming. Silver is not used enough in decorations; it is a relief from the classic gold, and forms admirable combinations with colors. The chapel, whose dome rises above the rest of the building, is no doubt pleasing to Protestants. It is well planned and well lighted, comfortable, reasonably decorated; but to one who has visited the Catholic churches of Spain, Italy, Belgium, and France, it is not very impressive. One thing in it surprised me—to see Melancthon and Theodore Beza, painted on gold backgrounds; however, nothing could be more natural.

Let us cross the square and take a look at the Museum, admiring, as we pass, an immense porphyry vase standing on cubes of the same material, in front of the steps which lead up to the portico. This portico is painted in fresco by various hands, under the direction of the celebrated Peter Cornelius.

The paintings form a broad frieze, folding itself back at each end upon the side wall of the portico, and interrupted in the middle to give access to the Museum.

The portion on the left contains a whole poem of mythologic cosmogony, treated with that philosophy and that erudition which the Germans carry into compositions of this kind; the right, purely anthropologic, represents the birth, development, and evolution of humanity.

If I were to describe in detail these two immense frescos, you would certainly be charmed with the ingenious invention, the profound knowledge, and the excellent judgment of the artist. The mysteries of the early creation are penetrated, and everything is faultlessly scientific. Also, if I should show you them in the form of those fine German engravings, the lines heightened by delicate shadows, the execution as accurate as that of Albrecht Dürer, the tone light and harmonious, you would admire the ordering of the composition, balanced with so much art, the groups skilfully united one to another, the ingenious episodes, the wise selection of the attributes, the significance of each separate thing; you might even find grandeur of style, an air of magisterial dignity, fine effects of drapery, proud attitudes, well-marked types, muscular audacities *à la* Michel Angelo, and a certain Germanic savagery of fine flavor. You would be struck with this free handling of great subjects, this vast conceptive power, this carrying out of an idea, which French painters so often lack; and you would think of Cornelius almost as highly as the Germans do. But in the presence of the work itself, the impression is completely different.

I am well aware that fresco-painting, even in the hands of the Italian masters, skilful as they were in the technical details of their art, has not the charm of oil. The eye must become habituated to this rude, lustreless coloring, before we can discern its beauties. Many people who never say so—for nothing is more rare than the courage to avow a feeling or an opinion—find the frescos of the Vatican and the Sistine frightful; but the great names of Michel Angelo and Raphael impose silence upon them; they murmur vague formulas of enthusiasm, and go off to rhapsodize—this time with sincerity—over some Magdalen of Guido, or some Madonna of Carlo Dolce. I make large allowance, therefore, for the unattractive aspect which belongs to fresco-painting; but in this case, the execution is by far too repulsive. The mind may be content, but the eye suffers. Painting, which is altogether a plastic art, can express its ideal only through forms and colors. To think is not enough; something must be done. The most beautiful design requires to be translated by a skilful pencil, and if, in these great works, we are willing to dispense with perspective, to have the details simplified, the coloring neutral and, so to speak, historic, at least we desire to be spared crude tints, outrageous discords, and a blundering, awkward, or heavy touch. However great respect may be due to the idea, the first merit in painting is to be painting, and a material execution like this is a veil between the spectator and the artist's conception.

The only French representative of this philosophic art is Chenavard, the author of cartoons destined to decorate the Pantheon, a gigantic work, rendered useless by the restoration of the edifice to divine worship, but for which a place should be found elsewhere, since the study of these fine compositions would certainly be profitable to our painters, who have the opposite fault from the Germans, and seldom offend through excess of ideal. But Chenavard, like a wise man, never exchanged the crayon for the brush. He wrote out his thoughts—

not painted them. However, if at any future time it should be proposed to execute them upon the walls of some public building, there will not be lacking expert patricians who will give them suitable coloring.

I shall not now give an inventory of the Museum in Berlin, which is rich in pictures and statues: to do this would require more space than is at my command. We find represented here, more or less favorably, all the great masters, the pride of royal galleries. But the most remarkable thing in this collection is the very numerous and very complete collection of the primitive painters of all countries and all schools, from the Byzantine down to those which immediately precede the Renaissance. The old German school, so little known in France, and on many accounts so curious, is to be studied to better advantage here than anywhere else.

A rotunda contains tapestries after designs by Raphael, of which the original cartoons are now in Hampton Court.

The staircase of the new Museum is decorated with those remarkable frescos by Kaulbach, which the art of engraving and the Universal Exposition have made so well known in France. We all remember the cartoon entitled "The Dispersion of Races," and all Paris has admired, in Goupil's window, that poetic "Defeat of the Huns," where the strife begun between the living warriors is carried on amidst the disembodied souls that hover above that battle-field strewn with the dead. "The Destruction of Jerusalem" is a fine composition, though somewhat too theatrical. It resembles a "close of the fifth act" much more than beseems the serious character of fresco painting. In the panel which represents Hellenic civilization, Homer is the central figure; this composition pleased me least of all. Other paintings as yet unfinished present the climacteric epochs of humanity. The last of these will be almost contemporary, for when a German begins to paint, universal history comes under review; the great Italian painters did not need so much in achieving their master-pieces. But each civilization has its peculiar tendencies, and this encyclopædic painting is a characteristic of the present time. It would seem that, before flinging itself into its new career, the world has felt the necessity of making a synthesis of its past.

These compositions are separated by arabesques, emblems, and allegorical figures having reference to the different subjects, and surmounted by a frieze in black and white, full of charming and ingenious devices.

Kaulbach constantly seeks effects resulting from the use of color, and if he does not always find them, he at least avoids harsh discords; he makes overmuch use of reflections, transparencies, high lights, touches of dazzling color, and his frescos sometimes resemble the pictures of Hayez or Théophile Fragonard. He makes a web of varied tints where one broad local color would have been enough; with his inopportune effects of light and shade he bores holes in the wall which he ought merely to cover, for fresco is a kind of tapestry, and it should never disturb by depths of perspective the general architectural lines. To sum up all, Kaulbach takes more pains with the execution of his work than do the pure thinkers, and his painting, though humanitarian, is human still.

This staircase, which is of colossal size, is ornamented with casts from the finest antiques. Copies of the metopes of the Pantheon and friezes from the temple of Theseus are set into its walls, and upon one of the landings stands the Pandrosion, with all the strong and tranquil beauty of its Caryatides. The effect of the whole is very grand.

"But," do you say, "what about the inhabitants? You have mentioned only houses and pictures and statues,—Berlin is not a deserted city!" Doubtless not; but I spent only a day in Berlin, and—especially as I am ignorant of the German language!—had not the opportunity to make any very profound ethnographic researches. At the present day there is no longer any visible difference between the people of one country and of another. The uniform domino of civilization is worn everywhere, and no difference in color, no special cut of the garment, notifies you that you are away from home. The men and women whom I met in the street escape description; the *flâneurs* of Unter den Linden are exactly like the *flâneurs* of the Boulevard des Italiens.

This avenue, bordered by splendid houses, is planted, as its name indicates, with lindens; trees "whose leaf is shaped like a heart," as Heinrich Heine remarks,—a peculiarity which makes Unter den Linden dear to lovers, and eminently suited for sentimental interviews.

At its entrance stands that equestrian statue of Frederick the Great, of which a reduced copy figured at the Exposition.

Like the Champs-Elysées in Paris, this avenue terminates at a triumphal arch, surmounted by a chariot with four bronze horses. Passing under the arch, we come out into a park in some degree resembling the Bois de Boulogne.

Along the edge of this park, which is shadowed by great trees having all the intensity of northern verdure, and freshened by a little winding stream, open flower-crowded gardens, in whose depths you can discern summer retreats, which are neither châlets, nor cottages, nor villas, but Pompeian houses with their tetrastylic porticos and panels of antique red. The Greek taste is held in high esteem in Berlin. On the other hand, they seem to disdain the style of the Renaissance, so much in vogue in Paris; I saw no edifice of this kind in Berlin.

Night came; and after paying a hasty visit to the zoölogical garden, where all the animals were asleep, except a dozen long-tailed paroquets and cockatoos, who were screaming from their perches, pluming themselves, and raising their crests, I returned to my hotel to strap my trunk and betake myself to the Hamburg railway-station, as the train would leave at ten, a circumstance which prevented me from going, as I had intended, to the opera to hear Cherubini's "Deux Journées," and to see Louise Taglioni dance the Sevillana.

"What! One day, and no more, in Berlin?" For the traveller there are but two ways: the instantaneous proof, or the prolonged study. Time failed me for the latter. Deign to accept this simple and rapid impression.

II.

HAMBURG.

TO describe a night journey by rail is a difficult matter; you go like an arrow whistling through a cloud; it is travelling in the abstract. You cross provinces, kingdoms even, unawares. From time to time during the night, I saw through the window the comet, rushing down upon the earth, with lowered head and hair streaming far behind; sudden glares of gaslight dazzled my eyes, sanded with the gold-dust of sleep; or the pale bluish radiance of the moon gave an air of fairy-land to scenes doubtless poor enough by day. Conscientiously, this is all I can say from personal observation; and it would not be particularly amusing if I should transcribe from the railway guide the names of all the stations between Berlin and Hamburg.

It is 7 A. M., and here we are in the good Hanse town of Hamburg; the city is not yet awake, or at most is rubbing its eyes and yawning. While they are preparing my breakfast, I sally forth at random, as my custom is, without guide or cicerone, in pursuit of the unknown.

The Hotel de l'Europe, at which I have been set down, is situated on the quay of the Alster, a basin as large as the Lac d'Enghien, which it still further resembles in being peopled with tame swans.

On three sides, the Alster basin is bordered with hotels and handsome modern houses. An embankment planted with trees and commanded by a wind-mill in profile forms the fourth; beyond, extends a great lagoon.

From the most frequented of these quays, a *café* painted green and built on piles, makes out into the

water, like that *café* of the Golden Horn where I have
smoked so many *chibouques*, watching the sea-bird
fly.

At the sight of this quay, this basin, these houses, I
experienced an inexplicable sensation: I seemed to
know them already. Confused recollections of them
arose in my memory; could I have been in Hamburg
without being aware of it? Assuredly all these objects
are not new to me, and yet I am seeing them for the
first time. Have I preserved the impression made by
some picture, some photograph?

While I was seeking philosophic explanations for
this memory of the unknown, the idea of Heinrich
Heine suddenly presented itself, and all became clear.
The great poet had often spoken to me of Hamburg, in
those plastic words he so well knew how to use—words
that were equivalent to realities. In his *Reisebilder*,
he describes the scene—*café*, basin, swans, and towns-
folk upon the quays—Heaven knows what portraits he
makes of them! He returns to it again in his poem,
"*Germania*," and there is so much life to the picture,
such distinctness, such relief, that sight itself teaches
you nothing more.

I made the circuit of the basin, graciously accompanied by a snow-white swan, handsome enough to make
one think it might be Jupiter in disguise, seeking some
Hamburg Leda, and, the better to carry out the decep-
tion, snapping at the bread-crumbs offered him by the
traveller.

On the farther side of the basin, at the right, is a
sort of garden or public promenade, having an artificial
hillock, like that in the Labyrinth in the Jardin des
Plantes. Having gone thus far, I turned and retraced
my steps.

Every city has its fashionable quarter—new, expensive, handsome—of which the citizens are proud, and
through which the *valet de place* leads you with much
complacency. The streets are broad and regular, and

cut one another at right angles; there are sidewalks of granite, brick, or bitumen; there are lamp-posts in every direction. The houses are like palaces; their classically modern architecture, their irreproachable paint, their varnished doors and well-scoured brasses, fill with joy the city fathers and every lover of progress. This is neat, orderly, salubrious, full of light and air, and resembles Paris or London. There is the Exchange! It is superb—as fine as the Bourse in Paris! I grant it; and, besides, you can smoke there, which is a point of superiority. Farther on you observe the Palace of Justice, the bank, etc., built in the style you know so well, adored by Philistines of every land. Doubtless that house must have cost enormously; it contains all possible luxury and comfort. You feel that the mollusk of such a shell can be nothing less than a millionnaire. Permit me, however, to love better the old house with its overhanging stories, its roof of irregular tiles, and all its little characteristic details, telling of former generations. To be interesting, a city must have the air of having lived, and, in a sense, of having received from man a soul. What makes these magnificent streets built yesterday so cold and so tiresome, is that they are not yet impregnated with human vitality.

Leaving the new quarter, I penetrated by degrees into the chaos of the old streets, and soon I had before my eyes a characteristic, picturesque Hamburg; a genuine old city with a mediæval stamp which would delight Bonington, Isabey, or William Wyld.

I walked slowly, stopping at every street-corner that I might lose no detail of the picture; and rarely has any promenade amused me so well.

Houses, whose gables are denticulated or else curved in volutes, throw out successive overhanging stories, each composed of a row of windows, or, more properly, of one window divided into sections by carved uprights. Beneath each house are excavated cellars, subterranean recesses, which the steps leading to the front door bestride like a drawbridge. Wood, brick, stone, and slate, mingled in a way to content the eye of a colorist, cover what little space the windows leave on the outside of the house. All this is surmounted by a roof of red or violet tiles, or tarred plank, interrupted by openings to give light to the attics, and having an abrupt pitch. These steep roofs look well against the background of a northern sky; the rain runs off them in torrents, the snow slips from them; they suit the climate, and do not require to be swept in winter.

It was a Saturday. Hamburg was at her toilette. Servants, perched aloft, were cleaning windows, and the sashes, which opened outward, projected into the street from both sides of the way. A light mist, gilded by the sun, gave a warm, brownish tint to the picture; and the sunshine, taking the houses in profile, struck full upon the opened window-sashes. It would be difficult to imagine the strange, rich coloring which these panes of glass assumed, placed one behind another all the way down the rows of houses, and pierced by level rays of the sun, darted the length of the street. Those windows, with the glass so green and full of bubbles, which belong to the mysterious interiors where Rembrandt delights to lodge his alchemists, had not, under their glaze of bitumen, warmer, more transparent, more splendid tints.

The windows being shut, all this disappears of course; still remain, however, signs and signboards, which compel the attention of the passer-by with their symbolic devices, and their letters detached from the wall and invading the sidewalk. Strict municipal regulations no doubt should forbid this projecting beyond the alignment; but all this agreeably interrupts the monotony, amuses the eye, and varies the prospect by unexpected angles. Here we have a shield in glass of various colors, flashing in the sunshine, with ruby, emerald, and topaz light; this announces an optician, or, in some places, a confectioner. Here, suspended to a great ornamental specimen of locksmith's work, a lion, holding in one paw a compass, and in the other, a mallet, emblem of some guild of coopers. Elsewhere, the copper basins of the barber, bright enough to make Membrinus' famous helmet look like verdigris; boards on which are painted oysters, lobsters, herrings, soles, and other produce of the sea, indicating a fish-dealer; and so on, indefinitely.

Some houses have doors ornamented with rustic columns, scroll-work, recessed pediments, chubby-cheeked Caryatides, little angels and loves, stout rosettes and enormous shells, all glued over with whitewash renewed doubtless every year.

The tobacco-sellers in Hamburg cannot be counted. At every third step you behold a bare-chested negro cultivating the precious leaf, or a Grand Seigneur, attired like the theatrical Turk, smoking a colossal pipe. Boxes of cigars, with their more or less fallacious vignettes and labels, figure, symmetrically disposed, in the ornamentation of the shop-fronts. There must be very little tobacco left at Havana, if we can have faith in these displays, so rich in famous brands.

As I have said, it was early morning. Servant-maids, kneeling on the steps or standing on the window-sills, were going on with the Saturday scrubbing. Notwithstanding the keen air, they made a display of robust arms bare to the shoulder, tanned and sunburnt, red with that astonishing vermillion that we see in some of Rubens' paintings, which is the joint result of the biting of the north wind and the action of water upon these blond skins; little girls belonging to the poorer classes, with braided hair, bare arms, and low-necked frocks, were going out to obtain articles of food; I shivered in my paletot, to see them so lightly clad. There is something strange about this; the women of northern countries cut their dresses out in the neck, they go about bare-headed and bare-armed, while the women of the South cover themselves with vests, *haicks*, pelisses, and warm garments of every description.

To give the finishing touch to my gratification, Costume—which the traveller of to-day is forced to go so far to seek, and often fails of finding—appeared with much *naïveté* before my eyes in the streets of Hamburg, in the persons of milk-women, resembling somewhat the female water-carriers of Venice. Their dress consisted of a skirt, clinging close over the hips, and laid in very small plaits, held in place by transverse strings, and spreading out below, and a jacket of green or bluish cloth, buttoned at the wrists. Sometimes this skirt is striped lengthwise; sometimes it has a broad band of cloth or velvet around the edge; blue stockings, which the short skirt leaves well in sight, and shoes with wooden soles complete this attire, which is not lacking in character. The head-gear is, however, the striking point: upon the hair, which is tied together at the nape of the neck with a knot of ribbon resembling a great black butterfly, rests a straw hat in the shape of a huge saucer upside down, cut out in the top, so that a pitcher or other small burden can be balanced thereon. Most of these milk-women are young, and their costume makes nearly all of them good-looking. They carry their milk-pans in an original position. From a sort of yoke cut out to fit the neck, hollowed on the under side, so as to take in the shoulders like a mould, and painted scarlet, are suspended two buckets of the same color, making counterpoise on either side the bearer, who walks between, erect and alert. There is no better orthopedic training than the carrying of heavy burdens in this fashion; these milk-women would be distinguished anywhere for their ease and freedom, and the uprightness with which they carry themselves.

Walking on, still at random, I came to the maritime part of the city, where canals take the place of streets. As yet it was low water, and vessels lay aground in the mud, showing their hulls, and careening over in a way to rejoice a water-color painter. Soon the tide came up, and everything began to be in motion. I would suggest Hamburg to artists following in the track of Canaletto, Guardi, or Joyant; they will find, at every step, themes as picturesque and more new than those which they go to Venice in search of.

This forest of salmon-colored masts, with their maze of cordage and their yellowish-brown sails drying in the sun, these tarred sterns with apple-green decks, these lateen-yards threatening the windows of the neighboring houses, these derricks standing under plank roofs shaped like pagodas, these tackles lifting heavy packages out of vessels and landing them in houses, these bridges opening to give passage to vessels, these clumps of trees, these gables overtopped here and there by spires and belfries; all this bathed in smoke, traversed by sunlight and here and there returning a glitter of polished metal, the far-off distance blue and misty, and the foreground full of vigorous color, produced effects of the most brilliant and piquant novelty. A church-tower, covered with plates of copper, springing from this curious medley of rigging and of houses, recalled to me by its odd green color the tower of Galata, at Constantinople.

I will note at random a few characteristic things: carts, formed of a plank and two broad wheels, are driven *à la Daumont*, when they have two horses. The booted driver rides one of his animals, instead of walking beside the team, as in France. When the cart has but a single horse, the driver stands up, American fashion; the narrowness of the street, the necessity of waiting till the bridges which had been opened for the passage of boats are replaced, occasion frequent obstructions from which the phlegm of bipeds and quadrupeds takes away all danger. The mail-carriers, clad in red overcoats of antique cut, amuse the stranger by their eccentric appearance. Red has become so rare a color in these days; modern civilization is so fond of neutral tints, making it an ideal, as it seems, to render the painter's trade impossible!

In the market which I traversed, green vegetables and green fruits predominated. As has been said, baked apples are the only ripe fruit of cold countries! By way of compensation, flowers are abundant; wheelbarrows full, baskets full, very fresh, brilliant, and fragrant. Among the peasants who sell these various articles, I observed some in round jackets and knee-breeches. They come, as do also the milk-women, from one of the islands in the Elbe, whose inhabitants intermarry from generation to generation, and carefully preserve old customs.

Near this market I observed a flesh-colored omnibus, which makes the trip between Hamburg and Altona. Its construction differs from that of our omnibuses. The front is a sort of coupé with a glazed curtain which can be lowered at will, protecting travellers from rain or wind without depriving them of the view; the body of the vehicle, pierced with windows, is occupied by two lateral benches, and at the back a prolongation of the sides and of the imperial protects the conductor, and gives an opportunity to get out or in, in shelter. "These are fine things to observe," you say; "rather tell us the annual tonnage of the port, in what year Hamburg was founded, what is its population?" About these subjects I know absolutely nothing, and you can find them in the guide-book; but without me, you would never have known that, in this good Hanse town, there are flesh-colored omnibuses!

Since I am speaking of the peculiarities of Hamburg, I will not forget to mention that on some shops you see the following inscription: *Magasin de galanterie, Grand assortiment de délicatesses.* What! I said, my curiosity highly excited, is gallantry an article of merchandise in Hamburg? Can delicacy be bought over the counter? Is it sold by weight or by measure, in boxes or in bottles? It must be a very mercantile mind that could sell articles like these. More careful observation showed me that these "warehouses of gallantry" were shops for the sale of fancy articles, and toys to adorn an *étagère;* and that delicacy, when offered for sale, means only something to gratify the palate.

While thus exploring the streets, an idea frequently occurred to me. Rabelais often speaks of the sausages and the smoked beef of Hamburg, which he praises as marvellous stimulants to the appetite, and I expected to see them heaped up in mountains in the shop-windows of the pork-butchers. There is no more smoked beef now in Hamburg than Brussels cabbages in Brussels, Parmesan cheese in Parma, or Ostend oysters at Ostend. Possibly they might be found at Wilkins's, the Véry of Hamburg, where you may inquire for birds'-nests soup, mock turtle not made of calf's head, Indian *kari*, elephant's feet *à la poulette*, bear's ham, bison's hump, sterlet of the Volga, Chinese ginger, conserves of roses, and other cosmopolitan dainties! There is this excellent thing about a seaport: its people are surprised at nothing; it is the place which eccentricities should select, if they were not fond of exciting attention.

As the hour advanced, the crowd became more numerous, and it was largely composed of women. In Hamburg they seem to enjoy great license. Very young girls come and go alone without any one's noticing it, and—a remarkable thing!—children go to school by themselves, little basket on the arm, and slate in hand; in Paris, left to their own free will, they would run off to play marbles, tag, or hop-scotch.

Dogs are muzzled in Hamburg all the week, but on Sundays they are left at liberty to bite whom they please. They are taxed, and appear to be esteemed; but the cats are sad and unappreciated. Recognizing in me a friend, they cast melancholy glances at me, saying in their feline language, to which long use has given me the key: "These Philistines, busy with their money-getting, despise us; and yet our eyes are as yellow as their *louis d'or*. Stupid men that they are, they believe us good for nothing but to catch rats; we, the wise, the meditative, the independent, who have slept upon the prophet's sleeve, and lulled his ear with the whir of our mysterious wheel! Pass your hand over our backs full of electric sparkles—we allow you this liberty, and say to Charles Baudelaire that he must write a fine sonnet, deploring our woes."

III.

SCHLESWIG.

THE city of Altona, to which runs that flesh-colored omnibus that I have before mentioned, begins by an immense street whose broad side-alleys are edged with little theatres and shows of divers kinds, suggesting the Boulevard du Temple in Paris; a somewhat droll souvenir on the frontier of the states of Hamlet, Prince of Denmark! It is true, however, that Hamlet himself loved players, and gave them advice like a journalist.

At the end of the suburb of Altona stands the station of the railway which leads to Schleswig, where I had business.

Business at Schleswig! Why not? What is there surprising about that? I had promised, if I should ever pass through Denmark, to pay a visit to a fair Danish *châtelaine*, a friend of mine; and at Schleswig I was to obtain the necessary directions for reaching L——, distant by a few hours' drive.

Imagine me, then, seated in a railway-carriage somewhat at a venture, having had much trouble in making the ticket-seller understand whither I desired to go, the German at this point being somewhat complicated with the Danish. Fortunately, some young gentlemen whom I encountered came to my rescue with a Teutonic French much like that in which Balzac's Schmucke and his Baron de Nucingen express themselves, but which was, for all that, most delicious music to my ears. They were so kind as to play the part of dragoman. When you are in a foreign country, reduced to the condition of a deaf-mute, you cannot but curse the memory of him who conceived the idea of building the tower of Babel, and by his pride brought about the confusion of tongues! Seriously, at the present day when the human race circulate like generous blood through the arterial, venous, and capillary tubes of railways in all parts of the world, a congress of nations ought to assemble and decide upon a common speech—French or English—which should be, like Latin in the Middle Ages, the universal human language; all schools and colleges should be required to teach it, each nation of course at the same time retaining its own native and peculiar tongue. But I leave this dream, which will be accomplished, I doubt not, at some not far remote future by some method which necessity alone can devise, and, meantime, cannot but felicitate myself that our own noble language is spoken, at least in some fashion, by every man, all the world over, who prides himself on being well-bred and well-informed.

Darkness comes on early, in these short autumn days, shorter here than in Paris even, and the level landscape soon disappeared in that vague darkness which changes the form and character of all objects. I should have done well to fall asleep, but I am a most conscientious traveller, and from time to time I put out my head, striving to see something in the gray light of the rising moon. Fatal imprudence! My cap was not secured, and the fresh wind, increased by the rapid motion of the train, which was going at full speed, took it off with all the dexterity of a *prestidigitateur!* For one moment I saw its black disk whirl in the air, like a star hurled from its orbit; a second later, and it was but a point in space, and I remained bareheaded and forlorn.

A young man who sat opposite me began to laugh quietly, then resuming his gravity, he opened his travelling-bag and drew out a student's cap which he begged me to accept. It was not a time to stand on ceremony; it was impossible to stop the train in order to procure other head-gear, nor indeed did the landscape have the appearance of being enamelled with hat-shops. Thanking the obliging traveller as best I could, I perched upon my cranium the minute cap,—taking good care, this time, to make sure of the strap—which gave me the air of a "mossy-head" of Heidelberg or Jena, well-advanced in the thirties, to say the least. This tragi-comic incident was the only one which signalized my journey, and from it I augured well of the hospitality of the country.

At Schleswig, the railway, which is to be carried further, goes a few rods beyond the station, and stops short in a field—like the last line of an abruptly interrupted letter! The effect of this is singular.

An omnibus took possession of myself and my trunks, and, with the feeling that it must of necessity take me somewhere, I confidingly allowed myself to be stowed in and carried away. The intelligent omnibus set me down before the best hotel in the town, and there, as circumnavigators say in their journals, "I held a parley with the natives." Among them was a waiter who spoke French in a way that was transparent enough to give me an occasional glimpse of his meaning; and who—a much rarer thing!—even sometimes understood what I said to him.

My name upon the hotel register was a ray of light. The hostess had been notified of my expected arrival, and I was to be sent for as soon as my appearance should be announced; but it was now late in the evening, and I thought it better to wait till the next day. There was served for supper a *chaud-froid* of partridge—without *sucre candi* or *confiture*—and I lay down upon the sofa, hopeless of being able to sleep between the two down-cushions which compose the German and the Danish bed.

The messenger, sent off upon my arrival, did not return till late the next day, the distance being twenty-seven miles from Schleswig to L——; that is, fifty-four miles going and returning. He brought contradictory tidings: the lady of the house was at Kiel, or Eckenföerde; possibly at Hamburg,—if not in England. It is sad to pay a visit in Denmark, and to leave a card with the corner turned down, saying: "I shall not come this way again."

A triple telegraphic message was despatched to the three places designated, and while waiting for an answer, I explored Schleswig, which is a city quite peculiar in its appearance. One wide street runs the length of the town, with which narrow cross-streets are connected, like the smaller bones with the dorsal vertebra of a fish. There are the handsome modern houses, which, as usual, have not the slightest character. But the more modest dwellings have a local stamp; they are one-story buildings, very low—not over seven or eight feet in height—capped with a huge roof of fluted red tiles. Windows, broader than they are high, occupy the whole of the front; and behind these windows, spread luxuriantly in porcelain or faience or earthen flower-pots, plants of every description: geraniums, verbenas, fuchsias,—and this absolutely without exception. The poorest house is as well adorned as the best. Sheltered by these perfumed window-blinds, the women sit at work, knitting or sewing, and, out of the corner of their eye, they watch, in the little movable mirror which reflects the streets, the rare passer-by, whose boots resound upon the pavement. The cultivation of flowers seems to be a passion in the north; countries where they grow naturally make but little account of them in comparison.

The church in Schleswig had in store for me a surprise. Protestant churches in general, are not very interesting from an artistic point of view, unless the reformed faith may have installed itself in some Catholic sanctuary diverted from its primitive designation. You find, usually, only whitewashed naves, walls destitute of painting or bas-relief, and rows of oaken benches well-polished and shining. It is neat and comfortable, but it is not beautiful. The church at Schleswig contains, by a grand, unknown artist, an altar-piece in three parts, of carved wood, representing in a series of bas-reliefs, separated by fine architectural designs, the most important scenes in the drama of the Passion.

This artist, worthy of being mentioned with Michel Columbo, Peter Vischer, Montañez, Verbruggen, and other masters of the chisel, is named Bruggemann,—a name not often spoken, but which ought to be famous. By the way, have you observed how commonly it happens that sculptors of equal or even superior talent are often less known than painters? Their works, in heavy material, and connected with the building in which they stand, are not moved from place to place, are seldom bought and sold, and their serene beauty, destitute of the charm of color, fails to attract the notice of the crowd.

Around the church stand sepulchral chapels of fine funereal fancy and excellent decorative effect. A vaulted hall contains the tombs of the ancient Dukes of Schleswig; massive slabs of stone, blazoned with armorial devices, covered with inscriptions which are not lacking in character.

In the neighborhood of Schleswig are great saline ponds, communicating with the sea. I paced the high-road, remarking the play of light upon this grayish water, and the surface crisped by the wind; occasionally I extended my walk as far as the chateau metamorphosed into a barrack, and the public garden, a miniature St. Cloud, with its cascade, its dolphins, and its other aquatic monsters all standing idle. A very good sinecure is that of a Triton in a Louis Quinze basin! I should ask nothing better myself. Growing tired of waiting for an answer that delayed its coming, and having exhausted all the amusements of Schleswig, I order a post-chaise, and set off for L——.

We drove for some distance along a road bordered by mountain-ashes, whose bright red berries rejoiced the eye with those glowing tints which sometimes burn in the sunset; on either side were ponds or lagoons of considerable size. Nothing could be more pleasing than this avenue of trees with their crimson umbels; a coral avenue, you might say, leading to some Undine's madrepore chateau.

To the ash-trees succeeded pines and birches, and we arrived at the post-house, where the horses were fed, while, in the meantime, I took a mug of beer, and smoked a cigar in a low room with broad windows, where servant-women stood up in front of postilions who were puffing at their porcelain pipes, in attitudes and with effects of light and shade to inspire Ostade or Meissonier.

Twilight had now come on, and presently night, if a magnificent moonlight can so be called; the road—longer than I had supposed—was lengthened still more by my impatience to arrive; while the horses continued their peaceful little trot, amicably caressed upon the croup by a phlegmatic postilion.

At each group of houses, whose lights shone out like eyes through openings in the trees, I leaned forward to see if I were drawing near my place of destination, for I had a vignette of the chateau, engraved upon a card; but the limit of my journey seemed to recede before me, and the postilion, who had the air of being himself a little doubtful about his route, exchanged a few words with the peasants whom he met, or who came to their doors, attracted by the sound of wheels.

However, the road was superb, now overshadowed by great trees, still in full leafage, now bordered by hedges through which the moon sifted its thousands of silver arrows, and whose shadow outlined upon the sand the oddest chequer-work. Where the foliage opened and showed the sky, there stood Donati's comet, flaming, dishevelled, the stars entangled in its golden hair. I had seen it at Paris a few days earlier, but so feeble, vague, uncertain! In a week it had gained in a manner that would have filled with wild terror an age more superstitious than our own.

In this vague, bluish light, cut by deep shadows which the horses did not enter without a shiver, everything took a strange and fantastic appearance. The road went up hill and down, following the undulations of the ground; hedges or trees concealed the horizon, and I lost my bearings completely. Once I felt sure I was at the end of my journey. A beautiful house, silvered by the moonlight, stood out clear against a background of sombre verdure, casting a trembling shadow in an ornamental piece of water. It answered well to the description of my friend's chateau; but the postilion drove by.

Soon after this, the carriage entered an avenue lined with trees which were surely the growth of centuries. At the left there was a shimmer of water, and the outlines of large buildings could be discerned through the branches, but I saw nothing clearly. Suddenly the post-chaise turned, and its wheels resounded upon a bridge crossing a broad moat. At the end of this bridge was a sort of bastion with a low archway which only lacked a portcullis; passing through, we found ourselves in a circular court like the interior of a donjon, and another archway yawned black before us.

All this, seen by moonlight and flooded with shadows, had a feudal and mediæval air, the look of a fortress, which disturbed me a little. Had my postilion, perchance, made some mistake, and brought me into the demesne of Harold Harfagar, or Biorn of the Sparkling Eyes? The thing grew legendary and dream-like. Finally we came out into an immense open space, bounded on one side by large buildings forming an elongated semi-circle; in the darkness it was impossible to decide what they might be, but their appearance was certainly formidable.

The chord of this arc, which seemed to represent the hollow of a curved fortification, was formed by the manor-house itself, whose imposing mass, standing entirely isolated, emerged from a sort of lagoon, with its crenellated roof and its high façade, which the moon frosted with a bluish light, making here and there some window-pane glitter like the scales of a fish.

It was not yet late, but all in the chateau seemed sleeping. It was a fairy palace, you would have said, lying under some spell, at which arrives the prince, who is destined to break the charm.

The postilion stopped his horses before a bridge which must have been a drawbridge in other days, and then lights appeared at the windows; the door opened, servants came out to the carriage, said a few words in German, and took off my luggage, looking at me, meantime, with surprise and some distrust. It was impossible for me to question them, and I was by no means certain that I was really at L——.

The bridge traversed a second moat filled with water, whose surface was scratched by a few lines of silver, then ended at a portico flanked by two granite columns and giving access to a great vestibule with black and white marble floor, and with oaken panelling and pilasters with gilded capitals. Stags' horns were suspended from the walls, and a couple of small cannon, of polished copper, pointed their muzzles at me. This looked scarcely hospitable—cannon in a nineteenth-century vestibule! I was conducted into a drawing-room furnished in modern style and with the utmost elegance.

Among the paintings which adorned the walls, was a picture, the work of a distinguished artist, representing the fair *châtelaine* in oriental costume. I recognized it at once; I had made no mistake in the house. A young governess who came down to receive me, addressed me in unknown tongues, and seemed quite alarmed at this nocturnal invasion. I pointed to the portrait and mentioned the name, and gave her the vignette of the chateau. At this, all distrust vanished, and a charming little girl, perhaps ten years old, who till then had stood remote examining me with the dark, deep eye of childhood, came up to me and said: "I understand French." My difficulties were at an end. The mistress of the house, absent for two days, would return on the morrow, and had given orders accordingly.

Supper was served for me, and I was conducted to my room, up a majestic staircase as large as a whole Parisian house. The house-maid placed on the table two candlesticks bearing candles enormously long, after the German fashion; and withdrew.

This room, one of a suite of three or four, was somewhat fantastic in appearance: over the mantel-piece, loves, illuminated by a reddish light, and greatly resembling imps, were warming themselves around a brazier, supposed to be an allegorical representation of winter; through the windows, notwithstanding the candlelight, the moon poured in its wan radiance, which stretched in a ghostly way across the floor.

Moved by the same impulse which led Mrs. Radcliffe's heroines to wander, lamp in hand, down the corridors of ghost-haunted chateaus, I made a reconnoissance, before going to bed, into the region round about my room.

The last room of the suite, a kind of small *salon*, adorned with a mirror, and furnished with a sofa and arm-chairs, offered not a corner suitable to lodge phantoms. Engravings of Esmeralda and the Goat were reassuring by their modern air.

The room preceding my own, occasioned more anxiety. Old, dingy tapestry adorned the walls, representing formidable watch-dogs held in leash by negroes. Each animal's name was written beside him, as in the dog-portraits of Godefroy Jadin. All these dogs seemed, in the flickering candlelight, to wag their tails more and more furiously, to open and shut their ivory-toothed jaws in a mute bark, and to strain violently against their collars in the effort to spring upon me. The negroes rolled the whites of their eyes, and one dog, named Raghul, looked at me with special displeasure.

The rooms were enclosed by a corridor which turned back upon itself, one of its walls going off to form a gallery, and disappearing beneath portraits of ancestors and historic personages. These were men of fierce aspect, with folio perukes, with steel cuirasses starred with golden nails and traversed by the broad ribbon of some knightly order, the hand resting on the commander's *bâton*, like the stone statue in Don Juan, each having his helmet on a cushion at his side. Also high and puissant ladies in costumes of different reigns, displaying their faded charms and graces long gone by, from the depth of their frames. There were dowagers, imposing and crabbed, and powdered young women in grand court dress with tight-laced corset and enormous *panier*, spreading out their ample skirts of pink or salmon-colored damask flowered with silver, and indicating with a careless finger the coronet of precious stones lying upon the velvet-covered console.

These noble personages, rendered pale and wan by time, presented an alarmingly spectral appearance; in the coloring, certain tints had resisted the years better than others, and the disproportionate fading produced the oddest effects. One young countess, otherwise very lovely, had retained, in her bloodless pallor, lips of the most brilliant carmine, and blue eyes of unaltered azure; the mouth and the eyes thus living made a contrast not at all reassuring with her pallor as of the dead. It seemed as if somebody were looking at you through the canvas as through a mask.

The portraits, as numerous as those shown by Ruy Gomez da Silva to Charles V. in Hernani, extended as far as the angle of the corridor.

Having arrived there, not without experiencing that faint shudder, which is caused even to the bravest, in a sombre, unknown, and silent place, by the image of those who once lived, and whose form thus pictured has long since fallen to dust, I hesitated, observing that this corridor stretched away indefinitely, full of mystery and shadow. The light from my candle failed to penetrate to the end of it, and projected upon the wall my own grimacing silhouette, which ever followed like a black servant parodying with lugubrious buffoonery every gesture and movement which I made.

Not willing to seem a coward in my own eyes, I continued my walk. About half-way down the corridor, in a place where a projection in the wall appeared to indicate a chimney, a grated air-hole attracted my attention. Approaching my light to the aperture, I distinguished a circular staircase, plunging into the depths of the building and leading upwards, Heaven knows whither. The color of the plaster around this grating indicated that the opening had been made long after the construction of the staircase,—doubtless when the secret of it was discovered.

Decidedly, this chateau of L—— was full of mysterious mechanism, like a stage-scene of *Angelo, Tyrant of Padua*, and, by night, one might hear " footsteps in the walls " !

The corridor ended at a door, carefully fastened, more recent than the rest of the building; had I known the secret of the chamber thus condemned, I surely should have had bad dreams. Happily I remained in ignorance; however, it was not without a faint feeling of relief that I saw in the morning the pure light of day filter through the window-shades.

Nocturnal phantasmagoria being put to flight, the feudal manor showed itself simply an old chateau modernized. It was the ghost of the ancient building that I had seen in the moonlight the preceding evening, and the effect was not entirely an illusion. In this colony of fortresses the pacific life of our day had taken up its abode without destroying the principal outlines, and through the darkness my error was not unnatural. The semi-circle of tall buildings, worthy of being the residence of a prince, must have been casemates before they became stables and servants' quarters; the entrance, with its two low archways, its drawbridge changed to a bridge, and its broad moat, seemed capable even yet of resisting an assault. Above the first arch a bas-relief, blurred by time, showed faintly a Christ on the Cross surrounded by holy women, protecting two rows of stone blazons, set into the thick brick wall.

The chateau, surrounded by water on all sides, raised its red walls crowned with a roof of purple tiles and pierced with windows of suitable proportions, from a foundation of bluish-gray granite. On the opposite side of the building, the two moats are crossed by bridges, the house being completely encircled by these canals.

Beyond was the garden. Great trees, in vigorous old age, still keeping all their leaves, although it was already autumn, and artistically grouped, formed, so to speak, the green-room to this magnificent stage-scene. An immense lawn, green as English turf, relieved by clumps of geraniums, fuchsias, dahlias, verbenas, chrysanthemums, Bengal roses, and other late flowers, stretched in velvety expanse as far as a hedge of yoke-elms, through which opened a long avenue of lindens, ending at a shallow fosse surrounding the park and giving an outlook into extensive pasture-lands dotted with cattle.

A ball of burnished metal, placed on a truncated column, gave a summary of this prospect, adding a tint of green tinsel. It is a German fashion, for which the taste of the *châtelaine* must not be held responsible. A similar ball stands in the court-yard of the Castle of Heidelberg.

At the right, a rustic pavilion, festooned with clematis and aristolochia, presents its sofas and arm-chairs made of knotty or curiously mis-shapen branches, and a suite of hothouses lift their glass roofs to the mild noonday sun. These greenhouses, of different temperatures, open into one another. In one, orange trees, lemons, cedrats, all laden with fruit in different degrees of maturity, seemed to feel themselves in their native climate, and not, like the delicate Mignon, to regret

"Das Land, wo die Citronen blühn";

in another, cacti bristled with countless spines, bananas spread their broad, silky leaves, and orchidaceous plants balanced their frail festoons. A third contained tree-camellias, their shining foliage starred with buds; another was reserved for rare and delicate plants arranged upon a staging; cages, painted, gilded, and ornamented with colored glass, hung from the ceilings, filled with birds, who, deceived by the warmth, caroled and sang as in the spring-time. The last building, decorated with painted trellises, served as a gymnasium for the children of the family.

Behind the greenhouses, a bit of rock-work tapestried with climbing plants simulated a kind of fountain whose basin was formed by a monstrous shell. What could have been the mollusk, the primitive inhabitant of this conch, capable of bearing Aphrodite upon the waves!

Somewhat farther on peaches, quite well crimsoned, rounded their velvet cheeks upon branches trained upon espaliers; and chasselas grapes, whose stocks only were exposed to the out-door air, were maturing behind glass attached to the walls.

A fir-wood extended its sombre verdure along the garden's edge, united with it by a light foot-bridge which crossed a deep trench half full of water. Come what might, I must explore that region. As is well known, the lower branches of the fir wither, as the tree grows larger and pushes its green spire skywards. All the lower part of these woods resembled a landscape prepared in bitumen, where the artist has been interrupted before having had time to put in touches of green. Here and there, the sun flung a handful of his golden ducats into this warm russet darkness; they caught and rebounded among the trees, and at last lay scattered over the brown earth, bare as the floor of fir-wood always is.

A pleasant aromatic odor escaped from the trees, which were agitated by a soft wind, and the forest gave forth a vague murmur, like the sigh from a human breast.

A path led through to the other side of the wood, which was separated by a trench from the open ground, where cattle and horses were feeding. I returned upon my steps, and re-entered the chateau.

Some time after, the little girl who spoke French ran up to tell me her mother had come. I related to my fair hostess my nocturnal invasion of her manor, and expressed my regret that I had not had a dwarf to sound the bugle beneath her donjon tower; she begged to know if I had slept well, despite my surroundings, and whether " the lady who died of hunger" had appeared to me in dream,—or in reality.

"Every chateau has its legend," she said, " especially if it is ancient. You no doubt observed the mysterious staircase that might be taken for a chimney. It leads up to a room that is not visible externally, and it goes down into the cellars. In this room one of the lords of L—— concealed from the eyes of all, especially from his wife, a mistress, charming and devoted, who accepted this absolute seclusion that she might live under the same roof with the man whom she loved. Every evening the master of the house had a supper prepared for him which he brought up himself from the kitchens underground to the captive's room. One day, drawn away from the chateau upon some expedition, he lost his life; and the lady, no longer receiving her food, died of hunger. Long after, repairs and alterations brought to light the secret door of the cellar, and at the foot of the staircase was found a woman's skeleton, seated in an attitude of despair amid fragments of rich materials; they investigated further, and came upon the sumptuously furnished chamber which had become to the helpless woman a Hunger Tower, more fearful than Ugolino's prison, since he, at least, had his four sons to eat! At times, her ghost walks by night in the corridors, and if she meets a stranger, she seems to implore food with the gestures of one famishing. To-night you shall have a less lugubrious apartment."

Guided by my hostess, I visited the state apartments of the chateau, which were decorated in the style of the last century; in the dining-hall, massive antique silver-ware and services of Dresden china glittered behind the glass doors of curiously carved buffets. The immense drawing-room, with five windows on the front, showed royal portraits upon its panels of gold and white, and from the ceilings hung chandeliers of rock-crystal with transparent branches and foliage cut in open work. A smaller *salon*, hung with green damask, offered to the eye nothing of special interest save a portrait of a knight in armor, with a scarf floating over his shoulder, and on his breast the orders of the Elephant and of Danneborg. This gentleman wore a gracious smile, suggestive of Versailles, but by some inadvertence of the artist, his back was turned to his pendant, a lady in powder and in grand court-dress of apple-green, shot with silver; a mistake which seemed much to annoy him, for he was doing his best to look at her from over his shoulder. The lady would have been extremely beautiful but for a nose of curve too aristocratic, descending over her mouth like a paroquet who is going to eat a cherry. Her sweet, sad eyes seemed to deplore this nose, a caricature of the Bourbon feature, which spoiled a charming face, notwithstanding the artist's efforts to attenuate it.

While I was looking attentively at this singular face,—agreeable, and yet, for all its grand air, ridiculous,—the mistress of the house said to me: "There is a legend, also, about this picture; but don't be alarmed, it is nothing terrible. If any one sneezes while passing before the long-nosed countess, she responds with a nod, or a 'God bless you,' like portraits in the melodramas. Take care to avoid colds in the head, and the painting will give no sign of life!"

The sleeping-rooms contained beds covered with damask or tapestry, standing, the head against the wall, so as to make a lane on either side. The hangings of one of them, in accordance with an old fashion, consisted of great paintings in distemper, executed on canvas, and set in panels, representing pastoral scenes, in which the Teutonic artist had essayed to imitate the fanciful style of Boucher,—an attempt resulting in awkwardly affected postures and grotesque coloring. "Will you have this room?" I was asked. "This *rococo* will be an excellent antidote to nocturnal terrors." But I declined; it is not agreeable to see around you in the silence and solitude, by the faint light of a lamp or a candle, these figures which seem to try to come down from the wall, and beg from you the soul which the painter has neglected to give them! My choice rested on a pretty room with Persian hangings and a little modern bed, situated at the corner of the chateau, and lighted by two small windows. It had no dark corridor behind it, no spiral stairs; and its walls, struck by the hand, gave back no hollow sound. The only disadvantage about this room was that to reach it you were obliged to pass in front of the lady with the paroquet nose,—portraits which are too polite being, I confess frankly, not quite to my taste; however, I did not have a cold in my head, and the young countess remained undisturbed in her armorial frame.

The most curious thing in the chateau was a hall of the sixteenth century preserved intact, and it gave me reason to regret that the possessors of this manor, about the beginning of the last century, had felt bound to renew the decoration of their apartments in the style of Versailles. It is incredible how long and despotically this style reigned, and of how many beautiful things it caused the destruction.

The hall was wainscoted with oak in small panels, forming frames of equal size, relieved by some light arabesques in a dull gold, which harmonized with the tint of the wood. Each frame contained an emblematic painting in oils, accompanied by a device in Greek, Latin, Spanish, Italian, German, or French, suited to the subject represented. These sentences were moral, gallant, chivalrous, Christian, philosophic, haughty, resigned, plaintive, witty, obscure. *Concetti* vied with *agutezzas*. Puns rivalled epigrams. The Latin, scowling in its enigmatic conciseness, assumed the airs of a sphynx, and looked askance at the more limpid Greek. Platonism in the style of Petrarch, amorous subtleties like those of Scalion de Virblunean, by their explanations confused still further pictures already complicated and unintelligible.

Storied thus from plinth to cornice, this hall would furnish devices for the blazons of a tourney, or moral sentiments for an album, or mottoes for a confectioner's *papillotes;* and yet, among so many puerilities, platitudes, and over-wrought sentimentalities, flashed out suddenly some haughty phrase of unexpected and profound meaning, worthy to be inscribed upon a knight's ring, or upon the blade of a sword.

I know no example of similar decoration. Of course we often find legends and monograms interlaced with ornaments, but nowhere the allegoric figure and the motto taken for the sole theme of the ornamentation.

Now that we have examined the chateau, let us take a turn through the environs. Two ponies, black as ebony, harnessed to a light phaeton, shook their dishevelled manes, and pawed the ground impatiently at the end of the bridge. The *chátelaine* took the reins in her fair hands, and we were off. We crossed at full speed, without well-defined road, immense pasture-lands, where fed or ruminated more than three hundred head of cattle, in attitudes which would have delighted Paul Potter or Troyon. Bulls, more peaceful than those of Spain, suffered us to pass without other demonstration than a sidelong look, and went on grazing. Horses, excited by the speed of the ponies, raced beside us for a time, then deserted us. The fields spread wide around us, slightly undulating, and bounded by a kind of earth-work crowned with a hedge. A couple of stakes joined by a transverse bar serve as gate to each field, and one must alight from the phaeton, and let down the bar, which the fiery little steeds, I think, would have willingly leaped, taking the carriage with them.

In less than twenty minutes we reached a wood crowning the summit of a hill. Elms, oaks, beeches with mighty trunks and dense foliage, had developed those varied attitudes, those odd freaks, those vigorous twists, that sloping ground will cause in trees. This wood is full of fallow-deer, and the badger digs his hole here, almost safe from disturbance. Here and there pines stretched out their arms, and lifted their crosiers of sombre green, as if to remind me of the North.

The freshness of the vegetation astonished me, so near the ocean, whose salt breath usually burns away the leaves; but the trees find abundant nourishment in the moist earth, and are well able to resist the fierceness of the winds.

We emerged from the road, and before us lay the gulf, spreading to the open sea—the North Sea—which, at its other extremity beats upon the icy covering of the pole, and in winter, balances its fields of ice laden with white bears!

At this moment there was nothing polar about it; a clear sky dappled with a few clouds, was mirrored therein, coloring the gray water with a pale azure tint. A faint current made the seaweed undulate along the shore, cast up some fragments of shells, and left a long fringe of foam upon the sand.

Upon successive days I made longer excursions in a carriage; but great white Mecklenburg horses, of milder temper, took the place of the little black whirlwinds, and they were driven by a coachman of grave and martial air.

We visited a residence surrounded, like L——, by a double moat. Here I admired a hall whose ceiling was

ornamented with carvings in high relief, representing
muses, winged genii, and musical attributes. An organ,
standing upon an elaborate console, made me question
what might be the destination of the place: a concert-
hall, or a chapel? The artists of the eighteenth century
did not examine closely into this; they did not mind
confounding Angels and Loves,—Operatic glories, and
the glories of Paradise. The old lady, the mistress of
the house, received us in a drawing-room filled with
flowers, the ceiling curiously ornamented with armorial
bearings and arabesque figures, and offered us a tray
loaded with peaches, pears, and grapes, in accordance
with the hospitable fashion of the country of always
presenting some collation to visitors. Around the house
extended a garden, or rather park, cut by avenues of
lindens of prodigious height. In an artificial pond, entirely covered with water-lentils, a swan was moving
slowly about, cleaving the glassy surface which closed
again behind him. The sight of this swan reminded
me that there were none at L——, although they were
represented in the vignette. The preceding winter
they had been devoured in their house by foxes, who
came across upon the ice. Less melodious than their
brothers of the Meander, no song was exhaled from
their long throats in the last hour, and a few feathers
were all that was found of them.

Now and then we passed upon the road a humble
vehicle of odd construction; a stout fellow, his cap over
one eye, pipe in his mouth, booted like a cavalry-man,
sitting crouched in a child's wagon, was slothfully drawn
along, not by watch-dogs, mastiffs, or bull-dogs, but by
three or four curs, real *tou-tous*, to borrow a child's
word,—so disproportionate to the weight they drew, that
one could not but laugh at seeing them. The poor animals were having a dog's life of it, in the sad meaning
of the phrase.—Since I am speaking of dogs, let me say
that in Denmark I have not seen a single Danish dog,
that is, the kind with white hair regularly spotted with

black, often offering the grotesque peculiarity of one eye blue and the other brown. These are generally animals without pedigree, without character, crossed by chance, curs, of no special type, resembling street-dogs, whose only merit is to conscientiously perform escort-duty, by barking from one end of a village to the other.

The villages are hamlets of a neatness and comfort which it is difficult to imagine without seeing them. The houses, built of brick in accordance with a regular plan, covered with tiles usually, sometimes with thatch, with their clean window-panes, behind which rare plants are growing in porcelain flower-pots, look like ornamental cottages, rather than peasants' dwellings. The suburban pavilions and villas which Parisians hire at so great expense do not compare with these bright, pretty houses, with their background of verdure, and the little pond which usually adjoins them.

Nor are the inhabitants out of keeping with the rest of the picture. Their clothing is neat and comfortable; the men wear the cap with Prussian visor, boots outside the trowsers, short waistcoats, and redingotes with long skirts. The women wear short-sleeved dresses, a good deal cut out in the neck, and go about bareheaded for the most part. It made me chilly to look at them in this cool weather, with their light dresses. Not perfectly white, it is true, but of striped calico, lilac, blue, or pink. Their red arms, in which the blood circulates with a vigor reminding one of Jordaens' pictures, were robust as any part of the body becomes on long exposure to the air, and yet you could see by their color that they were not insensible to atmospheric effects. This style is followed only by servants and women of the poorer class. Here, as everywhere else, ladies are dressed after the French fashion.

Another day was taken up by an excursion to Eckernfoëde, a small town some miles distant. The road thither lay betweed hedges dotted with berries of every color,—mulberries, mountain-ash, wild plums, barberries,—not to count the handsome coral knobs that remain after the wild rose is out of flower. It was charming. At other times we passed under great trees, through little villages, or fields ploughed in wavy lines by teams of superb horses. At last we came to the seashore and drove along a road, laved on one side by the waves, and on the other lined with handsome cottages, half-buried in flowers, which are hired by the season; for Eckernfoëde is a sea-shore resort like Trouville or Dieppe, in spite of its somewhat northern latitude. Carriages and bathing-houses, standing along the beach, bear witness that the courageous of both sexes do not fear to expose themselves to the shock of the icy waves. Some few trading-vessels lay in the harbor, and along their sides floated, contracting and dilating, a great quantity of those transparent or pearl-colored sea-mushrooms, which are animals, though they do not look like it, and which I saw once in the Gulf of Leparto, on my return from Corinth—"whither," as saith the local proverb, "everybody is not allowed to go!"

Eckernfoëde, save for the stamp which is impressed upon every city by the masts of ships rising among the trees and the chimneys, does not differ materially from Schleswig in point of architecture. There are the same brick churches, the same houses with broad windows, behind which you perceive flower-pots, and women in low-necked dresses, who sew industriously. An unwonted animation was enlivening the tranquil streets of Eckernfoëde at the time I saw it; great wagons were carrying home to their respective districts soldiers on leave, or discharged from service. Though crowded and ill-seated enough, the men seemed intoxicated with delight; perhaps, also, with beer!

At the chateau the days passed agreeably, diversified by walking, fishing, reading, conversation, and the cigar; and the nights were haunted by no unpleasant phantoms. "The woman who died of hunger" never came to ask for food; the countess with the paroquet's nose never had the opportunity to say to me, "God bless you!" Only once, a rain-storm, driven by a fierce wind, scourged the window panes, with noises sinister as the flapping of owls' wings. The sashes shook, the woodwork cracked strangely, the rushes in the moat smote one another vehemently, the water dashed up at the foot of the walls. From time to time the gale gave a thump at the door, like one who was urgent to come in, and had not the key. But nobody did come in; by degrees the sighing, murmuring, groaning—all the inexplicable noises of the night and the tempest—died away in a *decrescendo* which Beethoven himself could not have graduated more perfectly.

The morrow, it was radiant weather, and the wellswept sky showed more brilliant than ever before. I should have been glad to remain longer; but though it is admitted that all roads lead to Rome, it is less sure that they all conduct a man to St. Petersburg; and I had for a moment lost sight of my journey's aim amid the delights of the enchanted castle; the phaeton took me as far as Kiel, whence I was to return by rail to Hamburg, and thence to Lubeck, to embark upon the "Neva" for St. Petersburg.

IV.

LUBECK.

IT is necessary to go to Kiel in order to reach the railway; we made the distance in an open carriage without other incident than a halt at the post-house half-way, to let the horses breathe. I took a mug of beer in the hall of the inn, and on the glass I saw, engraven with a diamond, the Spanish name, Saturnina Gomez. At once, all the castanets of my imagination were set playing; doubtless she who bore this name was young and beautiful; and thereupon in my brain a little romance built itself up, wherewith Mérimée's "*Espagnols en Danemark*" had much to do. At Kiel, rain began to fall; at first fine, afterwards in torrents. This, however, did not prevent me from walking, umbrella in hand, across its beautiful promenade by the sea, while I was waiting for the Hamburg train to be ready.

Hamburg is worth revisiting, and I was much pleased to make some further expeditions through its animated, lively, picturesque streets. As I walked, I observed some little details which had before escaped me; for example, the wooden boxes, iron-bound and fastened by chains at the ends of bridges, accompanied by a picture where, to excite popular sympathy, all imaginable accidents at sea are united with amusing simplicity; storms, thunderbolts, fires, enormous waves, sharp-toothed rocks, capsized vessels, sailors clinging to masts, or translating, amid the foam, Virgil's lines:

"Rari nantes in gurgite vasto."

Frequently a sailor, bronzed by the sun of every

clime, is seen to fumble in his tarry pocket, and throw a shilling into the box; or a little girl stands on tiptoe to entrust to it her bit of money. The whole goes, I suppose, to form a fund in aid of the families of shipwrecked sailors. This box, destined to receive the alms for the victims of Ocean, a few steps distant from ships about to set sail, and to run all these risks, has something religious and poetic about it. The human brotherhood abandons no one of its members, and the sailor can go his way more tranquilly.

I must mention also the "beer tunnels," a kind of subterranean *estaminet*, purely local. The customers descend, as tuns into a cellar, by a few steep steps, and take their seats amid a fog of tobacco-smoke, through which faintly glimmer gaslights from the extremity of little halls with arched ceilings. The beer that you drink is excellent, for Hamburg makes eating and drinking a specialty. This is abundantly proved by the numerous shops for the sale of "delicacies," where you will find eatables from all parts of the world.

There are also many confectioners. Germans, especially German women, have a childish taste for sweets. These shops are very much frequented. People go there to nibble *bon-bons*, to drink syrups, to take ice-creams, as in Paris we go to a *café*. At every step you see the shining gilt letters of the word, *conditorei;* I believe I do not exaggerate in putting the number of confectioners in Hamburg at three times that in Paris.

As the Lubeck boat was not to leave until the morrow, I went to Wilkins's to get my supper. This famous establishment occupies a low-ceiled basement, which is divided into cabinets ornamented with more show than taste. Oysters, turtle-soup, a truffled *filet*, and a bottle of Veuve Cliquot iced, composed my simple bill of fare. The place was filled, after the Hamburg fashion, with edibles of all sorts; things early and things out of season, dainties not yet in existence or having long ceased to exist, for the common crowd.

In the kitchen they showed us, in great tanks, huge sea-turtles which lifted their scaly heads above the water, resembling snakes caught between two platters. Their little horny eyes looked with uneasiness at the light which was held near them, and their flippers, like oars of some disabled galley, vaguely moved up and down, as seeking some impossible escape. I trust it is not always the same ones that are shown to the curious, and that the *personnel* of the exhibition changes occasionally.

In the morning I went for my breakfast to an English restaurant, a sort of pavilion of glass, whence I had a magnificent panoramic view. The river spread out majestically through a forest of vessels with tall masts, of every build and tonnage. Steam-tugs were beating the water, towing sailing-vessels out to sea; others, moving about freely, made their way hither and thither with that precision which makes a steam-boat seem like a conscious being, endowed by a will of its own, and served by sentient organs. From this elevation the Elbe is seen, spreading broadly like all great rivers as they near the sea. Its waters, sure of arriving at last, are in no haste; placid as a lake, they flow with an almost invisible motion. The low opposite shore was covered with verdure, and dotted with red houses half-effaced by the smoke from the chimneys. A golden bar of sunshine shot across the plain: it was grand, luminous, superb.

In the evening the train carried me to Lubeck, across magnificent cultivated lands, filled with summer-houses, which lave their feet in the brown water, overhung by spreading willows. This German Venice has its canal, the Brenta, whose villas, though not built by Sanmichele or Palladio, not the less make a fine show against the fresh green of their surroundings.

On arriving at Lubeck, a special omnibus received me and my luggage, and I was soon set down at the Hotel Duffcke. The city seemed picturesque as I caught a glimpse of it through the darkness by the vague light of lanterns; and in the morning, as I opened my chamber-window, I perceived at once that I had not been mistaken. The opposite house had a truly German aspect. It was extremely high and overtopped by an old-fashioned denticulated gable. At each one of the seven stories of the house, iron cross-bars spread themselves out into clusters of iron-work, supporting the building, and serving at once for use and ornament, in accordance with an excellent principle in architecture, at the present day too much neglected. It is not by concealing the framework, but by making it more distinct, that we obtain more character in our buildings.

This house was not the only one of its kind, as I was able to convince myself on walking a few steps out of doors. The actual Lubeck is still to the eye the Lubeck of the Middle Ages, the old capital of the Hanseatic League. All the drama of modern life is enacted in the old theatre whose scenery remains the same, its dropscene even not repainted. What a pleasure it is to be walking thus amid the outward life of the past, and to contemplate the same dwellings which long-vanished generations have inhabited! Without doubt, the living man has a right to model his shell in accordance with his own habits, his tastes, and his manners; but it cannot be denied that a new city is far less attractive than an old one.

When I was a child, I sometimes received for a New Years' present one of those Nuremberg boxes containing a whole miniature German city. In a hundred different ways I arranged the little houses of painted wood around the church with its pointed belfry and its red walls, where the seam of the bricks was marked by fine white lines. I set out my two dozen frizzed and painted trees, and saw with delight the charmingly outlandish and wildly festal air which these apple-green, pink, lilac, fawn-colored houses with their small window-panes, their retreating gables, and their steep roofs, brilliant with red varnish, assumed, spread out on the carpet. My idea was that houses like these had no existence in reality, but were made by some kind fairy for extremely good little boys. The marvelous exaggeration of childhood gave this little parti-colored city a respectable development, and I walked through its regular streets, though with the same precautions as did Gulliver in Liliput. Lubeck gave back to me this long-forgotten feeling of my childish days. I seemed to walk in a city of the imagination, taken out of some monstrous toy-box. I believe, considering all the faultlessly correct architecture that I have been forced to see in my traveller's life, that I really deserved that pleasure by way of compensation.

As I was emerging from the hotel, a bas-relief, set into a wall, claimed my attention. Sculpture is rare in countries where brick abounds; this represented some kind of nereids or sirens, quite defaced by time, but of an imaginative and ornamental character which gave me pleasure. They accompanied great heraldic devices in the German taste; an excellent theme for decoration when well managed, and the Germans thoroughly understood it.

A cloister, or at least a gallery, a fragment of an ancient monastery, presented itself to view. This colonnade ran the whole length of a square, at the end of which stood the Marienkirche, a brick church of the fourteenth century. Continuing my walk, I found myself in a market-place, where awaited me one of those sights which repay the traveller for much fatigue: a public building of a new, unforeseen, original aspect, the old Stadt-haus in which was formerly the Hanse hall, rose suddenly before me.

It occupies two sides of the square. Imagine, in front of the Marienkirche, whose spires and roof of oxydized copper rise above it, a lofty brick façade, blackened by time, bristling with three bell-towers with pointed copper-covered roofs, having two great empty rose-windows, and emblazoned with escutcheons inscribed in the trefoils of its ogives, double-headed black eagles on a gold field, and shields, half-gules, half-argent, ranged alternately, and executed in the most elaborate fashion of heraldry.

To this façade is joined a *palazzino* of the Renaissance, in stone and of an entirely different style, its tint of grayish-white marvellously relieved by the dark-red background of old brick-work. This building, with its three gables, its fluted Ionic columns, its caryatides, or rather its Atlases (for they are human figures), its semi-circular windows, its niches curved like a shell, its arcades ornamented with figures, its basement of diamond-shaped stones, produces what I may call an architectural discord that is most unexpected and charming. We meet very few edifices in the north of Europe of this style and epoch. The movement of the Reformation seldom harmonized with this return to Pagan ideas and classic forms modified by a graceful fancy.

In the façade, the old German style prevails: arches of brick, resting upon short granite columns, support a gallery with ogive-windows. A row of blazons, inclined from right to left, bring out their brilliant color against the blackish tint of the wall. It would be difficult to form an idea of the character and richness of this ornamentation.

This gallery leads into the main building, a structure than which no scene-painter, seeking a mediæval decoration for an opera, ever invented anything more picturesque and singular. Five turrets, coiffed with roofs like extinguishers, raise their pointed tops above the main line of the façade with its lofty ogive-windows,— unhappily now most of them partially bricked up, in accordance, doubtless, with the exigencies of alterations made within. Eight great disks, having gold backgrounds and representing radiating suns, double-headed eagles, and the shields, gules and argent, the armorial bearings of Lubeck, are spread out gorgeously upon this quaint architecture. Beneath, arches supported upon short, thick pillars yawn darkly, and from far within there comes the gleam of precious metals, the wares of some goldsmith's shop.

Turning back towards the square again, I notice, rising above the houses, the green spires of another church, and over the heads of some market-women, who are chaffering over their fish and vegetables, the profile of a little building with brick pillars, which must have been a pillory in its day. This gives a last touch to the purely Gothic aspect of the square which is interrupted by no modern edifice.

The ingenious idea occurred to me that this splendid Stadt-haus must have another façade; and so in fact it had; passing under an archway, I found myself in a broad street, and my admiration began anew.

Five bell-towers, built half into the wall and separated by tall ogive-windows now partly blocked up, repeated, with variations, the façade I have just described. Brick rosettes exhibited their curious designs, spreading with square stitches, so to speak, like patterns for worsted work. At the base of the sombre edifice a pretty little lodge, of the Renaissance, built as an afterthought, gave entrance to an exterior staircase going up along the wall diagonally to a sort of *mirador*, or overhanging look-out, in exquisite taste. Graceful little statues of Faith and Justice, elegantly draped, decorated the portico.

The staircase, resting on arches which widened as it rose higher, was ornamented with grotesque masks and caryatides. The *mirador*, placed above the arched doorway opening upon the market-place, was crowned with a recessed and voluted pediment, where a figure of Themis held in one hand balances, and in the other a sword, not forgetting to give her drapery, at the same time, a coquettish puff. An odd order formed of fluted pilasters fashioned like pedestals and supporting busts, separated the windows of this aërial cage. Consoles with fantastic masks completed the elegant ornamentation, over which Time had passed his thumb just enough to give to the carved stone that *bloom* which nothing can imitate.

The building extended in a more simple style, decorated only with a frieze of stone representing masks, figures, and foliage, but so gnawed by time, blackened, and filled up, that it could not be well discerned. Under a porch sustained by Gothic colonnettes of bluish granite, I noticed two benches, whose exterior supports were formed by two thick plates of bronze, representing, one, an emperor with the crown, globe, and hand of justice; the other, a savage, hairy as a wild beast, armed with a club, and a shield with the blazon of Lubeck; the whole of very ancient workmanship.

The Marienkirche, which stands, as I have said, behind the Stadt-haus, is well worth a visit. Its two towers are 408 feet in height; a very elaborate belfry rises from the roof at the point of intersection of the transept. The towers of Lubeck have the peculiarity, every one of them, of being out of the perpendicular, leaning perceptibly to the right or left, but without disquieting the eye, like the tower of Asinelli at Bologna, or the Leaning Tower of Pisa. Seen two or three miles away, these towers, drunk and staggering, with their pointed caps that seem to nod at the horizon, present a droll and hilarious silhouette.

On entering the church, the first curious object that meets the eye is a copy of the Todtentanz, or Dance of Death, of the cemetery at Basle. I do not need to describe it in detail. The Middle Age was never tired of composing variations upon this dismal theme. The most conspicuous of them are brought together in this lugubrious painting, which covers all the walls of one chapel. From the Pope and the Emperor to the infant in his cradle, each human being in his turn enters upon the dance with the inevitable Terror. But Death is not depicted as a skeleton, white, polished, cleaned, articulated with copper wire like the skeleton of an anatomical cabinet: that would be too ornamental for the vulgar crowd. He appears as a dead body in a more or less advanced state of decomposition, with all the horrid secrets of the tomb carefully revealed.

The Greeks respected the modesty of Death, and represented him only under the form of a beautiful sleeping youth. But the Middle Age, less refined, plucked away the shroud, exposing him with all his terrors and wretchedness, in the pious intention of edifying the living. In this mural painting so much of graveyard mould still clings to the figure of Death, that a careless eye would take him for a consumptive negro.

Very rich and ornate tombs with statues, allegorical figures, attributes, blazons, long epitaphs attached to the walls or hung from the pillars, forming a burial chapel, as in the church Dei Frari, in Venice, make the Marienkirche an interior worthy of Peter Neef, painter in ordinary to cathedrals.

The Marienkirche has two pictures by Overbeck: "The Descent from the Cross," and "The Entrance into Jerusalem," which are greatly admired in Germany. The pure religious sentiment, the fervor, and the suavity of this master are exhibited in these pictures; but, for myself, their effect is destroyed by his archaic affectations and his forced simplicity. Their delicacy of execution shows that Overbeck has studied the charming primitive painters of the Umbrian school. In his own work, as well as in the picture by him in the Pinacothek at Munich, blonde Germany comes to ask from dark-eyed Italy the secrets of art.

There are also in this church a few pictures of the old German school, among them a triptych by Jean Mostaërt, the examination of which I was compelled to relinquish to go and place myself, at the instance of a beadle desirous of a *pourboire*, before one of those very complicated mechanical clocks which mark the course of the sun and moon, and the date,—year, month, day, and even hour,—that I might witness the procession of the painted and gilded figures representing the Seven Electors, which defile before a Christ in Glory. As the clock strikes twelve a door opens, and the electors, advancing around a semi-circle, each in his turn, bow their heads with a motion so sudden and energetic, that, in spite of the consecrated place, one cannot but smile. The salute made, the figure recovers itself with a jerk, and disappears by another door.

The cathedral, which is called in German the *Dom*, is quite remarkable in its interior. In the middle of the nave, filling one whole arch, is a colossal Christ of Gothic style, nailed to a cross carved in open-work, and ornamented with arabesques. The foot of this cross rests upon a transverse beam, going from one pillar to another, on which are standing the holy women, and other pious personages, in attitudes of grief and adoration; Adam and Eve, one on either side, are arranging their paradisaic costume as decently as may be; above the cross the keystone of the arch projects, adorned with flowers and leafage, and serves as a standing-place for an angel with long wings.

This construction, hanging in mid-air, and evidently light in weight, notwithstanding its magnitude, is of wood, carved with much taste and skill. I can define it in no better way than to call it a carved portcullis, lowered half-way in front of the chancel. It is the first example of such an arrangement that I have ever seen.

Behind, rises the pulpit-loft with its three arches, its gallery of statuettes, its mechanical clock, where the hour is struck by a skeleton and an angel bearing a cross. The baptismal fonts have the shape of a highly ornamented little building with Corinthian columns, the intervals between giving a view of a group representing Jacob and the Angel. The cover to the font is formed by the dome of the little building, which can be raised by a rope hung from the vault above. I will not speak of the tombs, the funereal chapels, and the organs; but I must mention two old paintings in fresco, or distemper, accompanied by a long inscription in Latin pentameters, where is seen Charlemagne's miraculous stag, with the collar on his neck bearing the date of his release, and captured four or five hundred years later by a hunter, on the very spot where now this cathedral stands.

The Holstenthor, a city gate close by the railway-station, is a most curious and picturesque specimen of German mediæval architecture. Imagine two enormous brick towers united by the main portion of the structure, through which opens an archway, like a basket-handle, and you have a rude sketch of the construction; but you would not easily conceive of the effect produced by the high summit of the edifice, the conical roofs of the towers, the whimsical windows in the walls and in the roofs, the dull red or violet tints of the defaced bricks. It is altogether a new gamut for painters of architecture or of ruins; and I shall send them to Lubeck by the next train. I recommend to their notice also, very near the Holstenthor, on the left bank of the Trave, five or six old crimson houses, shouldering each other for mutual support, bulging out in front, pierced with six or seven stories of windows, with denticulated gables, the deep red reflection of them trailing in the water, like some high-colored apron which a servant-maid is washing. What a picture Van den Heyden would have made of this!

Following the quay, along which runs a railway, where freight-trains were constantly passing, I enjoyed many amusing and varied scenes. On the other side of the Trave were to be seen, amid houses and clumps of trees, vessels in various stages of building. Here, a skeleton with ribs of wood, like the carcass of some stranded whale; there, a hull, clad with its planking, near which smokes the calker's chaldron, emitting light yellowish clouds. Everywhere prevails a cheerful stir of busy life. Carpenters are planing and hammering, porters are rolling casks, sailors are scrubbing the decks of vessels, or getting the sails half way up to dry them in the sun. A barque just arriving comes alongside the quay, the other vessels making room for her to pass. The little steam-boats are getting up steam or letting it off; and when you turn towards the city, through the rigging of the vessel, you see the church-towers, which incline gracefully, like the masts of clippers.

The "Neva," which was to take me to St. Petersburg, was quietly getting on board her boxes and bales, and gave no sign of being ready to sail on the appointed day. As it proved, she was not to go till one day later, a delay which would have been annoying in a city less charming than Lubeck. But I profited by it to go and see Don Giovanni performed in German, by a German troupe. The theatre is new and very pretty; the windows of the façade have for caryatides figures representing the Muses. I was not so well satisfied with the manner in which Mozart's great work was rendered in his native land. The singers were mediocre, and permitted themselves in many places strange license; for example, to replace the recitative by a lively, animated dialogue, doubtless because the music hindered the action! Leporello indulged in pleasantries in the worst possible taste, unrolling before the eyes of the weeping Elvira an interminable strip of paper, on which were pasted the pictures of the thousand and three victims of his master, these portraits being all exactly alike, and resembling a woman coiffed à la giraffe, in the fashion of the year 1828! Was it not a delightful idea!

V.

CROSSING THE BALTIC.

AT the designated hour the "Neva" set forth on her way, moderating her speed as she followed the windings of the Trave, whose banks are covered with pretty country-houses—*villégiatures* of the richer inhabitants of Lubeck. As we approach the sea the river widens, its banks are lower, the channel is marked by buoys. I am very fond of these horizontal landscapes; they are more picturesque than is generally believed. A tree, a house, a church-tower, the sail of a vessel, assume importance, and are enough, with a vague, vanishing background, for the *motif* of a picture.

Along a narrow line, between the pale blue of the sky and the opalescent gray of the water, is designed the silhouette of a city or a large town,—Travemunde, probably. The shores recede farther and farther, grow faint, and disappear. In front of us the water assumes greener tints; undulations, at first feeble, increase by degrees and become waves. Here and there white caps are seen. The horizon ends with a hard blue line—the flourish that Ocean appends to his signature. We are at sea.

Marine painters usually seem to be anxious to produce an effect of transparency, and when they succeed in this are commended—the very word being an eulogium. But the ocean is heavy, dense, solid, so to speak, and, above all, opaque. No attentive eye can confuse its dense, salt water with that of a river or lake. Doubtless the light traversing a wave gives it a partial transparency; but the general tone of the sea is always dull, and its local power is so great that it deprives the adjacent parts of the sky of a portion of their color. By the solidity of its tints and by their intensity, you recognize that this is a formidable element, of irresistible energy and of prodigious bulk.

In going out to sea, a certain impression of awe comes over any one, even the most frivolous, the most courageous, or the most habituated. You leave the solid earth—where death may reach you, it is true, but where at least the ground will not yawn beneath your feet—to furrow the immense saline plains, the covering of that abyss which hides so many shipwrecked vessels. You are separated from the turbulent water only by a fragile board or a thin plate of metal, which a wave can beat in, a reef can tear open. A sudden gust, a flurry of wind, is enough to capsize you, and all your skill as a swimmer will but serve to prolong your death-struggle.

To these sombre reflections is added ere long the indescribable misery of sea-sickness; the affronted element seems resolved to cast you out as an impure thing among the algæ of its shores. Resolution disappears, the muscles are relaxed, the temples throb, headache sets in, and the air which you breathe is bitter and nauseous. Everybody's face is altered, grows livid and green; lips become violet; color deserts the cheek, and takes refuge upon the nose. Then each one resorts to his little pharmacopœia: this one nibbles Maltese *bonbons;* that one bites a lemon; another sniffs at his smelling-salts; another begs for a cup of tea, which a sudden lurch of the vessel lands in his shirt; a few courageous ones walk up and down, with reeling gait, an unlighted cigar between their lips; almost everybody ends by leaning against the netting. Happy they who have presence of mind to select the leeward side!

Meantime the vessel goes on her way, and pitches more and more every minute. You measure the masts and smoke-stack of the plunging boat against the horizon-line, and find changes of level of several yards; and your discomfort is aggravated. All around you waves follow one another, swell, burst, and fall in foam; the climbing water rushes down again with dizzy uproar; now and then a wave breaks over the deck, and is resolved into salt rain running over the floor, after having given the passengers an unexpected *douche*. The breeze freshens, and the pulleys in the rigging give out that sharp whistling sound which is like a sea-bird's cry. The captain declares that the weather is delicious, to the great surprise of inexperienced travellers, and he orders the jib hoisted; for the wind, which was dead ahead, now comes on our quarter. Thus supported, the vessel rolls less, and her speed is increased. Now and then brigs or barques pass us, their top-sails clewed up, a reef taken in the lower sails, only the jib out; they bury their noses in the foam, and execute such astonishing pyrrhics that you doubt whether the sea is quite so friendly-minded as they choose to say.

You are plucked from this contemplation by the servant, who comes to say that dinner is served. It is not so easy to descend to the saloon by a staircase whose steps are displaced from under your feet like the rounds of the mysterious ladder in the initiatory rites of freemasonry, and whose walls hit you alternately, as battledores a shuttlecock. At last you sit down at table with a few intrepid companions. The rest are lying on the deck, wrapped in cloaks. You eat, but with much circumspection, and at the risk of putting your fork into your eye, for the ship is dancing her best. If you try to drink, with the precaution worthy of an acrobat, your beverage plays to the life, Gozlan's comedy, "*Une tempête dans un verre d'eau.*"

This difficult exercise ended, you return to the deck rather on all fours, and the fresh breeze proves encouraging. You risk a cigar; it is not too offensive; you are safe! The uncivil sea-gods will demand no more libations from you!

Whilst you walk the deck, your legs far apart, using your arms for a balancing-pole, the sun goes down in a bank of gray cloud, reddening all the rifts of it, and presently the wind sweeps the whole away. The horizon is altogether a solitude; no more outlines of ships. Under a pale violet sky the sea grows dark and wicked-looking; later, the violet turns to a steel-blue. The water becomes perfectly black, and the white caps shine like flakes of silver on a funeral pall. Myriads of stars of a greenish gold, dot the immensity, and the comet, with wide-streaming hair, seems plunging head-foremost into the sea. For a moment its tail is cut transversely by a line of cloud.

The limpid serenity of the sky does not prevent the north wind from blowing with all its lungs, and it becomes very cold. Everything is saturated with the salt spray that the wind takes off from the crests of the waves. The idea of returning into the cabin, and breathing its hot, mephitic air, gives me nausea, and I go and sit down by the smoke-stack, leaning my back against the heated sheet-iron, and sheltered sufficiently by the paddle-boxes. Nor is it till late into the night that I seek my berth and fall into a broken sleep, traversed with wild dreams.

In the morning the sun rose, red-eyed, like one who has slept ill, and scarcely able to draw aside his curtains of fog. The breeze grew more and more fresh, and vessels appearing at intervals on the horizon-line were seen to describe extraordinary parabolas. Seeing me titubate along the deck like a drunken man, the captain felt it his duty to call out, to reassure me, "Superb weather!" but his strong German accent gave an ironical tone to his words of which he was quite unconscious.

We went below to breakfast. The plates were held in place by little bars of wood; the decanters and bottles were anchored fast; but for this precaution, the table would have been cleared without hands. In bringing on the dishes, the stewards gave themselves up to extraordinary gymnastic performances. They reminded me of mountebanks balancing chairs upon the tip of the nose. Possibly the weather was not so fine as the captain averred.

Towards evening the sky became overcast, rain began to fall—fine at first, afterwards heavier—and, according to the proverb, "Small rain beats down great wind," greatly reduced the violence of the gale. From time to time through the darkness shone the light, white or red, fixed or revolving, of some light-house indicating points of coast to be avoided. We were now in the gulf.

When daylight came, a low, flat stretch of land, an almost imperceptible line between sky and sea, which might be taken by the naked eye for a morning fog or the vapor from the water, was outlined on the right. Sometimes the ground itself, was hidden by the sloping sea, and half-blurred rows of trees seemed to emerge from the water. There was the same effect in regard to houses and light-houses, the white towers of the latter often being taken for sails.

At the left we passed an island of barren rock, or at least in appearance such. Vessels were in motion along its coasts, and having recourse to a marine glass, at first sight their sails, lighted by the rising sun, looked like façades of houses against the purplish background of the shore; on closer examination, the island was seen to be uninhabited, and to contain only a watch-tower raised upon a slope.

The sea was now somewhat pacified, and at dinner, from the depths of their cabins, emerged, like spectres from their tombs, unknown figures, passengers of whose existence we had not been aware. Pale, famished, with tottering steps, they dragged themselves to the table; but they did not all dine; the soup was still too stormy, the roast meat too tempestuous. After a spoonful or two, they rose and tottered back to the cabin stairway.

A third night overspread the waters; this was the last to be spent on board, for on the morrow at eleven, all going well, we should be in sight of Cronstadt. I remained late on deck looking out into the darkness, and devoured with feverish curiosity. After two or three hours of sleep I came up again, anticipating the rising of the sun, who seemed on this day—to me, at least—to be a sad sluggard.

Who has not experienced the wretchedness of the hour before the dawn? It is damp, icy, and shivery. The robust experience a vague discomfort; the sick feel themselves losing strength; every fatigue becomes more insupportable; midnight phantoms, nocturnal terrors, seem to brush one with their clammy batwings, as they take their flight. You think of those who are no more, of those who are absent; you perform doleful introspection; you regret the domestic hearth voluntarily deserted: but, with the first ray of sunshine, all is forgotten.

A steam-boat, her long feather of smoke streaming out after her, passes at our right; she is going westward, and comes from Cronstadt.

The gulf narrows more and more; the shores, level with the water, are now bare, now clad in sombre verdure; watch-towers rise in sight; barques, ships, come and go, following the channel marked out by buoys and stakes. The water, grown shallow, changes color from its proximity to the earth, and gulls, the first we have seen, are sweeping through the air in graceful evolutions.

With the glass we can see ahead of us two rose-colored spots, dotted with black points; a fleck of gold, one of green; a few lines slender as cobweb, a few spirals of white smoke rising into the pure, still air: this is Cronstadt.

At Paris, during the Crimean war, I frequently saw plans of Cronstadt, all more or less imaginative, with cross-fires of cannon represented by multifold lines like the rays of a star; and I have made many an unsuccessful effort to represent to myself the real aspect of the city. But the most detailed plans give no notion of the silhouette as it really appears.

The paddle-wheels, sweeping through the calm, almost motionless, water, carried us forward rapidly, and already I could distinguish clearly a rounded fortress with four stories of embrasures at the left, and at the right a square bastion commanding the entrance. Flanking batteries appeared at the water-level. The fleck of yellow changed to a golden dome of wonderful lustre and transparency; the light was concentrated on the salient point, and the parts in shadow assumed amber tints of incredible fineness. The fleck of green was a cupola painted of that color, that looked as if it were oxydized copper. A golden dome, a green cupola: at first sight, Russia shows herself in her characteristic colors.

From a bastion, rose one of those tall signal masts which look so well in marine pictures, and behind a granite mole were a crowd of war-vessels in winter trim. Countless ships with the flags of all nations encumbered the harbor, and formed with their masts and cordage a kind of half-grown forest.

A derrick for putting in masts, with its beams and pulleys, rose at the corner of a quay which was covered with hewn timber, and, a little in the rear, the houses of the city appeared, painted of diverse tints, some having green roofs, all lying very low, and only the domes and the little cupolas of the churches rising above the level of the rest. These famous strongholds offer as little to the eye and to the cannon as possible; the sublime in this regard would be to have them completely invisible; we shall come to it by and by.

From a building with Greek façade, custom-house or

police-station, came off boats, rowing towards us as we now lay anchored in the roads. It reminded me of the visits of health-officers in the eastern Mediterranean, where rascals, far more pestiferous than ourselves, inhaling evil-smelling vinegar, came out to take our papers by the aid of tongs. Everybody was on deck; and in a skiff which seemed to be waiting until, formalities ended, some traveller should wish to go ashore, I saw the first mujik. He was a man of twenty-eight or thirty, with long hair parted in the middle, a blonde beard slightly curled, like that which painters give to the figure of Christ, with well-knit limbs, and managing his two oars with ease. He wore a pink shirt, girt at the waist, and hanging outside the trousers with an effect of tunic or frock, not ungraceful. His trousers, of some blue material, loose and having many folds, were tucked into his boots; on his head a cap, or small flat hat, narrowed in the middle, spreading out above, and turned up all round the brim.

And now the employés of the police and the custom-house, clad in long redingotes, wearing the Russian fatigue-caps, and most of them having medals or decorations, came on board, and fulfilled their duties with much courtesy.

We went below to receive our passports, which had been placed in the captain's hands on starting. There were English, Germans, French, Greeks, Italians, and some even of other nationalities; to our surprise, the officer in command, a very young man, changed his language with each interlocutor, speaking English to the Englishman, German to the German, and so on, without making any mistake as to the nationality of each. Like Cardinal Angelo Maï, he seemed to know every possible idiom. When it was my turn, he returned to me my passport, saying as he did so, with the purest Parisian accent: "Il y a longtemps que vous êtes attendu à Saint-Pétersbourg." (You have been expected here for a long time.) The truth is, I had come like a boy on his way to school, and had been a month on a journey which could have been made in a week. To the passport was appended a trilingual paper, indicating certain formalities to be observed upon arriving in the city of the Czars.

The "Neva" was again under way, and standing upon the prow, I watched with eager eyes the wondrous panorama unfolding before me. We had entered that arm of the sea into which the Neva spreads out. It was rather like a lake than a gulf. As we kept in the middle of the channel, the shores on each side could scarcely be discerned. The water, spreading far away on either side, seemed higher than the land, which was like a fine pencil-stroke upon a flat-tinted water-color. The weather was magnificent. A light, dazzling but cold, fell from the clear sky; it was a boreal azure—polar, so to speak—with shades of milk, opal, steel, of which our sky gives no idea; a pure, white, sidereal radiance, which does not seem to emanate from the sun, which is what one sees in dreams, in some other planet than our own.

Under this milky vault the immense watery level of the gulf was stretched out, tinted with colors that no pen can describe, in which the ordinary tones of water went for nothing. Now they were opaline white tints, such as you see in certain shells,—now, pearly grays of incredible delicacy; further on, blues, lustreless or streaked like a Damascus blade, or else rainbow-hued reflections like those of the pellicle on molten tin; to a belt as smooth as glass, succeeded a broad band waved like moire antique; and all this light, soft, vague, limpid, clear, to a degree that no pen and no palette can render. The freshest tint from human pencil would have been a muddy stain upon transparency so ideal, and the words that I employ to give an idea of this marvellous pale splendor seem to me like blots of ink, falling on the finest tinted vellum from a spattering pen.

If some vessel sailed past us with its genuine color,

its salmon-colored masts, its outlines clear and sharply defined, it resembled, in the midst of this Elysian blue, a balloon floating in mid-air; one could dream of nothing more like fairy-land than this luminous infinity.

In the distance, emerged slowly between the milky water and the opaline sky, encircled by its mural crown crenellated with turrets, the superb silhouette of St. Petersburg, whose tints of amethyst drew a line of demarkation between these two pale immensities of sea and sky. Gold scintillated in scales and in needles upon this diadem, the richest, the most beautiful, that ever city wore upon its brow. Soon St. Isaac's outlined between its four bell-towers its cupola of gold, like a tiara; the Admiralty darted high in air its glittering arrow; the church of St. Michael the Archangel rounded its domes of Muscovite curve; that of the Horse-Guards lifted sharp pyramids, their tips adorned with crosses; and a crowd of more remote church towers gleamed with their metallic lustre.

Nothing exists more splendid than was that golden city, upon that horizon of silver, when the evening had all the white radiance of the dawn.

VI.

ST. PETERSBURG.

THE Neva is a fine river, nearly as large as the Thames at London Bridge; its course is not long; it rises in Lake Ladoga, and is the outlet from it into the Gulf of Finland. A few revolutions of the wheels brought us alongside of a granite quay, near which was lying quite a flotilla of little steam-boats, schooners, and barges.

On the opposite side of the river, on the right, that is, as you go up stream, were to be seen the roofs of immense sheds under which vessels were building; on the left, great structures with fronts like palaces, the buildings of the engineer corps and the School of Naval Cadets, stretched away in stately outline. It is no small affair to put on shore all the luggage,—trunks, valises, hat-boxes, packages of every description,—which load the deck of a steam-boat as she reaches her landing-place, and for each traveller to recognize his own out of all this mass. But a whole swarm of mujiks had soon carried it all away to the office of inspection on the quay, each piece followed closely by its anxious owner.

Most of these mujiks wore the pink skirt outside their trousers, like a jacket, wide trousers, and the boots halfway up the leg; others, though the weather was unusually mild, were already muffled in the touloupe, or sheepskin tunic. The touloupe is worn, the wool inwards, and when it is new the tanned skin is of a pale salmon color, rather pleasing to the eye; some coarse stitching simulates trimming, and the whole is not wanting in character; but the mujik is as faithful to his touloupe as the Arab to his burnouse: once assumed, it is never off his back; it is his tent and his bed; he lives in it by day and night, sleeps in it in all corners, on all benches, upon all stoves. Consequently the garment soon becomes greasy and shiny, and acquires those tints of bitumen which the Spanish painters affect in their characteristic pictures. Unlike Murillo's and Ribera's models, however, the mujik is clean under this greasy coat, for he goes through a Russian bath every week. These men with long hair and enormous beards, clad in the skins of animals, upon this splendid quay whence you see on every side domes and spires of gold, by contrast seize upon the stranger's imagination. Do not, however, fancy in their appearance anything savage or dangerous; their faces are gentle and intelligent, and their courteous manners put to shame the brutality of our porters.

My trunk was examined without other incident than the very easy discovery of Balzac's *Parents pauvres* and *Les Ailes d'Icare* of Charles de Bernard, lying upon my linen; they were taken away, but I was assured that I should receive them again on application at the bureau of censure.

These formalities over, I was free to wander at will through the city. A crowd of droschkys and little carts for transportation of luggage were waiting outside, sure of finding employment. I knew well enough in French the name of the place where I had been advised to stop, but it was necessary to translate it into Russian for the coachman. One of those *domestiques de place*, who seem no longer to have a mother tongue, and have created for themselves a kind of *lingua Franca* not unlike the jargon which the pretended Turks employ in the ceremony in the *Bourgeois Gentilhomme*, saw my perplexity; understood in a general way that I wanted to go to the Hotel de Russie, kept by M. Klie; piled up my luggage on a rosponsky; climbed up beside me, and we were off. The rosponsky is a low wagon of the most primitive construction : a couple of roughhewn logs placed on four small wheels,—it is no more complicated than this.

To one who has just come from the majestic solitudes of the sea, the whirl of human activity and all the tumult of a great city cause a kind of vertigo ; you pass, borne along as in a dream, among unknown objects, desiring to see everything, yet seeing nothing ; you seem to be still balancing upon the waves, especially when a vehicle, no better hung than a rospousky, makes you pitch and roll over the inequalities of the pavement, and on solid ground gives you a reminiscence of the malady peculiar to the sea. However, though rudely shaken about, I did not lose a single instant, devouring with my eyes the novel sights which presented themselves to me.

We soon came to a bridge which, later, I knew as the Bridge of the Annunciation, or, more familiarly, the Bridge Nicholas ; it is entered by two movable ways which are displaced to allow the passage of boats, and then reunited, the conformation of the bridge being a Y, with very short branches. At the point of junction stands a little chapel of extreme richness, of which, in passing, I could observe only the mosaics and the gilding.

At the end of this bridge, whose piers are of granite and the arches of iron, we turned and went up the English Quay, which is lined with palaces of the classic style, or with private residences not less splendid, all painted in gay colors, having balconies and porticos projecting over the sidewalk. Most of the houses in St. Petersburg, like those in London and Berlin, are of brick, covered with stucco tinted in different shades, so as to bring out the architectural outlines, and produce a fine decorative effect. As we passed along, I noticed with admiration, behind the glass of the lower windows, bananas and broad-leaved tropical plants, suggesting a conservatory in every house.

The English Quay debouches into the great square,

where the Peter the Great of Falconnet, one arm extended towards the Neva, reins back his rearing horse, at the top of the rock which serves for a pedestal. I recognized it instantly from Diderot's description, and from drawings which I had seen. Across the square I saw the grand outlines of St. Isaac's with its golden dome, tiara of columns, its four bell-towers, and its octostylic portico. Returning to the English Quay,—at the entrance of a street, are seen columns of porphyry, winged Victories of bronze holding palms. All this, half discerned through the rapidity of the drive and the surprise of novelty, formed a magnificent and Babylonian *ensemble*.

Continuing in the same direction, the immense palace of the Admiralty soon came in sight. From a square tower, in the form of a temple ornamented with colonnettes, which is placed upon the main roof, springs that slender golden spire, with a ship for a vane, that is seen at so great a distance, and that attracted my attention from the Gulf of Finland. The trees in the avenue surrounding the building had not yet lost their leaves, although the autumn was already far advanced (October 10th).

Still farther, in the centre of another square, springs from its bronze base the column of Alexander, a stupendous monolith of red granite, surmounted by an angel holding a cross. Of this I caught merely a glimpse, for the driver turned a corner and came into the Newsky Prospekt, which is to St. Petersburg what the Rue de Rivoli is to Paris,—Regent Street to London, —the Calle d'Alcala to Madrid,—the Strada di Toledo to Naples,—that is to say, the main artery of the city, the most frequented and most animated of all its streets.

What struck me especially, was the immense throng of carriages—and a Parisian is not apt to be astonished in this respect—which were in motion in the broad street; and, above all, the extreme speed of the horses.

The droschkys are, as everybody knows, a kind of small phaeton, low and very light, and containing at most but two persons; they go like the wind, guided by coachmen as bold as they are skilful. They brushed past our rospousky with the rapidity of swallows; they passed each other, they crossed each other's track, they went from pavement of wood to pavement of granite, without the least collision; what seemed inextricable confusion came out right as if by enchantment, and each one went his separate way at full speed, finding room for his wheels where a hand-cart could not have gone by.

The Newsky Prospekt is at the same time the street of shops and the fashionable street of St. Petersburg. Rents are as high as on the Boulevard des Italiens; it is a truly peculiar *mélange* of shops, palaces, and churches; upon the signs, glitter in gold the beautiful characters of the Russian alphabet, which retains many Greek letters and is exquisitely adapted for inscriptions of every kind.

All this passed before my eyes like a dream; for the rospousky went at a rapid pace, and, before I was well aware, I found myself at the foot of the steps of the Hotel de Russie, whose landlord scolded the *domestique de place* roundly for having installed my lordship upon so wretched a vehicle.

The Hotel de Russie, at the corner of the Place Michael, near the Newsky Prospekt, is nearly as large as the Hotel du Louvre in Paris; its corridors are longer than many streets; you might easily fatigue yourself in walking through them. The lower part is taken up by extensive dining-halls adorned with greenhouse plants; in the first of these is a kind of bar-room, where are served caviare, herrings, sandwiches of white or black bread, cheese of many kinds, bitters, kümmel, and brandy; with which, according to Russian fashion, the guests may stimulate their appetite before dinner. Their *hors d'œuvres* are eaten here before the meal itself; but I have travelled too much to find this custom strange. Every country has ways of its own; in Sweden do they not serve the soup with the dessert?

At the entrance of this hall, behind a screen, are hooks to receive outside garments, and each one hangs up his paletot, his scarf, or his plaid, and lays off his overshoes. But it was not cold, and in the open air the thermometer registered 48° or 50°. These minute precautions in so mild a temperature astonished me, and I looked out to see whether snow had not already whitened the roofs; but they were only colored by the pale rosy light of the setting sun.

However, there were double windows everywhere; enormous wood-piles encumbered the court-yards, and every preparation seemed to have been made for receiving the winter in good style. My own bedroom was also hermetically closed; between one sash and the other is placed a layer of sand, in which are little paper horns filled with salt designed to absorb moisture and prevent the frost from covering the panes with its silvery foliage; copper mouths, like the openings of Parisian street letter-boxes, were all in readiness to blow their hot-air blasts. Winter, however, seemed to delay; and the double window was sufficient to maintain in the room an agreeable mildness of temperature. The only thing peculiar in the furniture of my room, was one of those immense sofas covered with wadded leather, that you meet everywhere in Russia; which, with their numerous cushions, are more comfortable than the usually very poor beds.

After dinner I went out without a guide; as usual, trusting to my instinct to find the way back. A watchmaker's dial on one corner, a sentry-box at another, would serve as landmarks.

This first random stroll through the streets of a strange and long-dreamed-of city, is one of the keenest delights of the traveller, and repays him liberally for the fatigues of the journey. Is it extravagance to say that night, with its mingled light and shade, its mystery, its strange power of magnifying all objects, adds much to this gratification? The eye sees but in part; imagination does the rest. The reality is not yet too sharply drawn; the picture is, as it were, blocked in, to be finished later in detail.

Imagine me proceeding slowly along the sidewalk, and going down the Prospekt in the direction of the Admiralty. Now I looked at the passers-by, and now at the brilliantly lighted shops; and then my eye explored the underground regions, which reminded me of the cellars in Berlin and the "tunnels" of Hamburg. At every step, I beheld, behind the elegant windows, a show of fruit most artistically arranged: pine-apples, Malaga grapes, lemons, pomegranates, pears, apples, plums, water-melons. They are as fond of fruits in Russia as they are of *bon-bons* in Germany; the luxury is expensive, and all the more fashionable on that account. Along the sidewalk mujiks offer to the passers-by green apples which look as if they were sour. However, it must be that they find purchasers: they seem to be offered for sale at every corner.

This first reconnoissance made, I returned to the hotel. Children perhaps require to be rocked to sleep; but grown people have a preference for stationary slumber; and for three nights past the sea had shaken us about so thoroughly in our steam cradle, that I, for one, desired a more stable bed; but through my dreams the motion of the waves still made itself felt. I have noticed this often before. The change to solid ground is not so prompt a remedy as one might suppose for the miseries caused by the ever-changing level of the watery plain.

In the morning I was abroad early to examine by aid of sunshine the picture which the vague glimmer of twilight and of starlight had in part already revealed to me. As the Newsky Prospekt is in a sense a summary of St. Petersburg, you will suffer me to give you a somewhat lengthy and detailed description, whereby you may be at once admitted to a familiar acquaintance with the city. And in advance I beg you to forgive some observations that may seem puerile and trivial. It is these very trifles, neglected as too humble and too easily observed, which make the difference between one place and another, and certify to you that you are not in Piccadilly, nor in the Rue Vivienne.

The Newsky Prospekt starts from the Square of the Admiralty, and extends as far as the convent of St. Alexander Newsky, a distance of more than three miles, where, after a slight curve, it ends. Like all the streets in St. Petersburg, it is broad, and along the middle of the carriage-road is a rough stone pavement sloping a little from each side to the gutter, which runs directly down the centre. On either side a zone of wooden pavement accompanies the belt of fragments of granite; large paving-stones form the sidewalk.

The spire of the Admiralty, which resembles the mast of a ship planted in the roof of a Grecian temple, produces a fine effect, standing as it does at the end of the Newsky Prospekt. If there is a single ray of sunshine, it is sent back from that gilded spire, a spangle of vivid light, amusing the eye as far off as the spire can be seen. Two neighboring streets have the same advantage as the Newsky Prospekt, and by a skilful combination of lines show the same glittering needle. For the present, however, we will leave the Admiralty behind us, and go up the Prospekt as far as the Anitschkov bridge; that is to say, through the most animated and frequented section of the street. The houses on either side are high and wide; palaces, or town-houses of the nobility, it would seem. A few, the most ancient, recall the old French style a little Italianized, and present quite a stately combination of Mansart and Bernini; Corinthian pilasters, cornices, pediments, consoles, voluted circular windows, doors with grotesque ornaments, and the lower story representing hewn stone. Others present decorations in the style of Louis XV., and elsewhere the classic taste of the Empire shows the even line of its columns and its triangular pediments in white upon a yellow background. The most recent buildings are of the Anglo-German style, and seem to have taken for their type those stately watering-place hotels, which, in lithographic views, offer temptation to travellers. This *ensemble*—which must not be too closely examined, for nothing but the use of stone gives value to the execution of ornamental work in preserving the direct imprint of the artist's hand—this *ensemble*, I say, forms an admirable picture, to which the name Prospekt, which this street bears in common with many others, is remarkably well suited and appropriate. All is combined with a view to optical effect, and the city, created at a stroke, by a will which knew no obstacle, emerged, a finished whole, from the marsh it now covers, like a painted scene in a theatre at the machinist's whistle.

If the Newsky Prospekt is beautiful, I hasten to add that it turns its beauty to good account. At once the fashionable street and the busy street, its palaces and its shops alternate; nowhere, except perhaps at Berne, is there such display in the matter of signs. It is carried to so great a height that it almost makes a modern order of architecture, to be added to the five orders of Vignole. Golden letters trace their light and their heavy strokes upon azure fields, upon panels of black or red; they are cut out in open-work, they are applied to the window-glass, are repeated at every door, profit by the corners of streets, curve around arches, extend along cornices, take advantage of the projections of *padiezdas*, descend basement staircases, and seek in every possible way to compel the attention of the passer-by. But perhaps Russian is to you an unknown tongue, and the form of these characters signifies nothing more to you than an ornamental design, a pattern for embroidery! Here, close beside it, is the French or German translation. Still you do not understand? The courteous sign grants you pardon for not knowing any one of the three languages; it even supposes that you are completely illiterate; and it depicts, to the life, what is for sale in the shop to which it calls your attention. Golden grapes, carved or painted, indicate the wine-merchant; near by, hams, sausages, neats' tongues, boxes of caviare designate a provision-shop; boots, *brodequins*, overshoes, naïvely depicted, say to the feet that cannot read: " Enter here, and you shall be shod;" gloves, in high relief, speak an idiom intelligible to all. Mantles and dresses there are, too, surmounted by a hat or a bonnet, to which the artist has judged it needless to add the face; pianos invite you to try their painted keys. All this is amusing to the loiterer, and has its character.

The first object which attracts the eye of a Parisian, upon entering the Newsky Prospekt, is the name of Daziaro, the dealer in engravings, whose Russian sign adorns the Italian boulevard in Paris; and on the right, going up, you are tempted to stop at Beggrow's, the Desforges of St. Petersburg, who sells artists' materials, and always has some water-color or oil-painting in his window.

This Venice of the North, built on its twelve islands, is cut by numerous canals. Three of these cross, without interrupting, the Newsky Prospekt: the Moïka, the Catherine, and, farther on, the Ligawa, and Fontanka canals. The Moïka is crossed by the Police bridge, whose salient curve repeats the arch too exactly, and forces the rapid droschkys to slacken their gait. The two other canals are crossed by the bridges of Kasan and of Anitschkov. In traversing these before the season of ice, the eye explores with pleasure the gap which these waters, confined by granite quays and furrowed by boats, open between the buildings.

Lessing, the author of Nathan the Wise, would have delighted in the Newsky Prospekt, for his ideas of religious toleration are practised here in the most liberal fashion; there is scarcely any confession which has not, in this broad street, its church or temple where its rites are freely practised.

At the left, as we are going, is the Dutch church, the Lutheran place of worship, the Catholic church of St. Catherine, and an Armenian church, not to mention, in adjoining streets, the Finnish chapel, and temples of other reformed sects; at the right, the Russian cathedral of Our Lady of Kazan, another Greek church, and a chapel of some old faith, called Starovertzi, or Rosskolniki.

All these houses of God, except Our Lady of Kazan, which interrupts the alignment, its elegant semi-circular colonnade, imitated from St. Peter's at Rome, curving around an extensive square, are intermixed familiarly with the houses of men; their façades are only slightly set back from the street; they present themselves without mystery to the devotion of the passer-by, only distinguished by the special style of their architecture. Each church is surrounded by immense estates, conceded by the czars; the ground is now covered by elegant structures, which are a source of great revenue to the church.

Continuing our walk we reach the tower of the Douma, a kind of watch-tower for fire, like the Seraskier in Constantinople; upon its summit is a signal apparatus, where red and black balls indicate the street in which fire has broken out.

Near by, on the same side, is the Gastiny-Dvor, a great square building with two stories of galleries, reminding me a little of the Palais-Royal, containing shops of every description and of lavish display. Then comes the Imperial Library, with curved façade and Ionic columns, and then, the Anitschkov palace, which gives its name to the neighboring bridge, with its four bronze horses, held in by grooms, and rearing upon their granite pedestals.

"This is a fair sketch of the Newsky Prospekt; but," does somebody say, "your picture is like that of a Turkish artist: there are no people in it!" Wait a little, please; I am about to enliven my view, and fill it with figures. The writer, less fortunate than the painter, can present objects only successively.

From one o'clock till three, the crowd is greatest; beside those who walk rapidly along, going about their affairs, there are many whose sole object is to see, to be seen, and to take a little exercise; their coupés or droschkys await them at a designated spot, or follow them along, in case a sudden fancy should take them to return to the carriage.

You distinguish first the officers of the Guard, in gray capote, a strap on the shoulder indicating the rank; they are almost all decorated with stars and crosses, and they wear the helmet or the military undress cap; then you observe the tchinovniks, or officials, in long redingotes plaited at the back, and gathered in by the belt; they wear, for a hat, a dark-colored cap with cockade; young men in general, who are neither in the army nor in the civil service, have paletots trimmed with a fur whose price astonishes strangers and would alarm our men of fashion. These overcoats, of the finest cloth, are lined with marten or muskrat, and have collars of beaver costing from one to three hundred rubles, the price varying in proportion to the fineness of the fur, its depth of color, and the long white hairs that it has retained. A paletot worth a thousand rubles is not unusual; some even cost more than this; it is a Russian luxury of which we know little in Paris. The proverb "Tell me your associates, and I will tell you what you are," might have a Northern version in this wise: "Tell me what furs you wear, and I will tell you how much you are worth." A man is valued according to his pelisse.

"What!"—do you say, as you read this description,— "furs so early as this, the beginning of October, in a temperature exceptionally mild, which must seem really spring-like to a man of the North!" Yes; the Russians are not such as a vain people suppose. It is imagined, that, hardened by this climate, they delight, like the polar bear, in ice and snow. No mistake could be greater; on the contrary, they are extremely susceptible to cold, and take precautions against the least inclemency of the season, which strangers, on their first visit, neglect,— sure to adopt them later, after they have been ill. If you see any one pass lightly clad, by his olive skin and his luxuriant black beard and whiskers you will recognize an Italian, a man of some southern climate, whose blood has not yet been chilled. "Take your wadded paletot, put on your overshoes, tie a scarf round your neck;"—they said to me. "But the thermometer is at 45°." Very true, but here, as in Madrid, there is a little wind, that would scarcely blow out a candle, that can extinguish a man's life. In Madrid I have worn a cloak with the thermometer at 50°, and I had no reason to refuse to put on a winter paletot in the autumn in St. Petersburg. It is wise to do at Rome what the Romans do. The paletot lined with light fur is the suitable thing then for autumn; as soon as the snow comes, you wrap yourself in your pelisse, and do not lay it aside till May.

The Venetian women never go out save in a gondola; the Russian only in a carriage: scarcely are they willing to walk a few steps along the Newsky Prospekt. Their bonnets and their fashions in dress come from Paris. Blue seems to be their favorite color, and it goes well with their fair complexions and blonde hair. Of the elegance of their figures it is impossible to judge, at least in the street, for ample pelisses of black satin or some woollen material with large plaids, wrap them from head to heel. Coquetry gives way to considerations of climate, and the prettiest feet are unhesitatingly buried in enormous *chaussures;* an Andalusian would rather die; but at St. Petersburg the phrase "to take cold" is answerable for everything. These pelisses are trimmed with sable, Siberian blue fox, and other furs, of prices most extravagant to us of the South; luxury goes to an unheard-of degree in this direction. If the rigor of the sky forbids to women anything more than a shapeless sack, be content; that sack will be made to cost as much as the most elegant toilette.

At the end of fifty paces, these languid beauties return to their carriages and go to pay visits, or drive homeward. What I have said refers to women in society, that is to say, women of rank; others, though equally rich and beautiful, are more unpretending: in Russia, rank takes the precedence at every point. Here are Germans, wives of business men, to be recognized by the Teutonic type, the gentle, dreamy air, the neat dress of more simple material; they wear talmas and basquines and mantles of shaggy cloth. Here are French women, in loud toilettes, outside garment of velvet, hat covering all the top of the head, suggestive of Mabille and the Folies-Nouvelles, here on the sidewalk of the Newsky Prospekt.

You might possibly till this moment have believed yourself on the boulevard, or the Rue Vivienne;—patience a moment; you shall see truly Russian types. Observe this man in blue caftan buttoned at the corner like a Chinese robe, gathered upon the hips into regular folds, and exquisitely neat; this is an artelchtchik, or tradesman's servant; a flat cap with a visor completes his costume; he wears the hair and beard parted like the pictures of Christ; his face is honest and intelligent. He carries bills, collects money, and fulfils commissions of various kinds demanding integrity.

Just as you are lamenting the absence of the picturesque, a nurse in the old national dress passes at your side; she is coiffed with the povoïnik, a kind of bonnet in the shape of a diadem, of red or blue velvet, with gold embroidery. The povoïnik is open or closed; being open, it designates a young girl; closed, a matron;

that worn by nurses has a crown, and from beneath the povoïnik falls the hair in two long braids. With girls, the hair is gathered into a single tress. The robe of wadded damask, with a waist just beneath the arms, and a very short skirt, resembles a tunic, and shows a second skirt of more ordinary material. The tunic is red or blue, matching the povoïnik, and is trimmed with broad gold galoon. This costume, genuinely Russian, has style and elegance when worn by a handsome woman. The grand gala dress at court festivities is made according to this pattern, and, lavishly ornamented with gold and with diamonds, it adds not a little to their splendor.

In Spain it is also a mark of elegance to have about the place a nurse wearing the costume of the *pasiega*. I used greatly to admire these handsome peasant women in the Prado or the Calle d'Alcala, with their vests of black velvet and scarlet petticoats with gold stripes. It would seem that civilization, feeling the national stamp grow faint, desires to imprint on its children the memory of it, by bringing up from some distant village a woman in the ancient dress, to be to them, as it were, the image of the mother-country.

Speaking of nurses suggests children; the transition is easy. The Russian babies are very pretty in their little blue caftans, under broad-brimmed hats like *sombreros*, adorned with the tip of a peacock's feather.

There are always some dvorniks, or *concierges*, upon the sidewalk, sweeping in summer, clearing off the ice in winter. They are seldom in their lodges, if such they have in the Parisian sense of the word; they are awake all night, and must answer the door-bell in person whenever it rings; they never dispute that it is their business to open the door at three in the morning quite as much as at three in the afternoon. They sleep anywhere, and never undress. They wear blue shirts, loose trousers, and enormous boots, exchanging this costume at the first approach of cold weather for the sheepskin, worn wrong side out.

Now and then, a boy with a sort of white apron tied round his waist by a string, emerges from the shop of some mechanic or artisan, and runs across the street to a neighboring house or shop; this is a malchtchik, or apprentice, doing an errand for his master.

The picture would still be incomplete, if I did not add some dozens of mujiks, always in greasy touloupes, who sell apples or cakes, carry along provisions in karzines (a kind of basket made of braided pine shavings), mend the wooden pavements with hatchets, or, in groups of four or six, advance with measured pace, bearing upon their heads a table, a sofa, or a piano.

You will rarely see any female mujiks; possibly they remain in the country upon the estates of their masters, possibly are employed in-doors in domestic labors. The few whom we meet have nothing specially characteristic about them. A kerchief knotted under the chin covers the head; a wadded overcoat of some cheap material, neutral color, and doubtful cleanliness, descends as far as the knee and shows a petticoat of printed calico, with coarse felt stockings and wooden shoes. They are not pretty, but they have a sad and gentle air; no flash of envy lights up their faded eyes at the sight of a lady in her fine attire; coquetry seems unknown to them. They accept their inferiority,—which no French woman ever does, be her position as humble as it may.

Further, I notice the comparatively small number of women in the streets of St. Petersburg. As in oriental countries, only men seem to have the privilege of being out of doors. In Germany, it is quite different; there the feminine population are always in the street.

I have as yet filled with figures the sidewalks only; the roadway presents a spectacle not less animated and interesting. There flows an endless stream of carriages in the most rapid motion, and to cross the Prospekt is a task not less perilous than to go from one side to the other of the boulevard between the Rue Drouot and the Rue Richelieu. It is very unusual to walk in St. Petersburg; you take a droschky if the distance be ever so short. A carriage is considered as an object, not of luxury, but of prime necessity. Small tradesmen, clerks with moderate salaries, economize in every way, and stint themselves in order to keep a careta, droschky, or sledge. To go on foot is a kind of disgrace; a Russian without a carriage is like an Arab without a horse. People might doubt his station, might take him for a mechtchanine, for a serf.

The droschky, or drojky, as it is spelled in Russia, is, *par excellence*, the national vehicle; there is nothing like it in any other country, and it merits particular description. At this very moment, here is one drawn up at the sidewalk, awaiting its master, who is paying a visit within; it seems to be here expressly to have its picture taken. This is a fashionable drojky, belonging to a young man of rank who is dainty about his equipages. The drojky is a very low, small, open carriage; it has four wheels, those of the rear not larger than the front wheels of a victoria; those of the front, the size of a wheelbarrow. Four circular springs support the body of the carriage, which has two seats, one for the coachman, the other for the master. This latter seat is round, and in elegant drojkys admit but a single person; in others, there is room for two, but so narrow that you are obliged to pass your arm about your companion, lady or gentleman. On either side two fenders of varnished leather curve above the wheels, and meeting on the side of the little carriage, which has no doors, form a step coming within a few inches of the ground.

The color of the drojky is almost always about the same. It is deep maroon with trimmings of sky-blue, or it is Russian-green with fillets of apple-green; but whatever the color selected, the shade is always very deep.

The well-stuffed seat is covered with leather or cloth of some dark tint. A Persian or a moquette rug is under the feet. There are no lanterns to the drojky, and it spins along by night without the two stars shining in front. It is the business of the pedestrian to keep out of the way, when the driver cries: "Take care!"

There is nothing prettier, more dainty, lighter, than this frail equipage, which you could pick up and carry under your arm. It seems to have come from Queen Mab's own carriage-makers.

Harnessed to this nutshell, with which he could easily leap a fence, stands, impatient and nervous, and champing his bits, a magnificent horse, which may have cost six thousand rubles, a horse of the celebrated Orlov breed, an iron-gray, high-stepping animal, the luxuriant silvery mane and tail powdered with glittering specks. He moves restlessly about, curves his neck till his head touches his chest, and paws the ground, held in with difficulty by the muscular coachman. There is nothing on him between the shafts, no tangle of harness to conceal his beauty. A few light threads, mere leather strings not half an inch in width, and caught together by little silvered or gilt ornaments, play over him without being an annoyance to him or taking anything from the perfection of his shape. The mountings of the head-stall are encrusted with little metallic scales, and there are no blinders to conceal a horse's greatest beauty, his dilating, lustrous eyeballs. Two little silver chains cross gracefully upon his forehead; the bit is covered with leather, lest the cold of the iron should harm his delicate mouth, and a simple snaffle is all that is needed to guide the noble creature. The collar, very light and simple, is the only part of the harness which attaches him to the carriage, for they use no traces. The shafts go directly to the collar, fastened to it by straps carried back and forth many times, and twisted, but having neither buckles nor rings nor metal clasps of any kind. At the point where the collar and the shafts are fastened together, are also fixed by means of straps the ends of a flexible wooden arch which rises above the horse's back like a basket-handle whose extremities are brought quite near together. This arch, called the douga, which leans a little backward, serves to keep the collar and the shafts apart, so that they do not hurt the animal, and also to suspend the reins from a hook.

The shafts are not attached to the front of the drojky, but to the axle of the forward wheels, which extends beyond the hub, passing through it, and kept in place by an exterior peg. For more strength, a trace placed on the outside goes to the knot of straps at the collar. This style of harness makes it exceedingly easy to turn, the traction operating upon the ends of the axle as upon a lever.

This is doubtless very minute; but vague descriptions describe nothing, and possibly the lover of horses in Paris or London will not be sorry to know how a fashionable drojky is built and equipped in St. Petersburg.

I have said nothing of the coachman, but a characteristic personage, and abounding in local color, is he! Coiffed with a low-crowned hat, whose brim is turned up in wings on either side, and projects over the forehead and the back of the neck; clad in a long blue or green caftan, which is closed under the left arm with five silver clasps or buttons, belted in at the waist, and spreading in folds over the hips; his muscular neck rising from his cravat, his enormous beard spreading upon his breast, his arms extended and holding one rein in each hand, he certainly has, it must be owned, a stately and majestic air,—he is quite master of the situation! The stouter he is, the higher wages he can command; if he is thin when he enters your service, and presently should grow fat, he will require increase of pay.

As they drive holding the reins with both hands, the use of the whip is unknown. The horses are animated or restrained by the voice only. Like the Spanish muleteer, the Russian coachman addresses compliments or invectives to his beasts. At one time the most tender and charming diminutives; at another, shockingly bad language, which modern decorum forbids me to translate. If the horse slackens his pace, or goes wrong in any way, a little slap with the reins on his back is enough to bring him right. The coachmen warn you to get out of the way, crying "Bériguiss! bériguiss!" If you do not obey quickly enough, they say, accentuating each syllable forcibly, "Bériguiss—sta—ch!" It is a matter of pride with coachmen belonging to good families never to raise the voice.

But our young gentleman has finished his visit, and enters his drojky. The horse sets off at a great pace, stepping so high that he touches his nose with his knees; he dances along, you might say, but this coquettish gait takes nothing from his speed.

Sometimes another horse, called a pristiajka (an off-horse), is harnessed to the drojky; he is attached only by a single rein, and gallops while his mate trots. The difficulty is to maintain these two equal and dissimilar gaits. The second horse, who appears to caper alongside, accompanying his companion for the mere pleasure of it, has something gay, free, and graceful about him which has no counterpart elsewhere.

The hired drojkys are much the same as those I have been describing, though somewhat less elegant in shape and fresh in decoration; they are driven by a coachman whose blue caftan is more or less neat, who carries his number stamped on a copper medal suspended by a leather string and habitually thrown back over his shoulder, so that the fare, during the drive, may have the number of the vehicle constantly before his eyes, and may remember it in case of need. The mode of harnessing is the same, and the little Ukraine horse, though not of so good stock, goes quite as well. There is also a long drojky, which is more ancient and more national. It is only a bench, covered with cloth, and carried upon four wheels, which you must bestride, unless you take it sideways, as a woman sits on horseback. The drojkys drive up and down, or stand, at corners of streets or squares, before wooden horse-troughs which contain hay or oats. At any hour of day or night, in whatever part of the city you may be, it is enough to cry out, "Isvochtchik!" two or three times, to bring to the spot, on a gallop, some little vehicle,—come from one knows not what quarter.

The coupés, coaches, and phaetons which are perpetually driving up and down the Newsky Prospekt, have no special peculiarity of appearance. They seem, in general, to be of English or Viennese manufacture. The horses are frequently superb and very fast. The coachman wears the caftan, and sometimes beside him is seated a kind of soldier, whose copper helmet has a ball on its point, instead of a flame, as have the real soldiers. These men wear a gray cloak, the collar edged with red or blue bands, indicating the rank of their master, general or colonel. The privilege of having a *chasseur* belongs only to the carriages of an embassy. This equipage with four horses, having a groom standing at the back, clad in ancient livery, and holding in his hand a tall, straight whip, is that of the archbishop, and, as it passes, everybody salutes.

Amid this whirl of elegant carriages, not a few very primitive carts make their appearance; the rudest rusticity is contiguous to the highest civilization. This contrast is frequent in Russia. Rospouskys made of two beams slung on axles, the wheels kept in place by pieces of wood resting against the hubs, and supported by the sides of the rude vehicle, graze the rapid phaeton glittering with varnish. The principle of the harnessing is the same as with the drojky. Only a larger arch, of grotesque colors, replaces the light bow with its graceful curve; ropes are substituted for the fine leather straps, and a mujik in his tonloupe or coarse tunic is crouched among the bales and boxes. As to the horse, all bristling with a coat that has never known the curry-comb, he shakes, as he goes, a dishevelled mane that hangs almost to the ground. House furniture is moved with teams of this kind. They enlarge them with planks, and chairs and tables travel about, their legs in the air, held in place by ropes. At a little distance, a hay-stack seems to be moving off alone, drawn by a wretched nag who is almost hidden under it. A tun full of water goes along slowly by the same process. A téléga passes at full speed, regardless of the shocks its springless axles may inflict upon the officer who sits within. How far are they going? A thousand miles or more—to the Caucasus or to Thibet, perhaps. No matter; but be sure of this, the light cart, for it is nothing better, will go at headlong pace all the way. Provided the two front wheels and the driver's seat arrive in safety, nobody will complain.

At St. Petersburg you will never see those heavy wains which five or six elephantine horses, scourged by the whip of a brutal driver, can scarcely move. The loads are very light, speed rather than draught being required of the horses. All loads which can be broken up are distributed among several teams instead of being heaped on one, as with us; they move along in company and form caravans, recalling, in the midst of a great city, the habits of locomotion of the desert.

Every civilized city owes itself omnibuses; there are a few running from the Newsky Prospekt to the more remote portions of the city; they have usually three horses. However, the preference is generally given to drojkys, for the fare is not high, while they will take you whither you please. The long drojky costs fifteen kopecks the course; the round, twenty: somewhere from twelve to sixteen cents. It is not dear; a man who walks must be very poor, or very economical.

But it is growing dark; people are hurrying home to dinner, the carriages disperse, and from the fire-tower is lifted the luminous ball that gives the signal for gas-lighting. Let us go in.

VII.

WINTER.—THE NEVA.

WITHIN a few days the temperature has grown perceptibly colder. We have had a frost every night, and the north-east wind has swept away the last red leaves in the Admiralty Square. Winter, although tardy for this climate, is at last on his way from the polar regions, and by the shudder of all nature we are made conscious of his approach. Nervous people feel that vague discomfort which is caused to delicate organizations by the presence of snow in the air, and the isvochtchiks—who have no nerves, it is true, but who possess, by way of compensation, an atmospheric instinct infallible as that of the animal—raise their noses to this sky blurred with one broad, yellowish-gray cloud, and gladly make ready their sledges. Still the snow does not come, and people accost one another with critical observations upon the weather, but in a style quite different from that in which the Philistines of other countries utter their meteorological commonplaces. At St. Petersburg they complain that the weather is not severe enough, and, looking at the thermometer, they say: "How's this! only five or six degrees below the freezing-point! Decidedly, climates are becoming unsettled!" And old people tell you about those fine winters when they used to *enjoy* a temperature of from 25° to 35° below zero steadily, from October to May.

One morning, however, on raising my window-shade, I saw through the double glass, humid with nocturnal exhalations, a roof of dazzling whiteness against a pale blue sky, across which shot the slanting rays of the sun, gilding a few rosy clouds, and some little feathers of yellowish smoke. Salient portions of the palace opposite were sharply outlined with silver, like those drawings on tinted paper that are brightened with watercolor touches of white; and over all the ground was spread, like wadding, a thick layer of virgin snow, where there was as yet no imprint, save from the starred feet of the pigeons, quite as numerous in St. Petersburg as in Venice and Constantinople. The flock, —splashes of grayish-blue color on the immaculate white background,—were hopping about, fluttering their wings, and seemed to await with more impatience than usual, in front of the underground shop of the provision dealer, the distribution of corn which he makes them every morning with the charity of a brahman. In truth, though the snow was very like a table-cloth, the birds did not find their table set; and the pigeons were hungry. What joy, therefore, when the grocer opened his door! The winged band swooped fearlessly down upon him, and for an instant he disappeared in a feathery cloud. A handful or two of grain, flung off to a distance, restored to him a little more liberty, and he stood in the doorway, smiling to see his little friends eat with such glad avidity, making the snow fly left and right. You will readily believe that a few uninvited sparrows profited by this boon,—saucy parasites, —and did not suffer a crumb to be wasted;—after all, everybody must live.

The city awoke. Mujiks going out to buy food, their karzines on their heads, plunged into the snow with their great boots, and left tracks as of elephants' feet. A few women, a kerchief tied under the chin, wrapped in quilted paletot, traversed the street with a lighter step, bordering their petticoats with silvery mica. Gentlemen in long cloaks, the collar turned up over their ears, were stepping airily along on their way to their places of business; and suddenly appeared in sight the first sledge, driven by Winter in person, under the figure of an isvochtchik, coiffed with a four-sided red velvet cap, clad in a blue caftan lined with sheepskin, and having an old bear-skin across his knees.

Waiting for a fare, he was sitting on the back seat of his sledge and looking idly about; with his great leather mittens he held the reins, which lay across the box, and the little Kasan horse trotted along, almost sweeping the snow with its mane. Never since my arrival in St. Petersburg had I felt so distinctly that it was Russia: it was like a sudden revelation, and a crowd of things, which till then had remained obscure, suddenly became clear to me.

As soon as I had perceived the snow, I had dressed in all haste; at sight of the sledge, I put on my pelisse and my overshoes, and a minute later I was in the street, calling: "Isvochtchik! Isvochtchik!"

The sledge drew up by the sidewalk, the isvochtchik stepped into his place, and I inserted myself into the box filled with hay, carefully folding over the skirts of my pelisse, and drawing the skin covering over me.

The construction of the sledge is very simple. Imagine two bars, or runners, of polished iron, the anterior end curved upward like the point of a Chinese shoe. On these runners, a light iron brace makes fast the driver's seat and the box in which the passenger is seated; this box is ordinarily painted mahogany color. A sort of dash-board, curving up and backwards like a swan's breast, gives grace to the sledge, and protects the driver from the particles of snow which the frail and rapid equipage throws up before him like silver foam. The shafts are attached to the collar, as in the drojky, and the traction comes upon the runners. All this weighs nothing, and goes like the wind, especially when the snow has been hardened by frost, and the roads are well trodden.

Our destination is the Anischkov Bridge, at the other end of the Newsky Prospekt. This point occurred to me only because it would give a long drive, for, at this hour of the morning, I had nothing to say to the four bronze horses that decorate its abutments; then, too, I was very glad to see the Prospekt all powdered with white, in full winter toilette.

It is incredible how much the street had gained by it; this broad strip of silver, unrolled as far as eye could reach, between the two lines of magnificent buildings, was a wonderful picture. The colors of the houses,—rose, yellow, fawn-color, warm gray,—which might seem in bad taste on ordinary occasions, became most harmonious in tone, relieved in this way by sparkling fillets and specks of brilliant white. The Cathedral of Our Lady of Kazan had undergone a most pleasing change; it had coiffed its Italian cupola with a cap of Russian snow, outlined all its cornices and its Corinthian capitals with pure white, and placed upon the terrace of its semi-circular colonnade, a balustrade of massive silver like that which adorns its iconostase, and the steps which led to its portico had a carpet of ermine, fine, fleecy, splendid enough for a czarina to tread with her golden slippers.

The statues of Barclay de Tolly and Kutusov seemed to rejoice upon their pedestals that the sculptor Orlovski, taking into consideration the climate, had not attired them as Romans, but had, on the contrary, accorded to them substantial bronze cloaks. Unhappily, however, he had not given them hats, and the snow ruthlessly powdered their bare heads with its cold *maréchale* powder.

Near Our Lady of Kazan, the Catherine Canal crosses, under a bridge, the Newsky Prospekt; it was completely frozen over, and the snow lay in drifts at angles of the quay, and on the steps leading down to it. One night had sufficed to make all solid. The floating ice which the Neva had been bringing down for a few days had caught, and surrounded with a transparent mould the hulls of the vessels ranged in their docks.

Before house-doors, the dvorniks armed with broad

shovels, were clearing the sidewalks and disposing the snow upon the road, like the heaps of small stones upon a macadamized pavement. From all sides sledges were making their appearance, and—strange to say—the droschkys, so numerous the evening before, had vanished entirely; you could not see a single one in the street. It appeared that, between one night and the next morning, Russia had returned to the most primitive condition of social life, that in which the use of wheels had not yet been invented. The rosposniks, the télégas, carts of every description, glided along on runners. The mujiks, harnessed with a small rope, dragged their karsines on microscopic sledges. The low-crowned, broad hats had all suffered eclipse, and velvet caps appeared in their stead.

When the track is good and the snow is frozen hard, an immense economy of force is produced by the use of runners. A horse can draw without difficulty, and at twice the rate of speed, a weight three times as great as he could under ordinary conditions. In Russia, during six months out of the year, the snow is like a universal railway, whose white tracks extend in all directions, wherever you may wish to go. This iron road made of silver, has the advantage of costing nothing per mile, a most economical rate, to which the best engineers will never attain; this is, perhaps, the reason why genuine railways have drawn as yet but two or three furrows across the immense territory of Russia. I came home much pleased with my expedition, and after having breakfasted and reduced to ashes a cigar—delicious sensation in St. Petersburg, where smoking in the street is prohibited under penalty of a ruble's fine!—I went out on foot, to enjoy still further the results of this scene-shifting which had taken place in the night. The great river, which I had seen so lately spreading its broad waves wrinkled by their perpetual fluctuation, changing their tint at every instant with new play of light upon their surface, furrowed by the never-ceasing motion of tug-boats, barges, ships, skiffs, and flowing down into the Gulf of Finland, itself as broad as a gulf, had totally changed its appearance; to animation the most lively, had succeeded the immobility of death. The snow lay, a thick covering, over the cemented ice-blocks, and between the granite quays stretched away, as far as the eye could see, a white valley whence rose here and there, the black tops of masts above half-buried vessels. Stakes and fir-branches indicated holes which are made in the ice for the purpose of drawing water, and mark out from one shore to the other, the road that may be safely followed; for already people on foot are crossing, and they are preparing slopes of planking for sledges and carriages; these slopes, however, are as yet barricaded, the ice not being solid.

The better to command the view, I went out upon the bridge of the Annunciation, more commonly designated as the Nicholas Bridge; of this I have already said a few words in speaking of my arrival in St. Petersburg. This time I had leisure to examine in detail the beautiful chapel raised in honor of St. Nicholas the Thaumaturgist, at the point where the two movable parts of the bridge are connected with each other. It is an exquisite little building, in that Byzantine-Muscovite style which is so well suited to the orthodox Greek ritual, and which I should be glad to see generally adopted in Russia. It consists of a sort of pavilion of bluish granite, flanked at each corner by a column with a composite capital, encircled by a moulding in the middle, and grooved in flutings, not straight, but deflected at top and bottom. The base, which is double, and supports the pilaster of an arch, is hewn diamond-shaped. Three bays open upon three sides of the building, whose rear wall within is resplendent with a mosaic of precious stones, representing the patron saint of the chapel, draped in his dalmatic, a golden halo behind his head, a book open in his hand, and surrounded by celestial figures in adoration. Iron lattice-work, richly wrought, closes the two lateral bays; that of the front, at which ends a flight of steps, gives access to the chapel. The cornice, covered with inscriptions in the Slavonic language, punctuated with stars, has for its acroteria a series of ornaments in the shape of hearts with their points upward, alternating with triangular notches. The roof, a little pyramid with a nervure at each angle, is entirely covered with golden scales. It bears on its summit one of those Muscovite belfries, which can only be likened to a tulip bulb, with gilt stars, and surmounted by a Greek cross, whose foot is set in a crescent, which is itself supported upon a ball. These gilded roofs have a strange charm for me, especially when the snow has strewn them with its silver filings and gives them the look of old silver-gilt whose gilding is partly worn off. The tones are incredibly rare and soft, effects absolutely unknown elsewhere.

A lamp burns, day and night, before the picture of the saint. The isvochtchik, as he drives past, gathers the reins in one hand and raises his cap, making the sign of the cross with the other. Mujiks prostrate themselves upon the snow. Soldiers and officers say a prayer, standing bareheaded and motionless, with an air of rapt devotion, meritorious when the thermometer is nearly at zero; women go up the steps and enter, to kiss the feet of the sacred figure, with many genuflections. It is not the common people only, as you might suppose, who do this, but also persons of the higher classes; no one crosses the bridge without some sign of respect, a salutation, at least, to its patron saint, and the kopecks rain into the two boxes placed one on either side of the chapel. But let us return to the Neva.

At the right, if you look towards the city, you will observe, a little behind the English quay, the five pointed bell-towers of the church of the Horse-Guards, their gold slightly frosted with white; farther away, the dome of St. Isaac's, like the diamond-starred mitre of some magian king; the glittering needle of the Admiralty; and a corner of the Winter Palace. In the background, and more to the left, springs from an island in the river, the bold, slender spire of the church of St. Peter and St. Paul, rising above the low walls of the fortress, its golden angel sparkling against the rose-streaked turquoise sky. On the left, looking up the river, the horizon is not so richly notched with gold; there are fewer churches on the left side, and they are more remote from the river, quite in the interior of Vassili-Ostrov, as this quarter of the city is called. But the palaces and other elegant buildings which border the quay present far-stretching, stately lines of frontage, felicitously accentuated by the snow. Just before the bridge at the Exchange, the Academy, a grand, classic edifice, containing within its square a circular court, leads down to the river by a colossal staircase, ornamented with two great human-headed Egyptian sphinxes,—sphinxes, surprised and shuddering to find caparisons of snow upon their red granite backs! From the centre of the square springs the obelisk of Roumianzov.

If you cross the river and go up, passing the Winter Palace and the Hermitage, as far as the Marble Palace, then turn just before reaching the Troitski Bridge, you will discover a new aspect well worth observation. The river divides into two arms, the Great and the Little Neva, enclosing an island whose point—opposed to the current, when the water is flowing—is decorated in architectural and imposing fashion.

At each corner of the esplanade which borders the island on this side, rises a sort of tower or rostral column of red granite, with prows of ships and anchors in bronze, surmounted by a tripod or lantern of the same material, which stands on a base, against which seated figures are leaning. Between these two columns, whose effect is fine, stands the Exchange, which is, like the Bourse in Paris, a faint suggestion of the Parthenon.

a parallelogram surrounded by columns. Only here they are Doric instead of being Corinthian, and the main body of the building appears above the top of the colonnade which surrounds it, presenting a triangular roof like a great pediment, on which opens a large arched window, half concealed by a sculptured group placed on the cornice of the portico. At the right and left, the University and Custom-House, buildings of regular and simple architecture, balance each other. The two towers, with their giant outlines, relieve the cold and classic effect of these buildings. In the little Neva are crowded, for winter quarters, vessels of various descriptions, their unrigged masts drawing fine lines upon the background. Finally, to this hasty sketch on pearl-gray paper, add some touches of intense white, and you will have a very fair sketch to paste into your album.

To-day I shall go no farther; it is not warm on these quays and bridges, where a wind is blowing that has come straight from the pole. Everybody accelerates his pace. The two lions placed at the *débarcadère* of the imperial palace seem to find their paws benumbed with cold, and with difficulty to retain the ball which each holds with his claws.

To-morrow, on the English quay and the Newsky Prospekt, there is to be a very Longchamps of private sledges and open vehicles. It is certainly surprising that in a city where the thermometer is often ten or twelve degrees below zero, they go out so seldom in close carriages. It is only at the last extremity, sensitive to cold as they are, that the Russians take refuge in the careta. But the pelisse is a defence against cold which they so well know how to use, that with its aid they can laugh at temperature severe enough to freeze the mercury in the bulb. At most they only need to put on one sleeve, and hold the garment firmly together, inserting the hand into a little pocket made in the front. To wear a pelisse is an art which you do not acquire in a day. The Russian, by an imperceptible motion, gives it play, crosses it, doubles and clasps it around his body like the cocoon of a silkworm or the wrappings of a mummy. The fur retains for some hours the temperature of the room in which it has been hanging, and completely isolates you from the outside air; in the pelisse you have as much heat out of doors as in the house, and if, renouncing the vain elegance of the hat, you put on the wadded or fur cap, there is nothing to prevent you from turning up the collar, which then has its fur inside. The nape of your neck, your occiput, your ears, are all in shelter. Only your nose, pointing outwards through two furry screens, is exposed to the inclemencies of the season; but should it begin to grow white, some charitable passer-by will notify you, and on rubbing it with a handful of snow, it will quickly resume its natural red. Besides, these little accidents happen only in winters exceptionally severe. Some old dandies, rigid followers of the London and Paris fashions, not able to make up their minds to the cap, have hats made for them with no rim behind, merely a visor in front, for sometimes it is impossible to keep the collar down. The sharp wind will make your bare neck feel the edge of its icy blade, quite as unpleasant as the contact of real steel with the neck of a patient.

The most delicate women do not fear going out in an open carriage, and breathing for an hour this icy but refreshing and healthful air, which is a relief to the lungs, oppressed by the hothouse temperature within doors. All you can see are faces rosy with cold: the rest is a confusion of pelisses and muffs, out of which you could hardly disentangle a human figure. Over the knees extends a great bear-skin, white or black, trimmed with scarlet. The carriage is like a sort of boat heaped with furs, whence emerge two or three smiling heads.

Confusing the Dutch with the Russian sledges, I had

imagined something quite different from the reality. It is in Holland that those fantastic sledges glide over the frozen canals, figures of swans, dragons, sea-shells, contorted, panelled, gilded, painted by Hondekoeter or Vost, whose panels have been carefully preserved,— drawn by horses wearing *pompons*, plumes, and bells, but more frequently pushed by the hand of a skater. The Russian sledge is not a plaything, a matter of luxury and amusement, but an object of daily use and of the first utility. No change is made in its form, and the gentleman's private sledge is similar in every point, in the principle of its structure, to that of the isvochtchik. Only the iron runners are more polished and of more graceful curve; the box is of mahogany or wicker-work; the cushions are of wadded morocco; the apron is varnished leather; a foot-muff replaces the hay, an expensive robe the old skin gnawed by mites; the luxury consists in the coachman's attire, the beauty of the horse, and the speed at which he goes.

There is often a second horse harnessed to the sledge, but the height of style is the troïka, a vehicle eminently Russian, full of local color, and very picturesque. The troïka is a great sledge which holds four persons, sitting face to face, and a driver besides; it is harnessed with three horses. The one in the middle, who is in the shafts, has the collar and the wooden arch, the donga, rising above his withers; the two others are attached to the sledge by an exterior strap, and by another strap, loosely, to the collar of the thill-horse. Four reins suffice for the three animals, the two outsiders having only one rein apiece. Nothing is more charming than to see a troïka spin along the Newsky Prospekt at the hour of promenade. The thill-horse trots, stepping straight ahead, the other two gallop and pull fan-wise. One of these ought to have a wild, excited, indomitable air, to hold up his head and seem to start aside and kick: this one is called "the fury." The other should shake his mane, arch his neck, curvet and go sideways, touch his knees with the end of his nose, dance, and fling himself about at the caprice of the moment: this is the "coquet." These three noble steeds with metal chains on their head-stalls, with harness light as threads, spangled here and there with delicate gilt ornaments, are suggestive of those antique horses upon triumphal arches, drawing bronze chariots to which they are in no way attached. They seem to sport and gambol before the troïka entirely at will. The horse in the middle alone has a slightly serious air, like some wiser friend between two gay companions. You will easily suppose that it is no trifling matter to maintain this apparent disorder in the midst of great speed, each animal preserving a different gait. Sometimes the "fury" plays his part in good earnest, or the "coquet" takes a fancy to roll in the snow.— There is needed, therefore, in driving a troïka, the most consummate skill. But what a charming amusement! I am surprised no gentleman-jockey in London or Paris has taken a fancy to it. It is to be considered, however, that snow is not abundant enough in England or France.

The sleighing remains good, and, after a few days, coupés and coaches appear on runners. These vehicles, taken off the wheels, present a peculiar appearance— unfinished carriages, you would say, placed on trestles; the sledge has infinitely more grace and style.

At sight of pelisses, sledges, troïkas, carriages on runners, and the thermometer going two or three degrees lower every morning, I thought winter definitely established. But prudent old heads, habituated to the climate, performed sceptical mutations, saying: "No, this is not winter yet." And truly, this was not winter, the true winter, the Russian winter, the winter of the Arctic Circle, as I saw it some weeks later.

VIII.

WINTER.

THE weather this year has fallen short of Russian tradition, and Winter has shown himself as capricious as in Paris. Now a wind from the pole freezes his nose and makes his cheeks the color of wax, and now his mantle of ice melts under the south-west wind, and drips away in rain. To sparkling snow succeeds grayish snow; to a road creaking under the runner like powdered marble, a muddy slough worse than the macadam of the boulevards; then suddenly, in a single night, the capillary vein of spirits-of-wine goes down twenty-five degrees in the thermometer by the window; a new white mantle covers the roofs, and the droschkys disappear.

At from two to ten degrees below zero, the winter becomes characteristic and poetical; it is as rich in effects as the most splendid summer. But thus far, it has lacked poet or painter.

We have been having, for a few days, truly Russian cold, and I propose to note some of its aspects; for, at this strength, cold is visible, and you see it perfectly, although you do not feel it through the double windows of your well-heated apartment.

The sky becomes clear, and of a tint of blue which has no resemblance to the azure of the South—a blue of steel, a blue of ice, of a rare and charming tone which no palette, not even that of Aïvasovski, has ever reproduced. The light is brilliant, but it is not warm, and the icy sun reddens the cheeks of a few little rosy clouds. The diamonded snow scintillates; it sparkles like Parian marble, and grows twice as white under the frost which makes it hard. The trees, covered with crystallized rime, resemble great spreading ramifications of quicksilver, or the metallic splendors of an enchanted garden.

Draw on your pelisse, turn up the collar, pull your fur cap down to your eyebrows, and hail the first isvochtchik who passes; he will drive up quickly, and bring his sledge close to the sidewalk. However young he may be, his beard will be perfectly white. His breath condensed in icicles around his face, which is purple with cold, gives him the aspect of a patriarch. His stiffened locks scourge his cheek-bones like icy serpents; and the fur which he lays across your knees is sown with a million little white globules.

You are off; the air, keen, penetrating, icy, but salubrious, stings your face; the horse, heated by the rapidity of his motion, breathes out smoke like a fabled dragon, and from his reeking sides rises a little cloud of vapor which hangs about him. You notice, in passing, horses of other isvochtchiks standing to be fed; the sweat has frozen upon them; they are actually encrusted with ice, as a sugared almond with sugar. As soon as they are again in motion, this pellicle breaks; it melts or falls off, to be renewed at the next pause. These alternations, which would ruin an English horse in a week, have no bad effect upon the health of these hardy little animals. No matter how cold it is, only the most expensive horses are blanketed, and instead of those leather caparisons, embroidered in the corners with armorial devices, usual with us and in England, they merely throw over the smoking flanks of their blood-horses a Persian or Smyrna carpet of brilliant hues.

The caretas, which glide about on runners, have their glasses coated thick with ice, which prevents your being seen, but also prevents your seeing. If Cupid did not shiver in a temperature like this, he would find as much mystery in the caretas of St. Petersburg as in the gondolas of Venice.

They have begun to drive upon the river; the ice, two or three feet thick, in spite of some temporary thaws which melt the snow, will not break up until spring; it is strong enough to bear heavy wagons or even artillery. Pine branches designate the roads to follow and the points to be avoided. At certain places the ice is cut out, to give an opportunity of drawing up water, which is still flowing under this crystal floor. The water, warmer than the atmosphere, smokes through these apertures like a boiling caldron, but this is only by comparison, and it would not be wise to trust to its warmth.

In walking on the English quay, or on the river itself, it is curious to see the fish taken out from the tanks in which they are kept alive; when the scoop brings them up and they are thrown palpitating on the planks, they fling themselves about, writhing for a moment, but soon are still, stiffened, and, so to speak, are imprisoned in a transparent casing; the water with which they were wet has suddenly congealed upon them.

In this intense cold, freezing is marvellously sudden; place a bottle of champagne between the sashes of the double window, and in five minutes it will be iced better than in any cooler. Pardon a personal incident: I will not abuse your permission. Carried away by the force of habit, one day I had lighted an excellent Havana just at the moment of going out for a walk. In the door-way, the prohibition against smoking in the streets of St. Petersburg, and the fine of a ruble, suddenly recurred to me; and yet to throw away an excellent cigar after only two or three whiffs is a hard thing for a smoker. As I was going but a few steps, I concealed it in my hand. To *carry* a cigar is not against the law. When I opened my hand again, in the vestibule of my friend's house, the end moist from my lips had become a bit of ice, while at the other the generous *puro* was yet smoking.

As yet, however, it has been only six or eight degrees below zero; this is not the "fine cold weather," the "splendid cold weather," which comes usually by Epiphany. The Russians complain of the mild winter, and say that the climate is deteriorating. They have not yet deigned to light the great piles of wood prepared under wrought-iron pavilions, in front of the Imperial Theatre, and of the Winter Palace, at which the coachmen gather to keep warm while waiting for their masters; it is too mild. And yet a shivery Parisian cannot help feeling a certain arctic and polar impression, when, on coming out from the opera or the ballet, he sees in the dazzling, cold moonlight, in the great square white with snow, the line of private carriages, their coachmen powdered with mica, their horses fringed with silver, their lamps shining faint through frosted glass; and it is not without many anxious fears lest he freeze by the way, that he confides himself to his sledge. But his pelisse is thoroughly impregnated with heat, and keeps the atmosphere about him warm. If he lives at the Malaia Morskoia, or upon the Newsky Prospekt, in a direction which requires him to go near St. Isaac's, let him not forget to cast, in passing, a glance at the church. Pure white lines bring out sharply the great architectural divisions, and upon the cupola, whose outline is blurred by the darkness, there gleams, at the most convex point, one scintillating scale, just facing the moon, who seems to gaze at herself in this mirror of gold. This luminous point has a brilliancy so intense, you would take it for a lighted lamp. All the lustre of the dome is concentrated there. The effect is truly magical. There is nothing more beautiful than this great temple of gold and bronze and granite, standing on a carpet of ermine without its spots, in the blue radiance of a winter moon!

Can it be that they propose to construct, as in the

famous winter of 1740, a palace of ice, that long files of sleds are transporting these enormous blocks of water congealed into hewn stone, transparent as diamond, well suited for the walls of a temple, raised to the mysterious Genius of the Pole? By no means; it is only the supply for the ice-houses; they are providing for summer, cutting from the Neva, at the most favorable period, these great cubes of crystal, with their sapphire gleams, of which each sled carries but a single one. The drivers seat themselves on these blocks, or lean against them as if they were cushions, and when the file, hindered in the crowded streets, stands still, the horses bite, with a truly Northern greediness, at the block of ice which happens to be in front of them.

Notwithstanding all this ice and snow and frost, when a party to the Islands is proposed to you, accept without undue anxiety concerning your nose and ears! If you have the weakness to set store by these cartilages, is there not fur enough to keep them safe?

The troïka, the great sledge with three horses and seats for five persons, is at the door. Make haste to go down. With her feet in a bear-skin *chancelière*, wrapped to the chin in the satin pelisse lined with sable, pressing to her breast the wadded muff, the lowered veil already spangled with a thousand brilliant specks, your fair companion only waits for you, that the great fur covering may be buckled down at its four sides, and that the impatient horses may have leave to start. You will not be cold; two beautiful eyes can warm the iciest temperature!

In summer, the Islands are the Bois de Boulogne, the Auteuil, the Folie-St.-James of St. Petersburg. In winter they scarcely deserve the name of islands. The canals freeze, they are concealed by snow, and the islands become a part of the mainland. Through the cold season, there is but one element left, and that is, ice.

You have crossed the Neva, and passed beyond the

last avenue of Vassili Ostrov. The character of the buildings changes; the houses, of fewer stories in height, are separated from each other by gardens which are enclosed, as in Holland, with board fences. Whichever way you look, wood has taken the place of stone, or, rather, of brick; streets become roads, and you drive along beside a sheet of snow, spotless and perfectly level; it is a canal. Along the edge of the road, little guideposts, designed to secure travellers against losing their way in this white wilderness, look in the distance like kobolds or gnomes, coiffed with tall caps of white felt, and wrapped in narrow brown cloaks. Some little bridges of a single arch, whose beams are faintly outlined where the snow has been heaped above them by the road, are all that indicate that what is below is water, frozen solid and hidden from sight. Soon appears a great pine forest, on whose edge are restaurants and tea-houses, for this is a famous resort for pleasure-parties, especially in the evening, though the temperature be severe enough to freeze the mercury in its bulb.

Nothing is finer, stretching away between the black curtains of the pine woods, than these broad, white avenues, where the scarcely perceptible track made by the runners is like the scratch of a diamond upon ground glass. The wind has shaken down from the branches the snow which fell a few days ago, and there remains of it only here and there a brilliant touch upon the sombre verdure, like the high lights placed by a skilful painter. The great trunks of the trees reach up like columns, and justify the title of "Nature's Cathedral,"—which persons of a romantic taste have given to the woods.

When the snow is one or two feet deep, a person on foot becomes an impossibility; all the way down the long avenue, there are not to be seen more than three or four mujiks, wrapped in their toulonpes, and plunging with their boots, of felt or of leather, deep into the white, powdery mass. About as many black dogs, or dogs that seem black by contrast, run,—tracing circles like the poodle of Faust,—or accost one another with the signs of canine free-masonry common all the world over. I mention this trifling detail, for it demonstrates the rarity of dogs at St. Petersburg, since one finds them worth noticing.

This part of the Islands is called Krestovsky, and it contains a charming village of Swiss cottages, occupied during the summer by a colony of families, who are, for the most part, German. The Russians excel in working in wood, and carve in pine quite as well as do the Swiss and Tyrolese. They make from this material exquisite ornaments of all sorts, executed on the impulse of the moment with knife and saw. The cottages of Krestovsky, constructed in the Swiss-Russian style, must be delightful summer residences. A great gallery, a sort of open room, occupies the whole lower floor in the front of the house. Here they pass their time in the June and July days that have no end, living among their flowers and shrubs. Hither they bring their pianos, tables, sofas,—to enjoy the luxury of life in the open air, after having been for eight months shut up as in a hothouse. In the first five days after the ice breaks up in the Neva, the migration becomes general. Long trains of wagons loaded with furniture set forth from St. Petersburg for the Island villas. As soon as the days begin to shorten again, and the evenings to grow cold, they return to the city, and the cottages are shut up till the following year; but they are none the less picturesque for that, under the snow which changes their lace-work of wood into silver filigree.

If you go on farther, you will soon come out into an extensive clearing, where rise what are called in France, Russian mountains, and in Russia, mountains of ice. Russian mountains were the rage in Paris about the time of the Restoration. There were some constructed at Belleville and in other public gardens; but the difference of climate required a different construction.

Cars with wheels ran down in steep grooves, and went up again to a platform not so high as the point of departure, impelled by the momentum acquired in the descent. Accidents were not rare, for sometimes the little vehicle ran off the track; so, after a time, this amusement was relinquished as dangerous. The ice-mountains of St. Petersburg are surmounted by a light pavilion with a platform, to which the ascent is by flights of wooden stairs. The slope consists of planks, bordered by a raised edge and supported by beams and posts, over which, at intervals, water is poured, which, freezing, makes a slide as smooth as glass. The corresponding pavilion has a separate track, so that there is no danger of collision. The descent is made usually by three or four persons together, who are seated on a sled, which is guided by a man on skates standing up behind it; or else a solitary individual dashes down alone upon a little seat which he directs with his foot or hand, or with a long stick. Now and then some one has the courage to launch himself head foremost, lying flat on his breast, or in some other position seemingly dangerous, but really quite without risk. The Russians are very adroit in this eminently national amusement, to which they are accustomed from childhood; the rapid motion through the cold air gives them delight—a thing incomprehensible at first to one coming from a milder climate, but which he soon learns to understand.

Often, on coming out from the theatre or from a party, when the snow glistens like powdered marble, and the moon shines clear and icy, or, in the absence of the moon, the stars have that scintillating brilliancy which the frosty air occasions, instead of thinking of a return to their warm, well-lighted, comfortable dwellings, a little party of young men and women, well wrapped in furs, drive out to have supper at the Islands. They take a troïka, and the rapid equipage starts off with tinkling bells, raising a silvery dust. They wake up the sleeping tavern, lamps are lighted, the samovar is set heating, the Veuve Cliquot champagne is iced, and dishes of caviare, ham, sliced herring, *chaud-froids* of partridge, and small cakes are set on table. They nibble a bit, touch the lips to many different glasses, laugh, joke, smoke; then, for dessert, rush down the ice-mountains, lighted by mujiks holding lanterns; finally, return to the city at two or three in the morning, enjoying with keenest zest, in the whirlwind of motion, and in the sharp, pure, healthy air of the night, the very luxury of cold.

Let Méry, who will have nobody speak of "a fine, frosty day,"—maintaining that frost is always ugly,—shiver, and put on an additional overcoat as he reads this page, bristling with icicles! Yes, cold is a luxury, a new kind of intoxication, a kind of white vertigo, which I—a shiverer *par excellence*—even I, begin to enjoy like a native of the North!

If my reader's fingers are not frost-bitten under this icy description of the Russian winter, and he has yet courage left to brave with me still further rigors of the thermometer, let him come, after we have had a large glass of very hot tea, and take a walk upon the Neva, to visit an encampment of Samoyeds who have established themselves quite in the middle of the river, as being the only place in St. Petersburg cool enough for them. These polar creatures are like white bears. A temperature of four or five degrees above zero is quite like spring to them, and makes them pant with the heat. Their migrations are most irregular, obeying caprices or reasons unknown. For several years they have failed to put in an appearance, and I esteem it one of the lucky incidents of my journey that they have come during my sojourn in the city of the czars.

We will go down on to the river by the descent at the Admiralty, in the trodden, slippery snow, not without casting a glance at the Peter the Great of Falconnet, whom the frost has coiffed with a white peruke, and whose bronze horse had need be sharp-shod to keep his balance on the block of Finland granite which serves him as a pedestal.

The inquisitive group which has gathered around the hut of the Samoyeds forms a black circle on the white snow-covered surface of the Neva. I slip in between a mujik in his touloupe and a soldier in a gray capote, and, over a woman's shoulder, get a look into the tent made of skins stretched by pickets driven into the ice, and resembling a great paper horn with its point in the air. A low opening, through which one could enter only by going on all fours, allows me to see indistinctly in the darkness bundles of furs, which, perchance, are men or women—one could not say which. Outside, some skins are hung on ropes; snow-shoes are scattered about upon the ice; and a Samoyed, standing by a sledge, lends himself complacently to the ethnographic investigations of the crowd. He is clad in a sack of skin, the hair inwards, to which is fitted a hood, with an aperture made for the face, as in those knitted caps they call *passemontagnes*, or as a helmet without a visor. Coarse gloves, having only the thumbs separate, and covering the sleeves so as to leave no passage for the air, and boots of white felt, tied on with thongs, complete his costume; inelegant, doubtless, but hermetically sealed from cold, and, besides, not lacking character; the color is that of the skin itself, dressed by some primitive process. The face which is framed in this hood—tanned, reddened by the air—has prominent cheek-bones, a flattened nose, a wide mouth, steel-gray eyes, with light lashes; not ugly, and with a sad, gentle, intelligent expression.

While in St. Petersburg, these Samoyeds earn a little by charging visitors a few kopecks a trip for excursions upon the Neva in their sledges drawn by reindeer. The sledge, which is very light, has but a single seat, covered by a ragged piece of fur, on which sits the passenger. The Samoyed, standing at the side, on one of the wooden runners, guides the team by means of a stick, with which he touches the reindeer who happens to lag, or who is required to change his direction. The team is composed of three animals abreast, or of four, in two couples. It is strange and droll to see these pretty, delicate creatures, with their dainty limbs and their stag's horns, run with so much docility, and draw loads. The reindeer go very fast, or, rather, seem to go very fast, for their movements are prompt and rapid in the extreme; but they are small, and I think that a trotting-horse of the Orlov breed would distance them without difficulty, especially if the race were prolonged. However, nothing is more graceful than these light equipages, as they describe great circles upon the Neva —flying off and then returning to the point of departure, scarcely making any impression upon the icy surface. Those who understand the subject say that the reindeer are not seen at their best, because it is too warm for them (twelve or fourteen degrees above zero)! In fact, one of the poor creatures, on being unharnessed, seemed to be suffocating; and, to restore her, they covered her with snow.

These sledges and these reindeer carried my imagination away into their polar country with a kind of whimsical nostalgia. A strange passion for cold seized upon me—who have spent my life in seeking the sun! It was the spell of the North; and had not important work retained me at St. Petersburg, I should have gone away with the Samoyeds. What delight to fly with all speed toward the pole with its crown of auroras—first, through pine forests weighed down with snow; then, through half-buried birches; then, through the white, spotless immensity, over the sparkling snow,—strange region, by its silvery tint suggesting a journey across the lunar surface,—and in an atmosphere, keen, cutting, icy as steel, wherein nothing, not even death, can grow corrupt! I should have been glad to live for a few days under that tent varnished by the frost, half-buried in the snow which the reindeer scratch up with their feet, to find under it some small, infrequent moss. Luckily, the Samoyeds were off, one fine morning, and, going down to the river to see them again, I found nothing but the grayish circle marking where their hut had stood. With them, the spell vanished.

Since we are upon the Neva, let us notice the singular aspect which is given to it by these cubes of ice, cut from its thick-frozen crust, and left lying here and there, like blocks of hewn stone, waiting to be removed. You might fancy they had been working a crystal or diamond quarry. These transparent cubes take strange, prismatic tints, as the light traverses them, and put on all the colors of the solar spectrum; in some places where they lie heaped up, they suggest a fairy palace in ruins, especially at evening, when the sun is setting in a sky of golden green, streaked at the horizon with bands of carmine. These are effects astonishing to the eye, and which the painter dares not render, lest he be taxed with exaggeration or falsehood. Imagine a long, snowy valley, formed by the bed of a river, with rosy lights and blue shadows, strewn with colossal diamonds blazing like chandeliers,—the valley terminating with the deep red line of the horizon; to heighten the effect, in the foreground, some boat held in the ice, some pedestrian or sledge crossing from one quay to the other.

After nightfall, if you look down from the side of the fortress, you will see, stretching across the river, two parallel lines of stars; it is the light from lamp-posts erected in the ice, where the bridge of boats of Troizky has been taken up; for the Neva, as soon as it is frozen over, becomes a second Newsky Prospekt for St. Petersburg: it is like a main artery of the city. We, of temperate regions, accustomed to see only floating ice in our rivers even in the severe seasons, can hardly escape a slight feeling of anxiety when we traverse, in a carriage or sledge, an immense river, whose deep waters are flowing silently under the crystal floor, which might give way, and then close over you like an English trapdoor! But the perfect tranquillity of the Russians reassures you; enormous weights, indeed, would be required to break this layer of ice, two or three feet in thickness, and the snow which covers it gives it the appearance of a plain. Nothing distinguishes the river from the solid ground save where, along the great walls of the quays, winter a few scattered vessels, caught unexpectedly in the ice.

The Neva is a power at St. Petersburg; they do honor to it, and bless its waters with great pomp. This ceremony, which is called the baptism of the Neva, occurs on the Russian 6th of January. I saw it from a window of the Winter Palace, to which I was graciously given admittance. Although it was a very mild day for the season, which is ordinarily the time for the severest cold, it would have been hard for me, as yet not well acclimated, to stand an hour or two, bareheaded, upon this frigid quay where the biting wind blows incessantly. The vast halls of the palace were crowded with persons of distinction: high officials, ministers, the diplomatic corps, generals all gold lace and decorations, came and went between lines of soldiers in full uniform, before the ceremony began. First, divine service was celebrated in the palace-chapel. From the back of the gallery, I watched with respectful interest the rites of this worship new to me, and stamped with the mysterious majesty of the East. From time to time the priest, a venerable, long-bearded, long-haired old man, mitred like a magian, clad in a dalmatic stiff with gold and silver, and supported by two acolytes, came out from the sanctuary, whose doors opened to give him egress, and recited the sacred formulas in a voice senile but still perfectly distinct. While he was chanting the psalms, I saw, amid the glitter of gold and candles, the Emperor and the Imperial family within the sanctuary; then the doors were closed, and the service went on behind the dazzling screen of the iconostase.

The choristers, in superb dress of nacarat velvet, braided with gold, accompanied and sustained, with the marvellous precision of Russian choirs, hymns wherein surely must be more than one old theme of the lost music of the Greeks.

Mass being ended, the procession began to move, and defiled through the halls of the palace, on its way to the baptism, or, more properly, the consecration, of the Neva. The Emperor and the Grand-Dukes in uniform, the clergy with copes of gold and silver brocade, those fine sacerdotal robes of the Byzantine fashion, the particolored crowd of generals and great officers, traversing this compact mass of troops drawn up in line in the halls, formed a brilliant and impressive spectacle.

Upon the Neva, in front of the Winter Palace, and close to the quay, to which it was joined by steps covered with carpeting, a pavilion was erected, or rather a chapel, with light columns painted green supporting a latticed cupola, whence was suspended a Dove surrounded by rays.

In the centre of the floor, under this dome, opened the mouth of a well, guarded by a balustrade, and communicating with the water of the Neva, the ice having been cut away at that place. A line of soldiers, standing at considerable intervals from one another, kept the space free upon the river for some distance from the chapel; bareheaded they stood, their helmets on the ground beside them, their feet in the snow,—so motionless that they might have been guide-posts.

Under the palace-windows fretted, held in by their riders, the horses of the Circassians, Lesghines, Tcherkesses, and Cossacks, who compose the Emperor's escort; it is a strange sensation to see in the midst of civilization, elsewhere than at the Hippodrome or the Opera, warriors like those of the Middle Ages, with helmet and coat of mail, armed with bow and arrows; or clad in oriental fashion, having a Persian carpet for a saddle, for sabre a Damascus blade, engraved with verses from the Koran; and perfectly suited to figure in the cavalcade of an emir or a caliph.

How martial and fierce the faces,—what savage purity of type,—what slender figures, supple and nervous,—what elegant bearing, in these costumes so characteristic in cut, so well adapted to enhance human beauty! It is truly singular that the people who are called *barbarians* are the only ones who know how to clothe themselves becomingly. The civilized man has entirely lost the feeling for costumes.

The procession emerged from the palace, and as I stood at my window I saw, through the double glass, the Emperor, the Grand-Dukes, and the priests enter the pavilion, which became so full that it was difficult to distinguish the gestures of those officiating about the orifice of the well.

Cannon from across the river, ranged on the quay of the Exchange, fired successively, at the grand moment. A great ball of bluish smoke, cut by a flash of flame, burst out between the river, with its snowy carpet, and the grayish white of the sky; to it followed a detonation that shook all the windows of the palace. The reports succeeded one another with perfect regularity, and without the interval of a second of time. The cannon has something terrible, solemn, and yet, like all things strong, something joyous about it; its voice, which roars in battles, mingles equally well with festivities; it adds that element of joy unknown to the ancients, who had neither bells nor guns,—noise! It, only, can speak amid great multitudes, and make itself heard in the immensities.

The ceremony was ended; the troops defiled away, and the spectators withdrew peaceably, without confusion, without tumult,—as is the habit of a Russian crowd, the most quiet crowd in the world.

IX.

RACES ON THE NEVA.

"WHAT! are we not going home soon? Really, it is a sin to keep a man out doors so long, in a temperature like this! Have you sworn to make us freeze our ears and our noses?" I have promised to show you a Russian winter, and I am keeping my word — besides, the thermometer scarcely falls below 20° to-day; this is almost like spring; the Samoyeds who camped upon the frozen river, were obliged to go away because it was growing too warm. Don't be anxious, but follow bravely. The horses are fretting before the door, eager for the start.

They are racing to-day on the Neva; we must not neglect the opportunity of making acquaintance with these Northern races, which are as elegant, as extravagant, as characteristic, and as exciting, as anything of the kind in England or in France.

The Newsky Prospekt and the streets leading into the grand square, where rises the column of Alexander, —that gigantic monolith of red granite which surpasses the Egyptian enormities,—present a scene of extraordinary animation, almost equal to the Champs-Elysées when a steeple-chase at la Marche calls out the carriages of the fashionable world.

The troïkas go by, their little bells all vibrating, their three horses, pulling fan-wise, each with a different gait; the sledges spin along upon their steel runners, the coachmen, in four-sided velvet caps and blue or green caftans, with difficulty controlling the splendid steppers. Other sledges, double-seated and having two horses, coaches and open carriages, dismounted from their wheels and set on runners, are taking the same direction, and the crowd of vehicles grows every moment more and more dense. Now and then a sledge of the old Russian style, with its leather apron stretched like a studding-sail, and its little shaggy horse galloping alongside his mate the trotter, slips along, in and out, through the crowd, impatient and rapid, powdering its neighbors with white particles.

A gathering like this in Paris would produce a great noise, a prodigious uproar; but at St. Petersburg the picture is only noisy to the eye, if I may so express myself. The snow, which interposes its padding between the pavement and the vehicle, deadens the sound entirely. Upon these roads, which winter has so carefully wadded, the steel of the runner makes scarcely as much noise as the diamond scratching a pane of glass. There is no snap to the small whip of the mujik; the masters, wrapped in fur, do not talk, for their words would freeze, like those Panurge tells of in the neighborhood of the pole. Everything is astir with silent activity in the midst of a mute whirlwind. Although there is nothing it less resembles, all this has in a slight degree the same effect as Venice.

Pedestrians are rare, for, as I have said, nobody walks in Russia except the mujiks, whose felt boots help them to keep their balance on the sidewalks, which are kept clean from snow, but are often glassy with ice, and especially dangerous when one is shod with the indispensable overshoes.

Between the Admiralty and the Winter Palace is the wooden planking which goes down from the quay to the Neva; here the sledges and other vehicles, falling into line, are obliged to slaken their speed very considerably, and sometimes even to stop, waiting their turn to descend.

I profit by the pause to examine my neighbors. The men are in pelisses, and wear the military undress cap, or else a cap of some fur; there is scarcely a hat to be seen. At a temperature like this, one is naturally shy of exposing the base of the skull to the icy *douche* of the north-wind. The women are less warmly clad. It would seem that they feel the cold far less than men do. The black satin pelisse, lined with sable or Siberian blue fox is all that they add to their carriage dress, otherwise exactly resembling the most elegant Parisian toilettes. The white throat, which no cold air seems able to redden, emerges bare and free of tippet, and the head is shielded only by a dainty French bonnet, which does not cover the hair. I thought with alarm of the influenzas, the neuralgias, the rheumatisms, which these intrepid beauties were willing to risk for the pleasure of being in the fashion, and exhibiting their rich locks, in a country and a climate where to lift the hat in a salute is sometimes a perilous action; animated by the fire of coquetry, they do not seem to know what it is to suffer from the cold.

Russia, with its immense territory, includes many different races, and the type of feminine beauty varies much. One may, however, indicate as characteristic, an extreme fairness of complexion, grayish-blue eyes, blonde or chestnut hair, and a certain *embonpoint*, arising from the lack of exercise and the life in-doors, which is compelled by a winter lasting seven or eight months. They suggest the idea of odalisques, whom the Genius of the North keeps confined in the tropical atmosphere of a hothouse. They have complexions of cold-cream and snow, with tints from the heart of a camellia—like those ever-veiled women of the Seraglio whose skin the sunlight has not touched. By this extreme fairness, their delicate features are rendered even more delicate; and the softened outlines form faces of Hyperborean sweetness and polar grace.

At this very moment, as if to contradict my description, in the sledge which has just drawn up by the side of my troïka, shines a radiant Southern beauty; the eyebrows black and velvety, the aquiline nose, the lengthened oval of the face, the brunette complexion, the lips red as pomegranates, all betray the pure Caucasian type;—a Circassian, and, for all I know, a Mahometan. Here and there, eyes long and narrow, and rising a little at the outer angle, remind us that, at one extreme, Russia touches upon China; charming little Finns with eyes of turquoise blue, pale golden hair, and tint, pure red and white, contrast well with those handsome Greek women from Odessa, whom you recognize by the straight nose and great black eyes, like those of the Byzantine madonnas. It makes a charming picture,—these lovely heads emerging, like winter flowers, from a mass of furs, which is itself covered by the white or black bear-skin thrown over all.

We came down upon the ice by a broad wooden slope (resembling that which, in the ancient Olympian circus, united the theatre with the arena) between the bronze lions of the quay, whose pedestals, when the river is open, mark the landing-place.

On the day which I am describing, the sky had not that keen, intense color which it assumes when the cold reaches zero. An immense canopy of cloud of a very soft and fine pearl-gray, holding snow suspended, hung over the city, and seemed to rest upon the towers and spires as upon pillars of gold. This quiet and neutral tint set off to unusual advantage the buildings with their delicate coloring relieved by fillets of silvery snow. In front we saw across the river, looking like a valley half filled by avalanches, the columns of red granite ornamented with prows of ships, which stand near the classic Exchange. At the point of the island which divides the Neva into two streams, the needle of the fortress raised its aspiring golden point, rendered yet more vivid by the gray tint of the sky.

The course,—with its board stands, and its track marked out by ropes attached to stakes set in the ice, and by artificial hedges of fir-branches,—stretched diagonally across the river. The crowd of people and carriages is immense. Privileged persons occupied the stands, if it be a privilege to remain stationary in the cold in an open gallery! Around the track are crowded, two or three deep, sledges, troïkas, open carriages, and even simple télégas and other vehicles more or less primitive; for no restriction seems to hamper this public amusement: the river is free to all. Men and women, in order to have a better view, turn out their coachmen, stand upon the seats and the boxes. Nearer the barriers are the mujiks in their sheepskin touloupes and felt boots, soldiers in gray capotes, and other persons who have not been able to secure a better place. All this crowd, astir like a mighty ant-hill on the icy floor of the Neva, was a scene not to be witnessed without anxiety,—by me at least; for I could not forget that a deep river, as large, at least, as the Thames at London Bridge, flowed beneath this frozen crust, two or three feet deep at most, upon which was the weight of thousands of people closely crowded together, and a great number of horses, not to mention equipages of every description. But the Russian winter is to be depended on; it never plays the trick of opening trap-doors under the crowd and swallowing them up.

Outside the course, jockeys were exercising the horses who had not yet been on the track, or leading about, to cool them gradually under their Persian rugs, the noble animals who had furnished their share of the day's amusement.

The track is a kind of lengthened ellipse; the sledges do not start abreast, but are stationed at equal intervals; these intervals diminishing or increasing according to the speed of the horses. Two sledges take their position in front of the stands, and two others at the extremities of the ellipse, awaiting the signal of departure. Sometimes a man on horseback gallops at the side of the horse in harness to stimulate him through rivalry to the utmost exertion. The horse in the sledge only trots, but his pace is sometimes so rapid that the other can hardly keep up with him; and once under good headway, abandons him to his own impulse. Many drivers, sure of their animals, scorn to employ this resource, and make the race alone. Any horse who breaks into a gallop loses his chance, if he makes more than six bounds before being brought back to the prescribed gait.

It is marvellous to see these splendid creatures, for whom wild prices are often paid, spin along over the level ice, which, swept clear of snow, is like a belt of dull-colored glass. The vapor comes from their scarlet nostrils in long jets; their flanks are bathed in a kind of mist, and their tails seem powdered with diamond dust. The nails in their shoes bite into the level and slippery surface, and they devour the distance with the same proud security with which they would tread the best-kept roads of a park. The drivers, leaning backward, grasp the reins with their utmost strength; for horses so powerful as these having only a light weight behind them, and, not allowed to break into a gallop, require to be restrained rather than urged. And they find, too, in this tension, a point of support which allows them to abandon themselves to their headlong pace. What prodigious steps these creatures take, looking as if they would bite their knees!

I could not discover that any special conditions regarding age or weight were imposed upon the contestants, only an amount of speed in a fixed time, measured by a chronometer,—or, at least, so it appeared to me. Occasionally, troïkas enter the lists against sledges having one or two horses. Each man selects the vehicle and number of horses which seem best to suit him. Sometimes even a spectator, who has been sitting in his sledge and looking on, will take a fancy to try his luck, —and forthwith he enters the lists.

At the race which I am describing, a very picturesque incident occurred. A mujik,—from Vladimir, it was said,—who had come into the city bringing wood or frozen provisions, stood looking on from the height of his rustic troïka. He was clad in the usual greasy toulonpe, with an old matted fur cap, and felt boots white with hard service; a beard unkempt and lustreless bristled upon his chin. He had a team of three little horses, dishevelled, wild-looking, shaggy as bears, frightfully filthy, with icicles hanging down underneath them, carrying their heads low, and biting at the snow heaped up in masses on the river. A donga like a Gothic window, painted with glaring colors in stripes and zigzags, was the part of the equipage on which most care had been bestowed—doubtless was the work of the mujik's own hatchet.

This wild and primitive equipage offered the strangest possible contrast to the luxurious sledges, the triumphant troïkas, and all the other elegant vehicles which stood drawn up along the edges of the track. More than one laughing glance ridiculed the humble troïka. And, to tell the truth, in this brilliant scene it had much the same effect as a spot of wheel-grease on an ermine mantle.

But the little horses, whose hair was all matted with frozen sweat, looked out scornfully through their stiffened, shaggy fore-locks at the high-bred animals that seemed to shrink away from contact with them,—for animals—like the rest of us!—feel a contempt for poverty. A gleam of fire shone in their sombre eyes, and they struck the ice with the small shoes attached to their slender, sinewy legs, bearded like an eagle's quills.

The mujik, standing upon the seat, contemplated the course, without appearing in the least surprised by the prowess of the horses. Now and then, even, a faint smile gleamed below the frozen crystals of his mustache, his gray eyes sparkled mischievously, and he seemed to say : "We, too, could do as much."

Taking a sudden resolve, he entered the lists to try his luck. The three little unlicked bears shook their heads proudly, as if they understood that they were to maintain the honor of the poor horse of the steppes, and, without being urged, they went off at such a pace, that everybody else on the track began to take the alarm; they went like the wind, with their little, slender limbs, and they carried off the victory from all the others,—thorough-breds of English race, barbs, and Orlov horses,—by a minute and some seconds! The mujik had not presumed too much upon his rustic steeds.

The prize was adjudged to him, a magnificent piece of chased silver by Vaillant, the most fashionable goldsmith in St. Petersburg. This triumph excited a noisy enthusiasm among the crowd usually so silent and so calm.

As the conqueror came off, he was surrounded by amateurs, proposing to buy his three horses; they went so far as to offer him three thousand rubles apiece, an enormous sum for beasts and man both. To his credit be it said, the mujik persistently refused. He wrapped his piece of silver in a fragment of old cloth; climbed upon his troïka, and went back as he came, not willing at any price to part from the good little creatures who had made him for the moment the lion of St. Petersburg.

The races were over, and the carriages came off the river, and took their way to the several quarters of the town; the ascent of the wooden slopes which unite the Neva to the quays would furnish a painter of horses—Twertzkov, for example—with the material for an interesting and characteristic picture. The slope is very abrupt, and the noble animals curve their necks, and grasp the slippery planks with their hoofs, and crowd themselves down upon their sinewy houghs; it is a scene of confusion full of picturesque effects, and would become dangerous, were it not for the skill of the Russian coachmen. The sledges go up four or five abreast, in irregular line, and more than once I felt on the back of my neck the hot breath of some impatient thorough-bred, who would have made no difficulty about going straight over my head if he had not been held in with a vigorous hand; and now and then was heard a little scream, when some flake of foam dropping from a silver bit, rested on a lady's bonnet. The scene made me think of an army of chariots assaulting the granite quays, which had a considerable resemblance to the parapets of a fortress. Notwithstanding the tumult, there was no accident; the absence of wheels makes it difficult for a collision to occur, and the equipages dispersed in all directions with a rapidity which would have alarmed Parisian prudence.

It is a genuine delight, when a man has been in the open air for two or three hours, exposed to a wind which has blown across the snows of the pole, to return home, and get off your pelisse, take your feet out of overshoes, wipe the melting icicles from your mustache, and light a cigar,—which latter luxury can be enjoyed, it will be remembered, only within doors. The warm atmosphere of the stove wraps your torpid frame caressingly, and restores suppleness to your limbs. A glass of very hot tea—in Russia you do not drink your tea from a cup—completes the work of making you, as the English say, "quite comfortable." Suspended circulation is renewed, and you taste that in-door pleasure which the Southern man, living altogether in the open air, knows not of. But already the day is declining; night comes on early at St. Petersburg, and after three o'clock lamplight is required. Culinary vapors escape from the chimneys; in every house the kitchen-stove is in full blast, for they dine earlier in the city of the Czars than we do in Paris. Six o'clock is the very latest, and this only with people who have travelled, and borrowed French or English customs. But I am invited out to dinner in the city; toilette must be made, the pelisse drawn on again over the black coat, and thin boots plunged anew into the heavy furred overshoes.

With the coming on of night, the air has grown colder; an absolutely arctic wind drives the snow like smoke along the sidewalks. The road creaks under the runners of the sledge. In the depths of a sky swept clear of all vapors shine the stars, large and pale, and through the darkness, upon the gilded dome of St. Isaac's, shines a point of intense light, a lamp of the sanctuary never extinguished.

Drawing the collar of my pelisse up to my eyes, and pulling the bear-skin of the sledge over my knees, I find myself soon, by means of the mystic words *na prava, na leva* (to the right! to the left!) in front of the house where I am expected—not having at all suffered by the difference of seventy degrees from the warmth of my apartment to the cold of the street. At the foot of my friend's staircase, the atmosphere, like that of a heated conservatory, seizes upon me; it thaws out my beard, and in the ante-chamber, the servant, an old soldier who still keeps his military capote, relieves me of my fur garments which he hangs up among those of the other guests, who are already all arrived—punctuality is a Russian virtue. In Russia, Louis XIV. would never have had reason to say: "I almost had to wait!"

X.

DETAILS OF INTERIORS.

THERE is something very peculiar in the appearance of a Russian ante-room. Pelisses hanging from the rack, with their limp sleeves and straight, heavy folds, vaguely suggest the human figure; the overshoes placed beneath, simulate feet; the general effect of all these furry objects, seen by the uncertain light of a small lamp suspended from the ceiling, is fantastic in the extreme. Achim von Arnim would discern with his imaginative eye the outside garments of M. Peau d'Ours, paying a visit within; Hoffman would ensconce grotesque phantoms of archivists or of aulic councillors behind their mysterious folds. I, who am but a Frenchman, and reduced to Perrault's tales, only see therein the seven wives of Bluebeard in the black closet! Hanging in this way near the stove, these fur garments become impregnated with heat, which they retain for an hour or two in the outside air. The servants have a marvellous instinct for identifying them; even when the number of guests is so great that the ante-room looks like Michel's or Zimmerman's shop, they never mistake, and lay upon the shoulders of each man the garment which belongs to him.

A comfortable suite of rooms at St. Petersburg gathers all the luxuries of English and of French civilization; at the first glance you would think yourself in the West-end, or the Faubourg St. Honoré; soon, however, the local character betrays itself by a multitude of curious details. First of all, the Byzantine Madonna and Child—the brown face and hands showing through apertures cut in the veneering of silver or silver-gilt, which represents drapery—glitters in the light of an ever-burning lamp, and notifies you that you are neither in Paris nor in London, but in orthodox Russia—in Holy Russia! Occasionally, an image of Christ takes the place of the Virgin, and frequently a saint is to be seen,—the patron saint of the master or mistress of the house,—covered with plates of gold or silver, like a tortoise in its shell, and having a golden halo about the head. Furthermore, the climate makes certain requisitions which cannot be evaded. The windows are invariably double, and the space between the sashes is covered with a layer of fine sand designed to absorb moisture, and prevent the frost from silvering the panes. Twisted horns of paper containing salt are set in it, and sometimes the sand is concealed by a bed of moss. There are no outside shutters or blinds, for they would be useless, since the windows remain closed all winter, being carefully filled in around the edges with a kind of cement. One narrow, movable pane serves to admit fresh air, but its use is disagreeable and even dangerous, so great is the contrast between the temperature without and that within. Heavy curtains of rich material still further deaden the effect of the cold upon the glass, a substance much more permeable than is generally believed.

The rooms are larger and higher than in Paris. Our architects—so ingenious in modelling cells for the human bee—would cut a whole suite, and frequently a second story, out of one St. Petersburg drawing-room. As all the rooms are hermetically sealed against the out-door air, and even the common halls and stairways are heated, the temperature never falls below 66° or 68°, so that ladies can be clad in muslins and have their arms and shoulders bare. The great copper mouths of the *calorifères* emit heat without cessation, by night as well as by day, and their hot-air pipes, and also huge porcelain stoves, white or painted in colors, and reaching to the ceiling, diffuse a steady, even warmth in places where openings cannot conveniently be made for the *calorifères* themselves. Open fireplaces are rare; when they do exist they are used only in spring and autumn. In winter they would carry off heat, and actually reduce the temperature of the room. They are closed, and filled with flowers—flowers, which are a truly Russian luxury! The houses overflow with them; flowers receive you at the door and go with you up the stairway; Irish ivies festoon the balusters, *jardinières* adorn the landings on every floor. In the embrasure of the windows, bananas spread out their broad, silken leaves; talipot palms, magnolias, camellias growing like trees, mingle their blossoms with the gilded volutes of the cornices; orchids hover like butterflies around lampshades of crystal, porcelain, and curiously wrought terra-cotta. From horn-shaped vases of Japanese porcelain, or of Bohemian glass, placed in the centre of a table or at the corner of a side-board, spring sheaves of superb exotics; and all this floral splendor thrives as in a hothouse. In truth, every Russian apartment is a hothouse; in the street you are at the pole; within doors, you might believe yourself in the tropics.

It would seem that by this profusion of verdure, the eye seeks to console itself for the implacable whiteness of winter; the desire to see something which is not white must become a sort of nostalgia in this country, where snow covers the ground more than six months out of the year. There is not even the satisfaction of looking at the green-painted roofs; they too must wear their white shirts until the spring. If apartments did not transform themselves into gardens, one would feel as if green had disappeared forever from the world.

In regard to furniture, it is much like our own, only larger, more ample, as beseems the size of the room; but one thing completely Russian is this little boudoir of delicate and costly wood, carved in open-work like the sticks of a fan, which occupies a corner of the drawing-room, festooned with the rarest climbing-plants,—a kind of confessional for confidential talk,—furnished with divans, where the mistress of the house, isolating herself from the crowd of visitors while yet remaining among them, may receive three or four guests of special distinction. Sometimes it is of tinted glass covered with engravings etched by fluoric acid, and mounted in panels of gilded copper. Nor is it rare to see, standing among the sofas, the *bergères*, the *dos-à-dos*, a huge white bear, suitably stuffed and arranged, offering to visitors a commodious seat; and sometimes little black cubs serving as footstools or ottomans. And so we are recalled, amid all the elegance of modern life, to the icebergs of the Northern Ocean, to the vast steppes covered with snow, and to the deep pine forests, the true Russia, which, at St. Petersburg, one is so tempted to forget!

The sleeping-rooms do not present, in general, the luxury and elegance which characterize them in France. Behind a folding-screen, or in one of those carved boudoirs of which I spoke just now, a little, low bed is hidden, a camp-bed or a divan it might be called; the Russians are of oriental origin, and, even in the higher classes, care little for luxuriously appointed bedrooms; they sleep wherever they happen to be, a little everywhere, like the Turk, often wrapped in a pelisse on one of their large green leather sofas. The idea of making a sort of sanctuary of one's bedroom never occurs to them; their ancient customs of the tent seem to have followed them into the very heart of civilized life,—all whose corruptions and all whose elegances, however, they perfectly understand.

Rich hangings adorn the walls; and if the master of the house prides himself on being an *amateur*, without fail, from the red India damask, from the brocatelle with its dull gold embroidery, stands out conspicuous, lighted by powerful reflectors and set in the most expensive of frames, a Horace Vernet, a Gudin, a Calame, a Koekkoek,—sometimes a Leys, a Madou, a Tenkate; or, if he will prove his patriotism, a Brulov or an Aïvasovsky; these are the painters most in fashion; our modern school does not seem to have reached them as yet. I have, however, met two or three Meissoniers and as many Troyons. The style of our painters does not appear sufficiently finished to the Russians.

This interior which I have been describing, is not that of a palace, but of a house—not *bourgeoise*,—that word has hardly any meaning in Russia,—but of a house *comme il faut*. St. Petersburg is crowded with the elegant residences of men of rank and with palaces, of which I hope later to give the reader some description.

And now having indicated the principal decorations, it is time to speak of the dinner. Before seating themselves, the guests approach a small round table where is set out caviare, bits of salted herring, anchovies, cheese, olives, slices of Bologna sausage, Hamburg smoked beef, and other relishes, to be eaten with biscuits in order to stimulate the appetite. This lunch is taken standing, and accompanied by a kind of absinthe, Madeira wine, *eau-de-vie de Dantzic*, Cognac, and *cumin*, a kind of anisette, which resembles the *raki* of Constantinople and the Greek islands. Inconsiderate or diffident travellers, who cannot resist polite urgency, allow themselves to be persuaded to taste of everything, not dreaming that this is but the prologue to the performance, and take their seats at the dinner-table, having already quite satisfied their appetites.

In all fashionable houses we find French cookery; and still the national taste is shown in some characteristic details. For example, by the side of the white bread is served a slice of the blackest rye bread, which the Russian guest crumbles with evident relish. They seem also to be very fond of certain salted cucumbers, called *agoureis*, and which I found at first far from delicious. During dinner, after great draughts of

Bordeaux and of Veuve Cliquot champagne, which is found nowhere but in Russia, they take porter and ale, and especially *kwas*, a kind of local beer made of the crusts of black bread fermented, which one must learn to like, and which, to strangers, scarcely seems worthy of the magnificent goblets of Bohemian glass or of chiselled silver, in which foams its brown liquor. And still, after a residence of several months, you come at last to like these *agourcis*, this *kwas*, and the *chtchi*, the Russian national soup.

The *chtchi* is a sort of stew, into whose composition enters breast of mutton, fennel, onions, carrots, cabbage, pearl barley, and prunes! This odd compound has a most original flavor, which you soon find agreeable, especially if you are an experienced traveller, a cosmopolite of the *cuisine*, whose gustatory papillæ are accustomed to surprises of every kind. Another favorite is the *potage aux quenéfes;* it is a clear soup, in which, as it boils, is poured, drop by drop, a kind of paste made of eggs and spices, which, surprised by the heat, forms into round or oval pellets, much like the dropped eggs of our Parisian *consommés*. With the *chtchi* are served little balls of pastry.

Everybody who has read Monte Cristo will remember that repast where the former prisoner of the Château d'If, realizing the marvels of fairy tales with his wand of gold, causes a sturgeon from the Volga to be served to him, a gastronomic wonder, unknown at even the most luxurious tables outside of Russia. And in truth, the sturgeon merits his reputation; 'tis an exquisite fish, the flesh white and fine, perhaps a trifle too rich in taste, midway between the smelt and the lamprey. He may attain very considerable dimensions, but those of medium size are best. Although not disdainful of such matters, I am neither a Grimod de la Raginère, nor a Cussy, nor a Brillat-Savarin, to speak with suitable lyric fire upon this theme, and I regret it, for the dish is worthy of the most accomplished epicure; to such a man, the sturgeon of the Volga would well repay the trouble of the journey.

Partridges, whose flesh, perfumed by the juniper berries on which they feed, emits a fragrance of turpentine at first quite surprising, appear frequently on Russian dinner-tables. The enormous moor-fowl also, and the bear's ham of fable, and the *filet* of elk, serve as proof that it is no bill of fare of Western Europe which is laid before us.

Every people, even though invaded by the monotony of civilization, retain some tastes absolutely peculiar, and still keep a few national dishes, whose flavor it is perhaps impossible for a foreigner to approve. For an example of this we may take the Russian cold soup, in which float crystals of ice amid bits of fish; its mixture of spices, vinegar, and sugar is as surprising to an exotic palate as the *gaspacho* of Andalusia. This soup, by the way, is served only in summer. It is very cooling, they say; and the Russians are enthusiastic about it.

As vegetables are for the most part raised under glass in this country, their maturity has no special date marked by the seasons, and they are always, or never, "early;" every month in the year you may eat green peas at St. Petersburg. The asparagus knows no winter. It is large, tender, succulent, and perfectly white; the stalks never have a green tip, as they do with us, and you may attack them at either end indifferently. In England they eat salmon cutlets; in Russia, cutlets of chicken. This dish has been in fashion since the Emperor Nicholas tasted it at a little tavern near Torjek, and found it good. The recipe had been given to the hostess by an unlucky Frenchman who could in no other way pay his scot; and it made her fortune.

In speaking of the Russian *cuisine* I have referred only to dishes that are peculiar and unlike our own; in general, however, in all great houses, it is purely French, and performed by Frenchmen. Without doubt, France supplies the world with cooks.

The great endeavor at St. Petersburg is to have fresh oysters; they come from so great a distance, that in summer the heat often spoils them, and in winter they are in danger of being frozen; they have been sold for a ruble apiece. Oysters so expensive are rarely good. They tell of a mujik who had become very rich, who, in return for a barrel of oysters furnished to his master at the season of their greatest scarcity, received his liberty, for which he had before vainly offered enormous sums—fifty or a hundred thousand rubles, it is said. I will not guarantee the truth of this story, but it proves at least, even though a fiction, that at certain times of the year oysters are extremely scarce at St. Petersburg.

On the same principle, there must always be a basket of fruit at dessert; oranges, pine-apples, grapes, apples, and pears are arranged in elegant pyramids; grapes come from Portugal usually, but sometimes they have rounded their pale amber globes in the rays of a *calorifère* in the cellar of the house, half buried under the snow. I have eaten strawberries too, in St. Petersburg, in January, which had vainly striven to grow red amid their green leaves, in a flower-pot. Fruits are a passion with people of the North; they import them at great expense, or they extort at least a semblance of them— for flavor and fragrance are wanting—from their own reluctant climate. The stove, however well heated, is but a poor substitute for sunshine.

I trust that the reader is very ready to pardon these gastronomic details; it may be worth while to know how a people is fed. "Tell me what you eat, and I will tell you what you are;" thus modified, the proverb is not the less true. Although they imitate the French *cuisine*, the Russian people preserve a relish for their national dishes, and these are the ones which at heart they prefer. It is the same with their character: although they conform to the highest refinements of western civilization, they still preserve certain primitive instincts, and it would not be so very hard for any of them—even the most elegant—to go back and live upon the steppes.

At table a servant in black coat, with white neck-tie and gloves, irreproachable in costume as an English diplomate, stands gravely behind your chair, ready to attend to your least wish. You might fancy yourself in Paris; but if you chance to look closely at this man, you will see that the color of his skin is yellow, his small black eyes are narrow and drawn up at the outer angles, his nose is flat, his cheek-bones are prominent, his lips thick; your host, whose eye has followed yours, remarks carelessly, as if it were the most natural thing in the world, that he is a Mongol Tartar from the confines of China.

This Tartar, a Mahometan, or perhaps an idolater, fulfils his duty with the regularity of an automaton, and not the most critical major-domo could find aught wherein to censure him. He has the appearance of a genuine European servant; but he would please me better if he wore the costume of his tribe, the tunic fastened at the waist with a belt of metal, and the lambskin cap; it would be more picturesque; but it would be less European, and the Russian does not like to have an Asiatic air.

The table-service as a whole,—porcelain, crystal, silver, *épergne*,—leaves nothing to be desired, but has nothing about it which is peculiar, save only charming little spoons of platina, ornamented with Niello-work of gold, wherewith one tastes the dainties of the dessert, the tea and coffee. Dishes of fruit alternate with baskets of flowers, and the more delicate pastry is often surrounded by a wreath made of little bouquets of violets, which the hostess gracefully distributes among her guests.

As to the conversation, it is carried on in French, especially when strangers are at the table. All Russians of any distinction speak our language very fluently, with all the whims of the hour, the phrases at the moment in fashion, as if they had learned it on the Boulevard des

Italiens. They even understand the French of Duvert and Lausanne, so peculiar and so intensely Parisian, that many provincials find it difficult. The Russians speak French without any foreign accent, yet may be recognized by a slight singing tone, not displeasing, and which you come at last to imitate yourself; also they fall into certain ways of expressing themselves, national perhaps, common to all persons who speak familiarly a language not their own. Thus they employ the word "*absolument*" oddly; you say, for example, "Is such a person dead?" and they will reply, "*Absolument;*" as we should say *oui*, or the Italian, *si*. The words *donc* and *déjà* occur often, placed where they do not belong in the sentence, with an interrogative significance: "*Avez vous donc déjà vu St. Petersbourg, ou Mme. Bosio?*"

The manners of the Russians are polite, caressing and extremely polished. One is surprised to find that they are minutely informed in regard to our literature; they read much, and many a French author is better known at St. Petersburg than in Paris. The gossip of the green-room, the *chronique scandaleuse* of the *demi-monde*, goes as far as the banks of the Neva, and I have heard there many a piquant detail, entirely new to me, concerning Parisian affairs.

Russian women have also much mental cultivation; with the facility characterizing the Slavic race, they read and understand many languages. They are familiar with Byron, with Goethe and Heine in the original, and when a writer is introduced to them, they are able by some adroit quotation to prove that they have read and remembered his works. As to their toilette, it is of the last degree of elegance, the very superlative of fashion. Diamonds sparkle upon bare and lovely shoulders, and only bracelets from Circassia and the Caucasus remind us by their peculiar oriental construction that we are in Russia.

After dinner we disperse through the drawing-rooms. On the tables lie albums, books of beauty, keepsakes, sketches of scenery, which may be useful to the embarrassed or diffident visitor. Stereoscopes offer the entertainment of their moving pictures; sometimes a woman rises, yielding to solicitation, and, seating herself at the piano, sings to her own accompaniment some Russian national air, or some gypsy song in which the melancholy of the North mingles with Southern ardor, —a strange melody, resembling a *cachuca* danced by moonlight upon the snow.

XI.

A BALL AT THE WINTER PALACE.

I PROPOSE to describe a *fête* which I attended without being there,—from which, in person, I was absent, while my eye was an invited guest,—a ball at court! Invisible myself, I saw everything, and yet I did not wear the ring of Gyges on my finger, or on my head the kobold's green felt hat, or any talisman whatever.

In the Square of Alexander—covered with its carpet of snow, and in a temperature cold enough to stiffen Parisian coachmen and horses, but which, to these Russians, did not seem severe enough to have the fires lighted under the Chinese-roofed kiosks of cast-iron, adjoining the Winter Palace—many carriages were standing. The trees of the Admiralty, diamonded with frost, had the appearance of great white plumes fixed in the ground, and the red granite of the triumphal column was coated with ice; the moon, rising pure and clear, flooded with its pale radiance all this whiteness of the night, gave a blue tint to the shadows and made the motionless equipages—whose ice-covered lanterns like polar glow-worms dotted with points of yellow light the immense expanse—suggest the figures of a phantasmagoria. In the background, the colossal Winter Palace flamed through all its windows, like a mountain pierced with holes and lighted by interior ignition.

Perfect silence reigned in the square; the severity of the cold kept away the curious crowd that in Paris is always sure to flock to witness such an entertainment, though seen only at a distance and from without; and even had there been a crowd, the approaches to the palace are of such enormous extent that it would have been scattered and lost in the immense space which nothing but an army could fill.

A sledge traversed diagonally the wide white plain across which stretched the long shadow of the column of Alexander, and disappeared in the sombre street which separates the Winter Palace from the Hermitage, a street whose aërial bridge gives it a certain resemblance to the Canal di Paglia, in Venice.

A few minutes later an Eye, which it is not necessary to suppose had any special belongings, hovered along a cornice just under the roof of a gallery in the palace. Lines of wax-candles fixed in the moulding of the entablature sheltered this Eye behind a hedge of flame, and no one from below could have perceived its feeble ray. Light concealed it more effectually than shadow could have done; it disappeared in the effulgence.

The gallery, broad and long, extended beneath, with its polished columns, its floor reflecting the lights and the gilding, and its pictures—whose subjects, seen from this point, could not be discerned. Already, brilliant uniforms were moving about below, and the long trains of court dresses swept hither and thither. Slowly the crowd increased; a many-colored, sparkling river, it filled its bed, and the broad gallery became too narrow for it.

The attention of this crowd was directed towards the entrance by which the Imperial family should appear. The doors opened; the guests fell back on either side, and the Emperor, the Empress, and the Grand-Dukes passed down the gallery, addressing occasionally with graceful and high-bred manner some remark to persons of distinction near whom they passed. Then the Imperial group disappeared through the opposite doors, followed at a respectful distance by the high officers of state, the diplomatic corps, generals, and persons of rank.

Scarcely had the procession entered the ball-room, when the Eye was again in position, and this time for nished with a good opera-glass. It was like a furnace of light and heat, so intense as to suggest a conflagration. Lines of fire ran along the cornices between the windows; thousand-branched *torchères* flamed like the burning bush; chandeliers by hundreds hung from the ceiling, blazing constellations in the midst of a phosphorescent mist; and the light from all these various sources, meeting and crossing, composed the most dazzling illumination *à giorno*, whose sun ever shone upon any *fête*.

The first impression—especially from a point so high, leaning over this gulf of light—is a sort of vertigo; for the moment, in the dazzling scene, it is impossible to distinguish anything whatever. A kind of incessant scintillation prevents you from seizing any outlines; but soon the eye becomes accustomed to the glare, and can drive away these black butterflies that dance before it, as when one has been looking at the sun; it takes in, from one extremity to the other, this hall of gigantic dimensions, all white marble and stucco, whose polished walls shine like the jasper and the porphyry in Martyn's engravings of Babylonian architecture, reflecting with vague outlines the lights and objects in the hall.

The kaleidoscope, whose colored fragments incessantly fall together and rearrange themselves, forming new designs; the chromatrope, with its dilations and contractions, where a bit of cloth becomes a flower, then changes its petals into the points of a crown, and ends as a whirling sun, passing from ruby to emerald, from topaz to amethyst, around a diamond centre, can only, millions of times enlarged, give an idea of this parterre in motion, where gold and gems and flowers renew with perpetual agitation its sparkling arabesques.

As the imperial family enter, this moving splendor becomes fixed, and, the scintillation for a moment abating, it is possible to distinguish faces and persons.

In Russia, court balls are opened with what is called a polonaise; it is not a dance, but a sort of moving in file, a procession, a *marche aux flambeaux*, which has a great deal of character. The guests fall back from the centre of the hall, leaving a sort of avenue of which they form the animated hedge. When everybody is in his place the orchestra plays an air with slow and stately cadence, and the promenade begins; it is led by the Emperor, who gives his hand to some princess or to some lady whom he desires to honor.

The Emperor Alexander wore, on the evening of which I speak, an elegant military dress, which showed to great advantage his tall figure and his free and graceful bearing. It was a kind of long military jacket, white, with gold *brandebourgs*, trimmed at the neck and wrists and around the edge with Siberian blue fox, and starred all across the breast with decorations. Light-blue trousers, closely fitting, ended at the narrow boots. The hair of the Emperor was cut very short, and showed his smooth, full, well-rounded forehead. His features, with their perfect regularity, seem modelled for the gold or bronze of the medal; the blue of his eyes is rendered particularly noticeable by the brown tints of the face, less white than the forehead, by reason of much exposure in the open air. The contours of the mouth are as clear cut as in the Greek sculpture; the expression of the face is one of majesty and gentleness, at times lighted by a gracious smile.

Following the Imperial family, come the high officers of the army and of the palace, each giving his hand to a lady. It is a crowd of uniforms embroidered with gold, epaulettes starred with diamonds, rows of decorations, whose enamel and precious stones form centres of flashing light. Some, the highest in rank and favor, wear about the neck an order more as a token of friendship than of honor, if possible—the portrait of the Emperor set with brilliants; but they are rare, these last,—one could count them.

The procession still moves, and is recruited as it goes; a gentleman comes out from the living hedge and extends his hand to a lady standing opposite, and the new couple join the others, taking their place in the ranks, who move on with measured step, slackening the pace or increasing it, according to the movement of the leader; it cannot be quite an easy thing to walk thus, holding your partner by the finger-tips under fire of a thousand critical eyes; the slightest awkwardness of bearing, the least embarrassment of the foot, the most trifling fault in keeping time, is noticed. Military drill has made many of the men safe; but what a difficulty for the women! Most of them acquit themselves admirably, and of one it can be said: *Et vera incessu patuit dea!* Lightly they walked, under their feathers and flowers and diamonds, modestly casting down their eyes, or letting them wander with an air of perfect innocence, manœuvring with a slight bend of the figure or a little backward motion of the foot, their waves of silk and lace, refreshing themselves with a flutter of their fans, and as much at their ease as if they were wandering among the solitary avenues of a park; to walk in a noble, graceful, and simple manner, when people are looking at you, is an art which more than one great actress has never been able to acquire!

What gives an air of originality to the Russian court, is, that now and then some wasp-waisted, broad-chested young Circassian prince, with his showy, elegant oriental dress, joins the procession, or some captain of the Lesghien guard, or Mongol officer, whose soldiers yet are armed with bow and quiver and buckler. Under the white glove of civilized life hides—that it may take the hand of some princess or countess—the small Asiatic hand, accustomed to grasp the straight handle of the kindjal in its brown, sinewy fingers. No one is surprised. In fact, what more natural than that some Tartar prince —Mahometan, perchance,—should walk the polonaise with a lady of rank in St. Petersburg, of the orthodox Greek confession! Are they not both equally subjects of his majesty, the Emperor of All the Russias?

The uniforms and the court dress of the men are so

splendid, so rich, so varied, so loaded with gold, with embroidery and decorations, that the women with their modern elegance, and the airy grace of the fashions of the present day, find it difficult to hold their own against this heavy splendor; more rich they cannot be; instead, they are more beautiful; their bare white arms and shoulders far out-value the gold embroidery. To match the masculine attire, the Russian women would need, like the Byzantine madonnas, robes of stamped gold and silver, stomachers of precious stones, halos striated with diamonds; but how to dance, enclosed in a shrine of jeweller's work!

Do not, however, imagine a simplicity too primitive! These simple dresses are of *point d'Angleterre*, and the two or three tunics worn outside are worth more than a dalmatic of gold or silver; the bouquets on the lace skirt are fastened with clusters of diamonds; this velvet ribbon has for its buckle a jewel which might have been taken from the crown of a czar. What more simple than a white robe,—silk, tulle, or *moire*,—and a few pearls in the hair,—a net-work, or two or three strings twisted among the braids? But the pearls are worth a hundred thousand rubles; never fisher brought up rounder or of purer color from the depths of ocean! Besides, this simplicity pays homage to the Empress, who prefers elegance to ostentation; but you may be sure Mammon loses nothing by it. Only, at the first glance, as they pass in rapid march, you would think the Russian women make less display than the men; it is a mistake. Like their sex everywhere, they know how to render gauze more costly than gold.

When the polonaise has made the circuit of the hall and gallery adjoining, the ball commences. There is nothing characteristic about the dances; they are quadrilles, the waltz, the redowa,—the same as in Paris, in London, in Madrid, in Vienna,—in fashionable society everywhere; I must except the mazourka, which is danced at St. Petersburg with an elegance and a perfection elsewhere unknown. Local peculiarities invariably tend to disappear, and first of all they vanish from the circles of high society. To recover them, we must go far away from the centres of civilization, and seek them in the depths of humble life.

As a whole, the scene was enchanting: the figures of the dance formed symmetrical centres in the midst of the splendid crowd which gave way to leave them room; the whirl of the waltz puffed out the skirts like the robes of dancing dervishes, and in the rapid evolution, the diamond clusters, the gold and silver laminæ, lengthened into serpentine flashes like those of lightning; and the small gloved hand of the lady, resting on the epaulette of her partner, was like a white camellia in a vase of massive gold.

Among the groups, the first secretary of the Austrian embassy was very conspicuous, with his magnificent Hungarian costume, and the Greek ambassador, also in his national dress.

After an hour or two of lofty contemplation, the Eye, through mysterious and Dædalian corridors, where the far-off sounds of the orchestra and the crowded ballroom died away in vague murmurs, made its way to another hall. Comparative obscurity reigned in this enormous apartment; here supper would be served. Many a cathedral is not so vast. Below, in the dim light, the white outlines of the tables could be discerned; at the corners great masses of silver glittered faintly, here and there flashing back some wandering ray of light which came, one knew not whence; these were the buffets. Steps led up to a velvet-covered estrade, where was arranged a semi-circular table. With silent activity, servants in gala livery went and came, majordomos and officers of the kitchen, giving the last touches to the preparations. A few scattered lights wandered about upon this sombre background, like the sparks in burnt paper.

However, countless wax-candles loaded the candelabra, and followed the border of the friezes and the outlines of every arch. They stood out white, like the pistils of flowers, but not the least luminous star trembled at any point of them. Congealed stalactites they seemed; and already could be heard, like tumultuous, advancing waves, the confused sound of the approaching multitude. The Emperor appeared at the threshold of the door; it was like a *fiat lux!* A subtle flame ran from point to point, rapid as a flash; in an instant all was brilliant as the day; torrents of light suddenly filled the immense hall as if by magic. This abrupt transition from a kind of twilight to the most dazzling illumination, is truly like a scene of enchantment. In our age of prose, every wonder must be explained; threads of gun-cotton connect all the wicks of the candles, which are, besides, soaked in some inflammable liquid, and fire, applied in seven or eight places, is propagated instantly. The great chandeliers in St. Isaac's are lighted in this way, a thread of gun-cotton hanging down from each like a cobweb above the heads of the faithful. With a row of connected gas-burners turned on suddenly, we can produce a similar effect; but gas is not employed in the Winter Palace; only genuine wax-candles burn there. Nowhere save in Russia does the bee still contribute the illumination.

The Empress seated herself, with several persons of the highest rank, at the semi-circular table, upon the raised platform. Behind her gilded arm-chair a great sheaf of white and red camellias spread, a giant bouquet, against the wall. Twelve negroes of great height, selected from the finest specimens of the African race, clad as Mamelukes,—with white, twisted turban, green vest with gold corners, wide red trousers girt with a cashmere scarf, the whole braided and embroidered on the seams,—went and came on the steps of the estrade, handing the plates to the servants, or receiving them, with that air of grace and dignity, even in a servile occupation, peculiar to orientals. These orientals, having forgotten Desdemona, fulfilled their duty with great majesty, and gave to this European entertainment an eastern stamp of the very highest taste.

Without any designation of places, the guests seated themselves at pleasure, at the tables destined for them.

Rich centre ornaments of silver and gilt, representing groups of figures or flowers, mythological or fantastic devices, adorned the tables; candelabra alternated with pyramids of fruit and ornamental structures of sugar. Seen from above, the sparkling symmetry of crystal, porcelain, silver, and bouquets, could be better appreciated than by those nearer. A double cordon of white shoulders, set in lace and scintillating with diamonds, surrounding the tables, betrayed their loveliness to the invisible Eye—whose gaze also followed the parting of the brown or the blond locks, amid the flowers, the leaves, the plumes, and the precious stones.

The Emperor went everywhere, addressing a few words to this person or that; sometimes seating himself for a moment and raising to his lips a glass of champagne; then going farther to repeat the same courtesy elsewhere. These brief visits are considered a great honor.

After supper, the dancing was resumed; but it had now grown late. It was time to go; the ball could but repeat itself, and to one only an eye-witness it no longer offered the same interest. The sledge which earlier in the evening has driven across the square and had stopped at a little door in the narrow street which separates the Winter Palace from the Hermitage, emerged again, taking the direction of St. Isaac's. It bore a fur pelisse, and a fur cap, which concealed the wearer's face; and, as if the sky were disposed to rival the terrestrial splendors, an aurora borealis was letting off its fire of polar pyrotechnics, its fusees of gold, of silver, of crimson, and of pearly tints, making the stars fade away before its phosphorescent radiance.

XII.

THE THEATRES.

THE theatres of St. Petersburg have a stately and classic appearance. In general, their architecture suggests the Odeon in Paris or the theatre at Bordeaux. Standing isolated in the centre of extensive squares, they offer great facilities of approach and departure. For my own part, I should prefer a style of more originality, and it seems to me it would have been possible to create one with a character suited to the country, from which many new effects might have been obtained. This fault is by no means peculiar to Russia. A mistaken admiration of antiquity has filled all the capitals of Europe with Parthenons and *maisons carrées*, copied more or less exactly with lavish use of building-stone, of brick, or of plaster. Only, nowhere do these poor Greek orders seem more out of place and more unhappy than at St. Petersburg: accustomed to the blue sky and the sunshine, they shiver under the snow which covers their flat roofs through the long winter. It is true these roofs are carefully swept after every new fall of snow, and this is the best criticism upon the inappropriateness of the style. Icicles among the acanthus leaves of a Corinthian capital! What do you say to that? A reaction from the classic style is now at work in favor of the Muscovite-Byzantine architecture, which I trust may prove successful. Each country, when it has not suffered violence in the name of a pretended good taste, produces its public buildings as it does its men, its animals, and its plants, in accordance with the necessities of its climate, its religion, and its origin; what is needed in Russia is the Greek of Byzantium, not the Greek of Athens.

This reservation being made, all the rest is praise. The grand theatre, or Italian Opera House, is superb, and of colossal size, rivalling La Scala or San Carlo: carriages draw up and drive away in the immense square without delay or disorder. Two or three successive vestibules with glazed doors, keep the biting cold from rushing into the main audience-room, and moderate a transition from the neighborhood of zero to something above 80°. Retired soldiers in uniform receive you as you enter, and remove your pelisse, furs, and overshoes. These are always restored to you without mistake, the memory for pelisses seeming to be, even in crowds like this, still an unfailing trait of the Russian. As in her Majesty's theatre in London, so in here in the Italian Opera, no gentleman is admitted, without the inevitable black coat, white neck-tie, and straw-colored or light gloves, unless he wear uniform of some kind, this being most frequently the case; the women are in full evening dress, *décolleté*, and with bare arms. This etiquette—of which I cordially approve—adds greatly to the brilliancy of the scene.

The parquette in the grand theatre is divided in the middle by a wide passage-way. A semi-circular corridor surrounds it, bordered on the outer side by a row of boxes, so that, during the interludes, it is easy to go and talk with any of one's acquaintance who may occupy these boxes. This arrangement, which is so convenient, and is in use in all the principal theatres of Europe except in Paris, ought to be imitated there when the Grand Opera is definitely reconstructed. In this way, a gentleman leaves his seat and returns to it without disturbing any one.

The first object which strikes your attention as you enter, is the Imperial box; it is not placed, as in Parisian theatres, close to the stage, but just in the centre of the house, opposite the performers. Its height cuts through two rows of boxes; enormous gilded staves, loaded with carving, support velvet curtains which are held back by heavy gold cords, and surmounted by a gigantic escutcheon bearing the arms of Russia represented in the proudest and most highly ornamented style of heraldry. A fine device is this eagle, his two heads topped with crowns, his wings displayed, his tail spread like a fan, holding in his claws the globe and the sceptre, beneath, the shield of St. George, and, like the decorations of orders, upon his scale-clad breast, the armorial bearings of the kingdoms, the duchies, and the provinces. No Greco-Pompeian decoration would be so satisfactory to the eye and so suitable as this.

The curtain does not represent velvet hangings with heavy folds and deep fringe, but it is a view of Peterhof, with its arcades and porticos, its statues, and its roof, painted green after the Russian style. The façades of the boxes, placed regularly one above the other in the Italian fashion, are ornamented with white medallions framed in gold, the figures painted in delicate and fresh color, resembling pastel, relieved against a rose-colored background. There are neither galleries nor balconies; instead of the columns either side of the stage as in Paris, the same great carved and gilded flag-staves are repeated, and the arrangement is graceful and novel.

It is not easy to define the style of the interior of the building, unless I borrow from the Spanish their word *plateresco*, which properly means a style of goldsmith's work, and is used to designate a sort of architecture in which ornamentation without rule or limit has free play in a thousand exuberant and lavish caprices. It is a mass of architectural embellishment whose gilding throws back the light of the chandeliers at a thousand glittering points; the general effect is gay, brilliant, and successful, and the luxuriously decorated audience-room is well suited to the luxuriously attired audience.

This mad extravagance in the decoration of a theatre pleases me better than a stupid correctness of taste. In a case like this, extravagance is better than pedantry. With velvet, and gold, and light in profusion, what more could any one desire!

The first row of boxes above the parquette is called the *bel-étage*, and, without any formal prohibition in regard to the matter, this *bel-étage* is reserved for the high aristocracy and the great court dignitaries. No woman untitled, whatever her wealth or position, would venture to be seen there; her presence in this privileged spot would astound everybody, herself most of all. In Russia, the possession of great wealth is not enough to destroy all social demarcations.

The first rows in the orchestra are, by custom, reserved for persons of distinction; in the one next to the musicians, you see only ministers of state, generals of the army, ambassadors, first secretaries of embassies, and other considerable and considered personages. Any celebrated foreigner of rank would be at liberty to sit there. The two rows next following are still aristocratic. In the fourth row you begin to find bankers, foreigners, functionaries of a certain rank, and artists; but no man of business would think of venturing beyond the fifth or sixth. It is a sort of tacit agreement, upon which nobody insists, but to which everybody yields obedience.

This familiar way of sitting in the orchestra at first surprised me, in persons of so high position; the very highest personages in the empire are seen there. To have his orchestra-stall does not prevent a man's having also his family box; but the former is the place preferred, and hence, no doubt, has arisen the discretion which keeps the ordinary public several benches off. One ought not to be shocked at this classification in Russia, where the Tchin divides society into fourteen well-marked categories, of which the first class contains rarely more than two or three individuals!

At the Italian Opera in St. Petersburg, the opera and the ballet are not performed on the same evening. They are two perfectly distinct performances, and each has its day. The subscription-price for the ballet is less than for the opera. As the whole entertainment consists in the dancing, the ballets are much longer than in Paris, extending to four or five acts, many tableaux and transformations; or perhaps two will be performed in the same evening.

The highest celebrities of song and dance have appeared at the Grand Theatre. Every star comes in turn to shine in this polar sky, and loses none of its brilliancy in so doing. By rubles and a welcome, all chimerical apprehensions of loss of voice and rheumatisms have been overcome. Not a throat, not a knee has suffered in this land of snow, where you see the cold without feeling it. Rubini, Tambarini, Lablache, Mario, Grisi, Taglioni, Elsler, Carlotta,—all have been in turn admired and appreciated here; Rubini has received decorations; imperial applause animates the artist, and shows him that he is understood and valued; though many of them have been late in venturing to undertake the journey.

The Russians are great *connoisseurs* in the ballet, and the fire of their lorgnettes is to be dreaded. Any one who has passed through it victoriously may feel henceforth secure. Their Conservatory of Dancing furnishes remarkable instances of talent, and a *corps de ballet* which has not its equal, for harmony, precision, and rapidity of its evolutions. It is a pleasure to see these lines which are so true, these groups, so perfectly defined, which break up at the given moment, to re-form under another aspect; all these little feet falling in cadence, all these choregraphic battalions which never become disorderly or confused in their manœuvres! It is a true world of pantomime, from which speech is absent; the action never goes beyond its limits. This *corps de ballet* is chosen with care from among the scholars of the conservatory; many are pretty, all are young and of good figure, and regard their employ seriously,—their art, if you prefer to call it so.

The decorations, which are very handsome and of great variety, are the work of German painters. The composition is frequently ingenious, poetic, and scientific, but at times overloaded with useless details distracting the eye and impeding the effect. The coloring is generally pale and cold; the Germans are not colorists, as everybody knows, and this fault is very marked when the observer is recently from Paris, where they carry the magic of scene-painting to such a height. As to the stage itself, the machinery is wonderful; the flights in air, the vanishings into the ground, the transformations, the plays of electric light, and all the illusory effects that a complicated *mise en scène* requires, are executed with the surest promptitude.

As I have said, the aspect of the house is most brilliant; the toilettes of the women are enchantingly set off by the crimson velvet of the boxes; and, to the stranger, the interlude is not less interesting than the performance. Turning his back to the curtain he can, without impropriety, hold under his opera-glass, for a few moments, these types of female beauty so varied, and, to him, so novel; and some friendly neighbor, having his Court Guide at his fingers' ends, will call by name, for his benefit, with their titles,—princess, countess, baroness,—these blondes and these brunettes, who unite the dreaminess of the North, with the tranquillity of the Oriental lands, as they mingle flowers and diamonds together.

In the half-light of the parquet boxes sparkle vaguely some few theatrical celebrities, two or three *Bohémiennes* from Moscow, and a certain number of Baronesses d'Ange, exported from the Parisian *demi-monde*, whose well-known faces have no need to be announced.

The Théâtre-Français, called also the Michael-

Theatre, stands in the square of the same name. The interior, commodiously planned but decorated poorly, has, like the Grand Theatre, its orchestra occupied in the first rows by Russians and foreigners of distinction. It is very much frequented, and comedy, vaudeville, and drama are played there with distinguished ability. The actors vie with each other in procuring novelties for their benefit nights, which are Saturdays and Sundays, and a new piece is brought out almost as soon at St. Petersburg as it is at Paris, and one cannot fail to feel a certain pride in seeing, in this far northern city, at so great a distance from Paris, that our language prevails sufficiently to support a theatre exclusively French, the " French colony" itself not filling more than one half the theatre at most.

During my sojourn in the City of the Czars, a celebrated American negro actor chanced to be there for a time, Ira Aldrigge by name. He was the lion of St. Petersburg, and it was necessary to go some days beforehand to obtain a good seat at one of his performances. He played Othello first, and his origin exempted him from all need of artifical coloring,—liquorice-juice, or coffee-grounds, or sleeves of chocolate-colored net. He had the right skin already, and was spared the trouble of assuming it. Consequently, his appearance on the scene was magnificent; it was Othello himself as Shakespeare has created him,—his eyes half-shut, as if dazzled by an African sun, his nonchalant oriental bearing, and that easy negro gait which no European can imitate. As there was no English troupe at St. Petersburg, but only a German one, Ira Aldrigge recited the text of Shakespeare, while his interlocutors, Iago, Cassio, and Desdemona, answered him in Schlegel's translation. The two languages, both of Teutonic origin, did not go badly together, especially to one who, like myself, understanding neither English nor German, gave his attention principally to the play of features, the gestures, and the attitudes of the actors. But it must have been a droll medley to those who were familiar with both idioms. I was anticipating a manner like that of Kean, energetic, violent, stormy,—a little savage, perhaps; but the great negro tragedian, doubtless wishing to appear as civilized as a white man, had a rational, moderate, classic, majestic style, much resembling Macready's. In the final scene, his fury never went beyond certain limits; he smothered Desdemona in the most considerate manner, and roared with decorum. In a word, so far as I could judge, under the circumstances, he seemed to have more talent than genius, more knowledge than inspiration. At the same time, he unquestionably produced an immense effect, and received endless rounds of applause. An Othello not so black and more ferocious would perhaps have had less success. After all, Othello has been living among Christians for some time; the lion of St. Mark must have tamed the desert lion.

The *repertoire* of a negro actor would seem to be limited to colored pieces; but, when you think of it, if a white comedian besmirches himself with bistre to play a black rôle, why should not a black comedian paint himself white to play a white rôle? It has been done. Ira Aldrigge, the following week, played King Lear, and all requisite illusion was perfectly produced. A flesh-colored skull-cap, whence hung some few locks of silvery hair, covered his woolly curls and came down to his eyebrows; a wax addition was made to his own flat nose, and a thick coat of paint covered his cheeks. For the rest, a great white beard concealed the lower part of his face, and fell upon his breast: the transformation was complete. Cordelia never could have suspected that her father was a black man! No make-up was ever better contrived. Through a kind of vanity, which is not to be wondered at, the actor had not whitened his hands, and they appeared below his sleeves as brown as the paws of a monkey. The King Lear was a better performance than the Othello, in my judgment. In the former he acted his part, in the latter he was simply himself. He had superb outbursts of indignation and fury, accompanied by attacks of weakness and senile tremblings, and a sort of somnolent babbling, as one would expect in an old man, almost a centenarian, passing from idiocy to madness, under the weights of intolerable woes. One thing in the performance was remarkable, showing how perfect was the actor's mastery over himself; although a man of robust strength and in the flower of his age, Ira Aldrigge never, through all the evening, allowed one youthful motion to escape him; voice, step, and gesture, all were those of extreme old age.

The successes of this black tragedian piqued to emulation the great Russian actor, Samoïloff; he also performed Lear and Othello, at the Alexander Theatre, with an energy and a power truly Shakespearian. Somoïloff is an actor whose style resembles Frederick; he is unequal, capricious, often sublime, full of flashes and inspirations. He is at once terrible and burlesque; he can represent with equal ability the hero or the drunken man, and is besides personally a gentleman of most pleasing manners. An artist to the finger-tips, he designs his own costumes, and draws caricatures that are as clever in the execution as they are in the idea. His performances were well attended, though not so successful as those of Ira Aldrigge. But Semoïloff could not make himself a negro!

XIII.

THE TCHOUKINE-DVOR.

EVERY city has its mysterious receptacle hidden somewhere, far away from the centre of the town, which the stranger, whose habits lead him day after day through the same net-work of fashionable streets, never sees; its rubbish heap, whereon are thrown the débris of luxury, soiled, faded, and past all recognition, yet still good enough to find purchasers at fifth or sixth hand. To this come at last the tasteful bonnets, the dainty triumphs of the milliner, now shapeless, torn, and soiled, fit to coif a learned donkey; to this, the fine black broad-cloth coat which was once starred with decorations, and figured at splendid entertainments; to this, the dresses of a single evening, thrown in the morning to the *femme de chambre*,—the yellowed blonde, the frayed lace, the worn fur; and here, too, are the countless pieces of cast-off furniture. It is, in short, the very humus and stratum of civilizations. Paris has its Temple; Madrid, its Rastro; Constantinople, its *Bazaar des poux;* St. Petersburg, its Tchoukine-Dvor,—a rag-fair most curious to visit.

Let us drive up the Newsky Prospekt, past the Gasthini-Dvor, a kind of Palais Royal with galleries and elegant shops, and just at this point say to the isvochtchik, "Na leva!" Turning to the left, you will cross two or three streets, and find yourself at your destination.

Let us enter—if your olfactory nerves are not too delicate—through the bazaar of shoes and leather. The strong odor of the leather combined with a musty smell of sour cabbage forms a perfume peculiar to the spot.

Strangers notice it more than do the Russians themselves, but I confess it is not easy to become accustomed to it. One must not, however, be fastidious, if he wishes to see everything.

The booths in the Tchoukine-Dvor, are made of ends of planks; they are paltry little sheds, and the snow, whose immaculate whiteness lay fresh on their roofs that day, made their filthy appearance even more offensive.

Festoons of old greasy leather boots,—and what boots!—stiffened skins of animals which recalled, in a sort of sinister caricature, the figure of the living creature, and touloupes, ragged and dirty, yet still keeping a vague impress of their former wearer, formed a composite decoration of the frontage of each booth. Hanging, as it was, in the open air, and with here and there a little snow resting on it, all this had the most wretchedly doleful aspect, under a lowering, yellowish-gray sky. The merchants were scarcely more attractive than their merchandise; and yet Rembrandt, had he seen them, could have made, with a few scratches on a plate of polished copper, some miracle of an etching of these bearded men wrapped in sheepskins, and given at one flash a redeeming character to all this sordid squalor. Art finds its wealth everywhere.

A multitude of narrow lanes intersect one another in the Tchoukine-Dvor, and each trade has its own special quarter. Numerous little chapels showing, by the lamp-light within, the silver and gilt of their miniature iconostases, shine at the corners of these lanes. Elsewhere throughout the Tchoukine-Dvor, light is forbidden; a spark might set in blaze this collection of rubbish. Only for the glorifying of their religious pictures, do they brave the danger, and the masses of goldsmith's work in this gloomy and squalid place gleam with strange splendor. Buyers and sellers, as they pass these chapels, make countless signs of the cross, in the Greek fashion. Some of the most devout, or the least busy, prostrate themselves, the forehead touching the snow, murmur a prayer, and, as they rise, throw a kopeck into the box fastened by the door.

One of the most curious streets in the Tchoukine-Dvor is that where religious pictures are sold. If one were not quite sure of the date, he might think himself in the Middle Ages, so archaic is the style of these paintings, for the most part the work of yesterday. In all this work, Russia preserves with the greatest fidelity her Byzantine traditions. Her religious painters seem to have served apprenticeship on Mt. Athos in the convent of Agria Lavria, in accordance with the manual of painting, compiled by the monk Denys, the pupil of Panselinos, the Raphael of this very peculiar form of art, in which too exact an imitation of nature is regarded as a sort of idolatry.

These shops are lined with sacred objects from floor to ceiling; brown-faced Madonnas, copies of St. Luke's portrait of the Virgin, in stamped drapery of gold or silver; Christs and saints, all the more appreciated by the faithful, the more primitively barbarous they are; pictures representing scenes from the Old and New Testaments, a multitude of figures in stiff attitude, the coloring purposely embrowned and covered with a yellow varnish, as are the frames of Persian mirrors, to simulate the smoke of centuries; plates of bronze, articulated like the leaves of a screen, framing a series of scriptural bas-reliefs; crosses of oxydized silver of a graceful Greco-Byzantine form, on which a world of microscopic figures, in the space left free by the old Slavonic inscriptions, represent the sacred Drama of Golgotha; ornamented covers for books, and a thousand other little devotional objects.

Some of these pictures, finished with more care, gilded or veneered more richly, rise to considerable prices. It is useless to look for any merit in them as works of art; but all, even the most coarsely executed, have an amount of character in them that is truly astonishing. Their rude forms, the crudeness of their coloring, and the mixture of goldsmith's work and painting, give them a certain officially religious stamp, better suited, perhaps, to stimulate devotion than a more skilful work of art would be. All these objects are identically similar to those which their ancestors revered. Immutable as dogma, they are perpetuated from age to age; art has had no bearing upon them, and to correct them, in spite of their rudeness and their simplicity, would have seemed a sacrilege. The blacker, more smoky, more rigid and ungraceful is the Madonna, the more confidence she inspires in the believer at whom she looks with her great sombre eyes, unchanging as eternity.

At the same time, it must be owned that a modern taste has invaded higher quarters in Russian society. At St. Isaac's, and in other chapels and churches of recent construction, while the general appearance and consecrated attitude is preserved, the artist has not been afraid to give to his Madonnas all the ideal beauty that he could; he has cleared the faces of his wild and bearded saints from their coating of bistre, and restored them to a human complexion. From an artistic point of view, no doubt this is better, but perhaps the religious effect may be weakened. The Byzantine-Russian style, with its gold backgrounds, the rigid symmetry of its forms and its use of metals and precious stones, lends itself admirably to church decoration; it has a mysterious and supernatural air that harmonizes well with the purpose for which it is designed.

In one of these booths, I discovered, arranged as a Greek Madonna, a little copy of the *Vierge à l'hostie* of Ingres. The hands joined in prayer, the fingers touching delicately at the tips, were not badly done, in spite of the difficulty of the *pose;* and the head preserved to a considerable degree the character of its original. I scarcely could have expected to find in the Tchoukine-Dvor, a souvenir of this illustrious master. How and by what paths did it come to serve as a pattern for a Russian sacred picture? I asked the price. They charged but ten rubles for it, because it had no silver ornamentation.

The dealers in sacred objects are more decent in their attire than their neighbors, the sellers of leather. They wear, in general, the old Russian costume, the caftan of blue or green cloth, fastened with a button near the shoulder, girt at the waist by a narrow belt; the hair parted in the middle is long on either side and cut short at the back, leaving the neck free, the blonde or brown beard thick and curled. The faces of many of them are beautiful, serious, intelligent, and gentle, and would serve as a model for the Christs they sell, did not Byzantine art forbid the imitation of nature in its sacred pictures. When they see that you stop before their booths, they courteously invite you to enter, and if you should buy nothing but the merest trifles, they will gladly show you everything, calling your attention, not without a certain pride, to their richest or most finely wrought wares.

Nothing is more curious to the stranger than these Russian shops. He can most easily deceive himself in buying for an antique something perfectly modern; in Russia, the ancient dates from yesterday, and the same forms, in religious representations, are repeated without variation. Pictures which a connoisseur, an expert even, would take for the work of some Greek monk of the ninth or tenth century, have often just come from an adjoining *atelier*, the gold varnish scarcely yet dry.

It is amusing to see the naïve and pious admiration of the mujik, passing through the street, which might be called the Holy Street of the Tchoukine-Dvor. Notwithstanding the cold, he stands still in ecstasy before the saints and madonnas, and dreams of possessing some such picture to hang up, with a lamp in front of it, in a corner of his cabin built of fir-logs. But he goes away, regarding the purchase as beyond his means. Now and then, one richer than the rest, enters, after having fingered the little roll of paper rubles stowed away in his purse, to see if it seems thick enough, and, after long discussion, emerges, bringing his purchase carefully wrapped up. They do their reckoning in the Chinese manner, with an abacus, a kind of frame crossed by iron wires, on which are strung balls that are moved up and down according to the figures to be added.

Not everybody is a purchaser in the Tchoukine-Dvor; its narrow lanes are crowded with a checkered population, for the most part idlers merely; the mujik in his touloupe, the soldier in gray capote, elbow the gentleman in his pelisse, and the antiquary hoping for some treasure,—a hope but seldom satisfied, for simplicity has taken its flight from this bazaar, and, to be on the safe side, the dealers ask extravagant prices for the least trifles. A regret for having parted cheaply with some rare object of whose value they were ignorant, has rendered them more jealous than the Auvergnats of the Rue de Lappe. A little of everything may be found in this bazaar; the old books have their quarter, French, English, German, from all countries in the world, they are stranded here upon the snow among Russian books, odd volumes, ragged, stained, and worm-eaten. Sometimes the patient investigator will find among heaps of trash, an *incunabulum*, a first edition, a lost book, long out of print, which has made its way at last to the Tchoukine-Dvor through a series of adventures strange enough to furnish material for a humorous Odyssey. Some of these booksellers do not know how to read, a circumstance which by no means prevents them from perfectly understanding their merchandise.

There are also booths for engravings and black or colored lithographs. You will frequently meet portraits of Alexander I., or the Emperor Nicholas, of grand-dukes and grand-duchesses, high dignitaries and generals of former reigns, drawn by hands more zealous than skilful, and giving a strange idea of their august models. It may be easily believed that there are numerons copies of the *Quatre Parties du Monde*, the *Quatre Saisons*, the *Demande en Marriage*, the *Noce*, the *Coucher et le Lever de la mariée*, and all the horrible daubs of the Rue Saint-Jacques.

Among the loiterers and the purchasers, women are in the minority; it would be the other way in Paris. The Russian women, although nothing compels them to do so, seem to have preserved the oriental habit of seclusion; they rarely go out. Scarcely will you see, at remote intervals, a solitary female mujik, her kerchief knotted under the chin, her overcoat of cloth or felt drawn around her heavy skirts like a man's redingote, with thick leather boots, stumbling through the snow, leaving tracks that could not, it would seem, belong to the more delicate half of the human race; the other women, those who stop before the shop-windows, are Germans or other foreigners. In the booths of the Tchoukine-Dvor, as in the bazaars of Smyrna or Constantinople, men are the dealers. I do not remember seeing a Russian shop-woman.

The street of second-hand furniture would furnish material for a series of lectures on domestic economy, and would throw much light upon Russian home life for any man who knew how to decipher from these fragments in various stages of preservation, the history of their former owners: all styles are represented here, fashions gone-by form regular stratifications; each period deposits its layer. The predominating objects are those great green-leather sofas, a truly Russian article of furniture.

Elsewhere are trunks, valises, *karsines*, and other articles of a traveller's outfit, extending into the middle of the street and half buried under snow; then old saucepans, ironware of every kind, broken-nosed jugs, wooden bowls, utensils out of use, no longer having names in any tongue, fragments of cloth that are nothing more than lint, coming only into the rag-pickers' province. If it were not near zero, an expedition through a region like this would have its perils, but all the swarming tribe perishes in such a temperature. Had it been warmer weather the danger for me would have been increased by the proximity of an organ-grinder, who followed me persistently in the hope of a few kopecks, which I was for some time reluctant to open my pelisse far enough to obtain for him. This organ-grinder was a most grotesque and characteristic object. A greasy rag fringed out at the edges surrounded his head like a mock diadem; an old bear-skin, once the apron of a droschky, covered his shoulders, and, projecting over the case of the organ, designed for the poor wretch a hump upon the lower part of his back, which contrasted oddly with his lean figure. Really it was not easy to account for this hump so unusually situated, for nothing but the crank of the organ came through the matted fur, and the hand turning it recalled the gesture of a monkey scratching himself eagerly.

A kind of baize tunic notched in saw teeth around the edge, and felt boots, completed the costume. The boots alone were a whole poem of poverty and dilapidation. Crushed, mis-shapen, wrinkled, they were half as long again as the foot, and their toes rose up like peaks of a Chinese roof, so that the legs seemed to curve under the weight of the torso and the organ, as if they had contained no tibias. The poor fellow had the appearance of walking upon two sickles.

As to the face, it suggested one of Gavarni's figures; a many-sided nose flattened between two projecting cheek-bones, over a wide mouth in a tangle of wrinkles, was the most perceptible feature, for the elf-locks of the hair and beard, glued together with morsels of ice, prevented me from catching the outlines of the face; however, from beneath the shaggy eyebrows gleamed a little steel-blue eye, expressing a kind of philosophic mischief. The Russian winter had illuminated with its northern red this copy in flesh and rags of a Parisian lithograph, till it was like a tomato surrounded with tow.

The organ, concealed under the bear-skin, when its master teased it with the crank, whined lamentably, seemed to beg for mercy, uttered asthmatic sighs, coughed, wheezed like one dying. Occasionally with the few teeth left on its wheel, it bit into two or three airs of a former age, wavering, feeble, tremulous, dolefully comic, false enough to make the dogs howl, but touching, after all, as those refrains of other days which the great-grandmother a hundred years old, fallen into her dotage, murmurs with broken voice and whistling breath. At last these spectres of songs came to be something fearful.

Sure of the effect of his instrument, and seeing that he had a stranger to deal with—for towards a Russian he would not have allowed himself such urgency—the rogue, with the volubility of a monkey, kept on turning his crank until, when he had made himself sufficiently intolerable, a great handful of copper reduced him to silence; he received my kopecks with a smile, and, to prove his gratitude, stopped short in a waltz just commenced. The organ uttered a deep sigh of relief.

I have described the picturesque side of the Tchoukine-Dvor. It was the one most amusing to me. There are, besides, covered passage-ways bordered with shops containing articles of daily consumption of all kinds: smoked fish for the long Greek Lent; olives; butter white as that which comes from Odessa; green apples; red berries, of which they make tarts; new furniture; clothing; boots and shoes; clothing materials, and jewelry for the common people;—all this is curious, but nothing is more singular than this oriental bazaar itself spread out in the midst of the snow.

XIV.

ZICHY.

IF you walk on the Newsky Prospekt in St. Petersburg—and it is as difficult to avoid doing this as it is, when you are in Venice, to keep away from the Plaza di San Marco; in Naples, from the Strada di Toledo; in Madrid, from the Puerta del Sol, or in Paris, from the Boulevard des Italiêns—you will doubtless observe Beggrow's shop. In front of it, the sidewalk is always blocked with a curious crowd, who, quite regardless of the cold, stand gazing with interest at the oil-paintings, water-colors, engravings, photographs, statuettes, even the color-boxes in the window. Above the group the vapor of many breaths is condensed into a cloud, and forms, so to speak, a permanent fog; to it you will not fail to add your own, as you wait your chance to reach the window when some spectator shall suddenly and most opportunely recollect that he has business at the other end of the city, over the Anischkov Bridge in the Ligowka, or across the river in the remotest avenue of Vassili-Ostrov. If, however, you are not yet quite acclimated, and the severity of the cold is alarming, boldly turn the handle of the door, and fearlessly enter this sanctuary. Beggrow is a young man of finished manners, and truly a gentleman; though you should make no purchase, he will treat you with faultless politeness, and will courteously show you all his treasures. The artist, the society man, the scholar, the amateur, frequent this shop, as they do Desforges' in Paris; it is the place to look over portfolios, to examine the new engravings, to air one's aesthetics, and to obtain the latest intelligence in the world of art.

One day when I was there looking over some heliographic proofs, a great water-color placed in a corner upon an easel drew my attention by its warm and brilliant coloring, although it was already too late in the afternoon for the light to be good. I have noticed, however, that paintings, especially those of a high order, sometimes at this hour have a magical phosphorescence. It would seem that they retain and concentrate for a moment the light that they are about to lose.

I drew nearer, and found myself in the presence of a work of art which it was impossible to ascribe to any known master, and yet one which any of them would have been glad to claim. It was not Bonington, it was not Louis Boulanger, it was not Eugene Lami, nor Cattermole, nor Lewis, nor Delacroix, nor Decamps, nor any of those who have carried into the use of water-colors all the strength and richness of oil; this manner was perfectly new, this handling original; it was a surprise, a discovery, an unclassified vintage in the domain of art of a taste, a bouquet, a flavor, unusual but exquisite.

The picture represented a Florentine orgie of the sixteenth century. Some old nobles, accomplished libertines, ancient wrecks of elegance, have been at supper with some young courtesans. Upon the pillaged and devastated table glitter water-jars, vases, dishes for sweetmeats, boxes for spicery, carved in the manner of Benvenuto Cellini; heel-taps of wine gleam with ruby and topaz lights at the bottom of cups and flagons; fruits and leaves together have rolled off the enamelled platters. In the background, whose transparent darkness concentrates the light full upon the groups of figures, you faintly discern the faded frescos and tapestries, side-boards, shelves, carved cabinets, here and there a bluish fillet marking the relief; and in the compartments of the ceiling you guess at rather than perceive the gilded and painted arabesques. The figures, with the ease of their motion, the variety of their attitude, their postures caught upon the instant, the bold foreshortening, the drawing so free and true, betrayed a talent long since sure of itself, nourished upon strong studies, knowing perfectly what great painting is, and bending the human figure into postures of every kind, even those which a model would scarcely know how to assume. The young women, their extravagant toilette a little disordered, laugh and throw themselves back, displaying the false gayety of the courtesan, and but half resisting the attack which they know is without danger; fatigue, disgust, and *ennui* pierce through the paint and the artificial laughter. One, turning away a little, seems to dream of her young lover, or of her years of innocence; another appears, through her scornful *abandon*, to be possessed with a mad whim to pluck off the wig of the superannuated libertine who kneels with difficulty at her feet, in the gallant fashion of a by-gone day; but the power of the yellow metal conquers and over-rules all these fancies; and in their gracious attitudes, full of a secret deference, one can see that women such as these, find no man, however old or ugly, utterly ridiculous, so long as he is rich. Besides, these old nobles, despite the traces of age and of evil living, rendered perhaps even more evident by the efforts made to conceal them, have a grand air still, in their garments whose elegance is extravagant, like Vittore Carpaccio's fine costumes, and whose youthful cut becomes unshapely on the broken-down figures, the withered or heavy limbs. In their plastered wrinkles more than one profound meditation, worthy of Machiavelli, may be read; and may be read, also, the wicked delight of the old man, profaning, at the price of gold, the delicate flowers of beauty and youth. Some of them seem happy—like slugs upon roses; others confess, by their air of dejection, the inconsolable sadness of exhausted nature, sinking under vice; and all this with a coloring, a spirit, a touch, a skill truly wonderful, with a light suggestion of caricature, arrested in time—for painting is a serious thing, and a grimace fixed and unchanging becomes intolerable.

In a corner of this picture was written an odd name, of Hungarian orthography and Italian sound: Zichy.

When I warmly expressed my admiration, Beggrow replied simply: "Yes, it is by Zichy;" taking it as a matter of course that a water-color by Zichy should be a magnificent thing; and he opened a portfolio containing several sepias by this young master, of character so varied, so contrasting, that it would have been easy to attribute them to different artists.

There was, first, a scene most pathetic and distressing, —a poor family who have lost their way upon the steppe. At the foot of a huge mass of ice, an ill-fated woman, exhausted with fatigue, overpowered by cold, scourged by the wind, blinded by snow, has sought temporary and insufficient shelter. To that irresistible desire to sleep which seizes a person suffering from intense cold, and which is the first step toward freezing, has followed death itself; the nose is pinched, the eyelids convulsed, and the mouth, stiffened in death, seems to breathe forth a frozen sigh. Near the mother is stretched out a little dead child, half wrapped in a ragged covering, and foreshortened in the drawing with incredible boldness and skill. A boy of thirteen or fourteen, more robust, whose warm young blood has been better able to resist the fatal torpor, is anxiously busied about his mother; frightened, desperate, with passionate tenderness and wild terror, he tries to awaken her from this obstinate slumber which is to him so mysterious. You feel that he has never seen any person die, and yet, by his intense alarm, by his secret horror, it is evident that he suspects the presence of death. Soon this adored mother will be to him as frightful as a spectre; instead of a human creature, will be a corpse; and yet soon, too, the white shroud of snow will have covered all.

We have, next, a Doge's wife, her Marino Faliero at her side, listening dreamily to a young musician who plays upon a dulcimer. They are seated in a rich Venetian apartment, opening upon a balcony with colonnettes and trefoils in the Moorish or Lombard style. Like Gustave Doré, Zichy understands and loves the mediæval; he knows the architecture, the styles of furniture, of armor, of costume, of decoration, peculiar to the Middle Ages, and reproduces it all, not with painful archaic labor, but with a free, careless hand, as if his models were before his eyes, or he had lived familiarly among them. He does not bring out, as does Doré, the grotesque and fantastic; he represents by preference the more elegant side, still avoiding the romanesque and troubadour style of Marchangy.

A third drawing made a complete conquest of me. The two former recall, one, the pathetic sentimentality of Ary Scheffer and Octave Taessert; the other, Chasseran's etchings illustrating Othello, and neither at all resembled the Florentine Orgie. The one now before me suggests the best, the most brilliant and clever of Gavarin's sepias. It is an officer of spahis, or African chasseurs, about to rejoin his regiment, and receiving with the most martial indifference the adieus of a too tender beauty who weeps and sobs upon his shoulder, in an attitude of grief that is certainly most touching. The chasseur, a Ulysses always on the point of departure, and habituated to the lamentations of Calypsos left behind in the garrison islands, is enduring the warm shower of tears, like rain at one's back, with a dull, patient, tired air,—knocking off with the nail of his little finger the white ash formed at the end of his cigarette, and turning in his toes, like a man who no longer cares about being elegant. It is impossible to imagine the wit, the finesse, the sparkle of this little water-color, done casually, but with incredible correctness, on the first bit of drawing-paper that came to hand. If, in order to give an idea of a painter unknown at Paris, I have been forced to seek resemblances, do not on this account think of copies or imitations. Zichy has that true genius which draws from itself only; in the pathways of art, he has never met those masters whom one might say he resembles. Some of these names, even, are unknown to him.

"How has it happened," I said to Beggrow, "that Zichy has sent nothing to the expositions; that we have seen no picture of his engraved; that we have met no painting or sketch of his in any collection? Does Russia guard with jealous care, for her exclusive gratification, the secret of this talent so subtle, new, and strange?"

"Yes," Beggrow said quietly, "Zichy paints a great deal for the court and for the city; none of his pictures remain very long in my shop, and it is by an accident that you had found so many of them here to-day. The frames were not quite ready. You came in opportunely: for the Florentine Orgie will be taken away this evening."

I left the shop, and—like La Fontaine, who, delighted and surprised on having lately read the book of Baruch, went about asking, "Have you read Baruch?"—I began every conversation by the question, "Do you know Zichy?"

"Certainly!" was always the reply; and one day, M. Luoff, director of the Conservatory of Design, said to me, "If you desire to know him yourself, I can procure you the pleasure."

There is in St. Petersburg a kind of club, called the Friday Society: it is composed of artists, and meets, as its name indicates, on Friday of every week. There is no particular place of meeting, every member receiving the brotherhood in turn, till the list is ended and they recommence at the top.

Shaded lamps stand in a row on a long table, which is covered with drawing materials, stretched paper, pencils, pastels, water-color palettes for sepia and for India ink,—everything, in short, which may be needed for the evening's work. Each member of the club takes a seat at the table, and is bound to execute in the course of the evening a picture of some kind, in pencil, crayon, or water-color, which becomes the property of the society, and is sold, or disposed of by lottery, the proceeds going to form a fund for the assistance of unfortunate artists, or those in a state of temporary embarrassment. Cigars and cigarettes—papyros, they are called in Russia—bristle from the horns of carved wood or varnished earth that are placed between the desks, and each man, without interrupting his work, takes to himself a cigarette or an Havana, as he may prefer, and is soon, work and all, wrapped in a cloud of smoke. Glasses of tea circulate, and some kind of small pastry; they sip the scalding beverage, and rest a little and talk. Those who do not feel themselves sufficiently inspired, rise and go to look at what others are doing, often returning suddenly to their seats, as if stung by emulation, or inspired by some lucky flash.

Towards one o'clock in the morning, a light supper is served, where the frankest cordiality prevails. It is enlivened by discussions on art, stories of travel, ingenious paradoxes, the wildest of jokes, and, sometimes, a mimicry truer than anything that is ever done on the stage, —a trick, this, whose secret artists attain through their incessant study of nature. Then everybody goes home having done a good work—in more senses than one— and having been amused—a rare thing! It would be well if some society like this existed in Paris, where, as a rule, artists seldom meet, and know one another only as rivals.

I had the honor of being admitted into the Friday Society, and it was at one of these meetings that I saw Zichy for the first time.

We were at the house of Lavazzari, a cosmopolite among artists, who has seen everything and sketched everything. Water-colors—in which I recognized the Alhambra, the Parthenon, Venice, the Pylons of Karnak, the tombs of Lycia—covered walls which were in some places half hidden by the leaves of tropical plants,

8

growing here, as in so many Russian houses, with the greatest luxuriance.

A young man of thirty or thirty-two years of age, with long fair hair falling in disordered curls, grayish blue eyes, full of animation and intellect, blonde, slightly curling beard, and harmonious, pleasing features, stood by a table, arranging his paper and brushes and glass of water; he was replying with a silvery laugh, a really boyish laugh, to some pleasantry which a comrade had, at the moment, addressed to him. This was Zichy.

On being presented to him, I expressed, as well as I was able, the ardent admiration with which his Florentine Orgie, and the sketches I had seen at Beggrow's, had inspired me. He listened with evident pleasure (for he could not doubt my sincerity), mingled, however, with a modest surprise which certainly was not assumed. He seemed to say, " Am I really so great a man as that?" —Not that Zichy is unaware of his own talents, but that he does not attach to them the importance that he ought. He believes that what he does so easily, is an easy thing to do, and he is a little surprised that people should be enraptured over what has cost him only three or four hours' work, all the time smoking and talking. The master-strokes of genius are done with ease, when one is a genius—and this he is.

Zichy paid me the compliment of improvising a composition upon a subject drawn from *Roi Candaule*, a recent antique of mine, which has already had the honor of inspiring one of Pradier's statues, and one of Gérôme's paintings. The moment chosen is when Nyssia, unable to endure that two living mortals should know the secret of her charms, introduces Gyges into the nuptial chamber and directs his poignard against the breast of the sleeping king. Under the sure and rapid hand of the artist, a splendid Græco-Asiatic interior was created as by enchantment. The Heraclid, with his athlete's muscles, already lies overpowered with sleep upon the cushions, and Nyssia, white and slender as a statuette cut in a column of Parian marble, lets fall her last garment, a gesture voluptuous, yet rendered terrible by its significance, for it is the signal agreed upon for the murder; Gyges advances with the step of a tiger, pressing the cold blade convulsively against his breast. The pencil ran unhesitating, as if it copied some invisible model.

All this time the other artists were at work too, with an ardor and rapidity almost incredible. Svertchkov was drawing, in colored crayon, a horse, resting his head sociably upon his companion's shoulder. Like Horace Vernet, like Alfred de Dreux, like Achille Giroux, Svertchkov excels in representing the play of light upon the satiny skin of the thorough-bred horse; he understands the steely springs of their sinewy legs; he knows how to interlace the veins upon the smoking neck, and to make the fire flash from their eyes: but he has a weakness for the little Ukraine horse, dishevelled, shaggy, unkempt, the poor beast of the mujik; him he paints, harnessed to the rosposnik, the télèga, or the sledge, pulling, in the ice or in the snow, through pine woods whose branches are bent under their wintry load. You feel how he loves these brave animals, so sober, so patient, so courageous, so inured to fatigue; he is the Sterne of these kind creatures, and that page, in the Sentimental Journey, upon the donkey, eating a leaf of artichoke, is not more pathetic than some of his sketches. Here too I found, busied with the foaming waters of a little cascade, my old friend Pharamond Blanchard, whom I have never chanced to meet in Paris, but with whom I have passed many an hour at Madrid, at Smyrna, and at Constantinople; and now I must needs come to St. Petersburg to see him again after six years.

Popaf, a Russian Teniers, was sketching with charming simplicity a scene of peasants drinking their tea; Lavazzari was guiding an *araba* drawn by oxen through the narrow streets of an oriental city; while Charlemagne, whose correct and faithful views of St. Petersburg are so much admired in Daziaro's window, was adding, upon his own authority, a new island to Lake Maggiore, and covering it with fairy structures enough to ruin the Borromeo princes, notwithstanding all their wealth. Farther on, Lwoff, the Director of the Conservatory of Design, was lighting up with warm sunshine the public square of Tiflis; Prince Maxintoff was launching at full gallop a detachment of firemen, before whom droschkys fled away in all haste, hugging the wall with their wheels; an Italian, Premazzi,—who has had the skill to give in warm and transparent water-colors all the charm of a Venetian landscape to the quay of the Admiralty,—to make a picture from the canal of Fontanka which Canaletto or Guardi would have acknowledged,—to render with a truly oriental magic of coloring the Byzantine splendors of the Kremlin and its motley, pagoda-like churches,—was rounding above its elegant columns the porch of a convent, its white façade relieved against the blue surface of a lake; Hoch, who was giving the finishing-touches to a woman's head, seemed to me to mingle with the pure Roman type, beloved of Leopold Robert, something of Winterhalter's peculiar grace; and Rühl, with a pinch of plumbago and a flock of cotton-wool was sketching vapory Gudins and Aivasovkys,—Rühl, who, after supper, can be, by turns, for his friends' amusement, Macaluso or Henri Monnier,—unless, running his agile fingers over the keys of the piano, he will prefer to play the last opera, or to improvise for us a new one.

In my turn I was forced to do my share, for, as a rule, no profane presence can be permitted at the club, with only the one exception of M. Mussard, who, for the sake of his exquisite taste, his wit, and his attainments, is excused from work of any kind, on express condition that he shall talk! A crayon-head, made to pass for an Ophelia, by the aid of some flowers and bits of straw in the hair, was kindly accepted as *morceau de reception;* and in the Friday cœnacula they were good enough to treat me as not a Philistine; at every meeting, I had my desk like the rest, and my small efforts were added to the common portfolio of the society.

Meanwhile Zichy had washed in the entire drawing, and was preparing to add that play of light and shade in which he is so skilful, when supper was announced, wherein a dish of macaroni, juicy, and of peculiar but unexceptionable flavor, held an honorable place. The charming profile of an Italian girl hanging upon the wall may perhaps account for the perfection of this classic dish.

The following day I received a note from Zichy, in which he informed me that, having re-read *Roi Candaule,* he had torn his sketch into a thousand fragments—the barbarian! the Vandal!—He also invited me to dine with him, that he might show me, while waiting for the soup to be served, things more worthy of my notice, and perhaps justifying the good opinion I had formed of him. The note was accompanied by a little plan from his own hand, destined to aid me in finding his house, a precaution by no means superfluous, considering my perfect ignorance of the Russian language. By aid of his plan, and with the four phrases that form the staple of the traveller's conversation with the isvochtchik: *pré-ama* (straight ahead), *na prava* (to the right), *na leva* (to the left), *stoi* (stop),—I arrived safely at the bridge of Vosnesensky, not far from the painter's house.

Although in my travels I have always made reticence upon some points a duty, I shall take the reader with me in paying this visit to Zichy, without feeling that I abuse, in so doing, the hospitality offered me; one ought, it is true, to stop before the threshold of domestic life,—but it may be permitted to open, part way, the door of the studio. Zichy will pardon me for bringing to see him a few visitors who have not been formally introduced.

A suite of rooms in Russia always begins with a sort of cloak-room, where the guest leaves his pelisse in charge of a servant, who hangs it up, and the overshoes are removed also, as in the east they lay aside their slippers before entering the mosque. That foreground of old shoes which so much surprised the Parisian eye in Gérôme's picture, the Prayer of the Arnauts, is to be seen here in every ante-room, if the master of the house be at all a person of consequence, a celebrity, or a favorite; which is to say, there is always an abundant supply of shoemakers' wares in the cloak-room at Zichy's. However, on this day, there was neither overshoe, nor furred boot, nor felt gaiter in position under the rack; Zichy had denied himself to other guests, that our conversation might be quite uninterrupted.

I traversed, first, a drawing-room of considerable size, one wall of which was adorned with a superb collection of arms and equipments used in hunting. There were guns, carbines, knives, game-bags, powder-horns,—suspended from antlers, and grouped with skins of lynx, wolf, and fox, trophies or models. It would have seemed the abode of some famous hunter, at least of some sportsman, had not a picture of a prophet in a cave, the heavy shadows suggesting Rembrandt, and proof engravings of the Hemi-cycle of Paul Delaroche, and the Smala of Horace Vernet, together with some empty frames awaiting pictures, attested that this was the home of an artist.

Vases containing hothouse plants were arranged along the window, keeping alive the tradition of green, a color for eight months lost in Russia, and which a painter, more than any other man, has need to preserve.

In the centre of the room stood the great round table of the Friday Club.

The next room was much smaller. Two sides of it were lined with divans, which bent away from each wall at an oblique angle at the back of the room, till they were met by one of those elegant carved-screens, like that of a choir or of a convent parlor, real masterpieces of Russian carpentry, in which the wood is bent and twisted like cast-iron, into leaves and volutes and trellis-work, with colonnettes, trefoils, arabesques, and caprices of every description; ivies and other climbing plants, springing from *jardinières*, hung their natural foliage among the carved leafage of the screen, producing the most charming effect imaginable.

With these elegant screens, cut in open-work, like a fish-knife or like paper lace, one may be partially isolated, in the centre or the corner of a drawing-room; you have at will a bedroom, a boudoir, a "retreat," as the Gothic nations express it; you are secluded, yet not solitary, and are still bathed in the general atmosphere of the apartment.

Upon consoles formed by salient parts of the carving, stood two of Pollet's graceful statuettes, The Morning Star, and Night, modelled in stearine; and through the lattice-work were visible characteristic costumes of Tchergesses, Lesghines, Circassians, and Cossacks, which, hanging against the wall behind, and quite in shadow, formed by their varied coloring a warm, rich background, against which stood out clear and light, the fine carvings of the screen.

Upon the walls I noticed, on one side, The Defeat of the Huns and The Destruction of Jerusalem, magnificent German engravings after Kaulbach's well-known frescos, and beneath, a row of medallions in pastel, portraits of the Friday Club, done by Zichy himself; on the other, the Assassination of the Duke of Guise, by Paul Delaroche, some bits of studies, some casts, and various artistic trifles.

In the last room of the suite, the one in which Zichy received me, my eye was caught, first of all, by a suit of armor for a child, of the sixteenth century, standing upon the mantel-piece in the place which the Philistine is wont to adorn with a clock. In the same taste, the mirror was replaced to advantage by a multifarious array of weapons. These were arms of every variety: swords of Toledo workmanship, the blue blades of Damascus, the *flissahs* of Kabyle, the yataghan, the *kriss*, daggers, guns with long barrels ornamented with niello-work and stocks incrusted with turquoises and coral. A second trophy composed of bows, quivers, pistols, and fowling-pieces, Georgian casques with gorgets of chain-work, steel *narghilehs* from Khorassian, Persian musket-rests, African *zagai*, and those thousand objects that the lover of the picturesque delights to gather, covered one entire wall. Zichy is a frequenter of the Tchoukine-Dvor of St. Petersburg and of Moscow; at Constantinople, he would never be able to get away from the bazaar of weapons; he has a passion for them, he hunts them out, buys them, barters for them, obtains them in exchange for his own sketches; and wherever a strange, fierce, savage instrument of destruction is unearthed, it is almost sure to find its way at last into his possession. In exhibiting all this *bric-à-brac*, Zichy might say with Rembrandt: "These are my antiques."

A second side of the room is occupied by a library, the books in many languages testifying to the good taste and learning of the artist, who reads in the original the best works in nearly all European literatures. The other two walls are pierced by windows, for the room makes the corner of the house; between the windows are various small objects, not important to describe.

But, does my reader say, a little wearied, perhaps, by these details, "You promised to show us Zichy's studio, and all that you have done is to give an inventory of the contents of three rooms more or less picturesquely furnished." It is no fault of mine, but there is no studio; neither Zichy, nor any other artist in St. Petersburg has one. No provision has ever been made for painters in this city, the "Athens of the North," though it is; no landlord has ever taken the matter into consideration; and so art finds lodging where it can, and seeks, often with fruitless labor, in suites of rooms planned solely for domestic life, a place for an easel and a favorable light; and yet neither space nor material was lacking.

Zichy was at work at a desk, on the corner of a table near a window, profiting assiduously by the last pallid rays of daylight. He was finishing a large drawing in India ink, destined to be engraved. It was a Werther at the supreme moment of the suicide. The virtuous lover of Charlotte, having condemned his love as hopeless and guilty, is making ready to execute his own sentence against himself. Upon a table covered with cloth, a sort of tribunal,—before which has been seated, to deliberate upon his own case, Werther, the judge of Werther,—burns a failing lamp, witness of this nocturnal debate. The artist represents Werther standing, like a magistrate rendering a decision, and, while his lips close, with corners a little drawn down, after pronouncing the sentence, his hand, delicate as that of a dreamer or an idler, fumbles among his papers for the handle of the pistol.

The head, lighted from below by the lamp upon the table, has all the scornful serenity which a man should have who is sure of escape from moral anguish, and who already looks at life from the other side. Everybody knows how little aid is given to the expression of tragic feeling by the powder and the curled hair and the styles of dress of 1789; and yet Zichy has been able to make of Werther, in spite of the vignettes of the time, and even the famous blue coat, an ideal creation, poetic and full of character. It has a vigor worthy of Rembrandt; the light, coming from beneath, strikes unexpectedly upon all objects, bringing them out in a strange, weird fashion; and behind Charlotte's lover rises to the very ceiling a shadow, magnified into a phantom. The spectre seems to stand ready to take the place of the man, who is about to disappear. It is not

8*

easy to imagine the strength of color obtained in this drawing in India ink, which is usually so cold.

As I have said, this artist has a multiform nature; you believe you understand him, you assign to him a rank, a manner and style characteristic, as you suppose; suddenly he places before you a new work which quite disconcerts you, and renders your former estimate incomplete. Who would have expected after this Werther to see three large water-colors of still life, representing the very same fox, wolf, and lynx whose skins hang in his drawing-room, and which he killed with his own hand? Neither Jadin, nor Barye, nor Delacroix could have done better. This talent alone would be enough to make its possessor famous in Paris, and this is but one of the least with which Zichy is endowed; there is a truthfulness of tone, a skill in the anatomical drawing, a free touch, a fortunate rendering, a comprehension of each animal's nature, of which one can have no idea. Each beast keeps his own individual characteristics perfectly in death. The fox, with half-shut eyes, his nose sharper than usual and making fine wrinkles at the corners of his mouth, seems meditating some last stratagem, which has, as it seems, proved unsuccessful. The wolf shows his fangs to their very roots, as if he had sought to bite the ball which went through him. The lynx is sublime with powerless ferocity and rage; his wide, gaping jaws open with a frightful grimace, stretched apart up to the very sockets of the glazing eyes, and forming skinny wrinkles like those which are made by a sardonic laugh; he is like some savage hero killed by the white man's treachery with an unknown weapon, and flinging out his scorn at his destroyer, even in the last agony of death.

Each one of these water-colors was executed in a single day. The rapid progress of decay required this celerity of work; but for all that, the artist has not sacrificed or falsified anything. His eye is so sure, his hand so certain, that every stroke tells.

If now you propose to class Zichy among painters of animals, you will be strangely in error; he is quite as much an historical painter; look at these magnificent pen-and-ink drawings, representing ancient Muscovite battles, and the establishment of Christianity in Russia, works of his youth, in which the influence of his German master, Waldmuller, may be distinctly observed. If you were told that these designs, so fine in their style, of so heroic cast, of such lavish invention, were Kaulbach's, you would be quite ready to believe it. I doubt even whether Kaulbach would have given all these curious barbaric details to the costumes of his Tartar warriors, for here the lack of historic documents has left the utmost latitude to the fancy of the painter. These drawings are so accurate, and so highly finished, that they only need to be enlarged by measurement to become admirable cartoons, and to be spread out as frescos upon the walls of some palace or public building.

And now what will you say, when to these severe compositions which, exposed in Goupil's window, engraved like the works of Cornélius or Overbeck, would seem to emanate from the serious school of Düsseldorf, succeeds some light fantasy, some impossible dream of love, flying away into the blue, borne by a chimæra with black, waving hair,—drawn with a pencil as delicate, as aërial as that of Vidal,—a rosy cloud shaped in the azure by the caprice of the libertine winds! Ah! you exclaim, our young Russian is a modern Watteau, a Boucher with English graces, and all the elegance of a Book of Beauty; he shall be engraved by the Robinsons or the Findens. And again your judgment is rash; for Zichy, with his fresh, boyish laugh, will draw from his port-folio and lay before you a sombre sepia, improvised one evening by lamplight, which is equal in gloomy force to the most powerful and dramatic masters.

The scene is laid in a cemetery; it is night. Feeble

rays of moonlight pierce through banks of clouds heavy with rain. Black wooden crosses, funereal monuments, columns truncated, or surmounted by an urn shrouded in crape, figures representing the Genius of Death treading out the torch of life, all the doleful forms of sepulchral architecture detach their sombre outlines from an horizon filled with mysterious terrors.

In the foreground, where the earth has been thrown up, two picks are vibrating, struck into the turf, and a hideous trio appear, busy—like the witches in Macbeth—at a deed without a name. Plunderers of churchyards, hyenas in human form,—who rifle graves to steal from death its last treasures,—the woman's gold ring, the silver rattle of the child, the lover's medallion, the reliquary of the devout,—they have disinterred a rich coffin, whose covering of black velvet with silver trimmings is pushed aside, showing the figure of a young woman, the head lying on a pillow of lace. Through the parted shroud you see the chin resting on the breast, in one of those meditations upon eternity which employ the leisure of the tomb, and one arm lying across the heart whose beating has ceased forever, and at which the worm already gnaws in secret. One of the robbers,—the face brutal, the expression that of a galley-slave, on his head a filthy cap,—holds a bit of candle which he shelters with his hand against the night-wind. The flickering light falls wan and livid upon the pallor of the dead face. Another bandit, standing half in the grave, and whose ferocious features have the effect of a wild boar among swine, is lifting in his paw the slender hand, white as wax, which the corpse abandons to him with spectral indifference. He plucks from the ring-finger, rudely separated from the rest,—broken, perhaps, under this sacrilegious handling,—a ring of value: the wedding-ring, no doubt. A third villain, on picket-duty upon the mound of a new-made grave, listens, making an ear-trumpet of his cap, to the far-off baying of a dog, disturbed by the movements of the band, or the scarcely audible step of the watchman going his rounds. A spasm of the most ignoble fear contracts his face black with shadows, and his baggy trousers, moist with dew, heavy with the crass earth of the cemetery, betray limbs and articulations like the monkey's.

Romantic horror can go no further. This drawing which I thus extol shall be seen by all Paris; it is now my own; Zichy has done me the honor to present it to me; I esteem it one of his greatest works and a work of the greatest genius. In looking at it, one is reminded of the Lazarus of Rembrandt, of the Suicide of Descamps, of the Hamlet and the Grave-diggers of Eugene Delacroix; nor does it suffer by the comparison. What magic of light and shade,—what immense effect produced by means so simple! In the foreground a little red sepia; in the distance, a few shades of India ink! The richest palette could not give more wondrous results!

To this frightful scene, which looks at first sight like a banquet of ghouls, the artist offers, by way of contrast, a Bacchante surprised by a Satyr; so pure in style, so classic, that you ask yourself from what intaglio, from what cameo, from what Pompeian fresco, from what Grecian vase of the Studii, this beautiful group is borrowed?

From antiquity we come down at once into the very heart of the mediæval period, with a composition entitled "The Jewish Martyrs,"—a work of great value, wherein Zichy has depicted, in a manner as picturesque as it is profound, the two-fold persecution, political and religious, which, under pretext of avenging the death of a God, forever whetted its sword against the unhappy nation of Israel.

In the depths of a cellar, or rather, perhaps, of a subterranean back-shop,—an insufficient asylum, a precarious hiding-place,—is gathered a family of Jews, the very embodiment of desolation and terror. The solid doors of this vault have given way, in spite of their bolts and bars and locks, under the pressure from without, and, torn from their hinges, have fallen in upon the steps. A flood of light penetrates this mysterious retreat, and reveals all its secrets. At the head of the stairs are seen, appearing with brilliant refulgence, powers spiritual and temporal; the cross and the sword shine out in the midst of the sudden light before the dazzled eyes of the poor Jews, forced in their last retreat. Amid the tumultuous ingress of the soldiers, the procession of monks advances,—gently inexorable, tranquilly fanatic, implacable as a dogma. The temporal power, the seigneur, the feudal baron, has lent to the church the means at his disposal; he has delivered over the body; the Inquisition shall now take possession of the soul. Here he stands, proud and scornful in his *pourpoint* stiff as a cuirass; a striking personification of the mediæval time. That monk with his broad, square face,—notwithstanding an *embonpoint* worthy of Friar John of the Entommeurs,—has an air of irresistible authority, and bears, like a diadem, the crown of his tonsure; one feels that he is the representative of a grand Something. Behind him, the flat face of a beadle, crushed by the fist of triviality, leans forward and regards with a rude gaze of stupid hate and curiosity, this frail human covey caught in the nest and palpitating like doves in the talons of a vulture. This man, without being more wicked than anybody else, will not fail to witness the *auto-da-fé;* and how it will make him laugh when he sees the scorched flesh shrivel in the flame! But the truly frightful figure in the picture, the one concentrating in himself its idea, is a monkish spectre, a frock like a shroud, a cowl which, like the mouth of a Gothic gargoyle, swallows up the emaciated, fleshless head, livid even in the shadow, and as terrible as that of the monk in the St. Basil of the elder Herrera. A light like the glitter of a vulture's beak reveals his thin, bony nose. Tawny, phosphorescent gleams shine vaguely under the cowl, indicating the eye, wherein all the life of this dead face has taken refuge. From this living death's-head, covered with skin, where coldly seethe so many hot passions, comes the leading thought which directs all.

The father of the family, a stately Jew, whose grand oriental features recall the Old Testament prophets, seeing all hope lost, has risen to his full height; he will degrade himself by no useless falsehood, and his half-opened cymar shows upon his breast the phylacteries, whereon are written in Hebrew characters verses from the Old Testament, and sentences from the Talmud. He will confess his faith, the old faith of Abraham and Jacob, and,—martyr without the crown,—he will die ignominiously for Jehovah,—who is, too, his persecutors' God as well as his own. His wife, once beautiful as Rachel, but whose noble features have grown withered, yet not ugly, amid terrors and humiliations, throws herself back, clasping her hands and closing her eyes, as if to shut out the frightful reality; upon her knees lies her little grandson, asleep in the midst of this tumult with the peaceful sleep of childhood; a nursling, beautiful as the Infant Jesus in his manger. The lovely young mother lies upon the ground almost fainting, her hair dishevelled, her head sinking upon her breast, her arms lifeless, without strength or thought or will,—mad with terror. Her pure Hebraic type makes real one's dreams of the Rebecca of Ivanhoe.

In the foreground, in an attitude of the boldest foreshortening, a boy rolls upon the ground, overpowered with fear. Just behind creeps the grandfather, in whom are centred all the sordid instincts of the race; with his old trembling hands and his bent body he tries to protect the vessels of gold and silver which Israel never forgets to bring out of Egypt; at this supreme moment he has but a single thought: to save the strong-box.

The execution of this drawing is both broad and finely finished; the stump and the crayon are the means employed. To strong, silvery lights are opposed shadows as velvety as those of the best English engravings. The Jewish Martyrs will itself be magnificent as an engraving, and such is, no doubt, its destination.

If Meissonier painted in water-colors he would use them as Zichy has done in a picture of his, representing a *lansquenet*. The old soldier is seated at a table, on which he has placed his helmet beside a pot of beer and a large mug; he has been drinking, and now wipes his long gray mustaches and twists them to a point. The picture is about large enough for one of Frederick the Great's snuff-boxes; but do not look for the minute, patient finish of the miniature; all is done with a firm, free touch. The hand that twists the mustache is a wonderful bit of work: muscles, bones, veins, nerves, even to the rough, sunburnt skin of the soldier,—all is there. The cuirass deceives your eye with its metallic lustre, and on the leather, defaced by long use, the rubbing of the steel has left its bluish trace. In the veteran's eyes, scarcely as large as the head of a pin, the luminous speck, the pupil, the iris, are all to be discerned: no detail of his jovial visage, reddened by sun and wind, is omitted or sacrificed. The microscopic face has the relief and the strength of an oil painting the size of life, and when you have looked at it for a few minutes, you know the man's character by heart. He is passionate, but a good boon companion, with a little knavery about him, very much addicted to liquor, and a great forager. Some enemies he has killed, no doubt; but what an Achilles of the poultry-yard is this,—how many times his rapier has served as a spit!

No one resembles Meissonier less than does Eugène Lami; Zichy reproduces both equally well, and, which is singular, has seen nothing by either of them. The flexible character of his own genius and the exigencies of the subject alone lead him to find these different modes of expression. His sketches for pictures representing scenes of coronation are marvels of brilliancy, grace, and aristocratic elegance. No painter of high life has ever rendered with more splendor of effect, the procession, the ceremonial, the gala; the pencil of the artist seems to sparkle when he represents the sparkling tumult of *fêtes*; it assumes dignity when he has to paint interiors of Byzantine churches, with their gold mosaics and velvet drapery, against which august and consecrated heads are thrown into relief, like statues of saints.

This sketch of a state performance in the Court Theatre at Moscow, is a wonderfully adroit instance of getting round an impossibility. The view is taken from the balcony, and the curved lines of the galleries rise, one above another, crowded with women bestarred with diamonds, and high dignitaries covered with orders and crosses; specks of white and yellow spangle the flat color, and make a scintillation of gold and precious stones that is fairly dazzling. Here and there, certain persons of historical or official importance are indicated, the likenesses being unmistakable, and all these beauties and splendors are bathed in a golden, diamonded, glowing atmosphere, the atmosphere of illuminations *à giorno*, so difficult to render with the means which a painter has at his command.

Finally, to complete the list of transformations, you will see Zichy emulating the successes of Grant, of Landseer, of Alfred de Dreux, and other painters of the chase. Our artist has prepared for a magnificent Game-Book, which is to be offered to the Emperor of Russia, a series of borderings for the pages, designed with the most exquisite taste. Each page has a space where is to be written the number of pieces killed, and an ample margin left free for the painter's design. Each design represents a different hunting-scene, and the difficulties of arrangement are surmounted with wonderful skill. There is the chase of the bear, the lynx, the elk, the wolf, the hare, the moor-fowl, the partridge, the snipe, the crane; each with the equipment peculiar to it, and the landscape which is its customary background: sometimes snowy, sometimes foggy; a daybreak, a twilight; a thicket or a heath, according to the haunts and the habits of the game. Deer of every kind, and creatures of fur and of feather, blood-horses, hunting-dogs, guns, knives, powder-horns, spears, and all implements of the chase, are rendered with a skill, a truth, and an accuracy almost incredible, and in a light tone which never goes beyond the gamut of ornament and harmonizes with the silvery, russet, or bluish tints of the landscape. Each hunt is led by a great officer of the palace, some noble, whose head—no larger than your finger-nail—is an exquisite portrait in miniature. The collection ends with a stroke of wit in the best taste. Among all these Nimrods, mighty hunters before the Lord, ought to be found Count A., who never hunts! Zichy has represented him descending the palace stairs, coming to meet the Emperor, on the latter's return from the chase. Thus Count A. has his place in the picture, and still no violence is done to the truth.

I stop, for one must not go on forever; but I have not said all. A chapter might be employed in the description of this Hunting-Book, with its fifteen or twenty leaves, and there are other pictures, which I have not even mentioned. Like Gustave Doré, Zichy is a very phenomenon of genius,—a *portentum*, to use a Latin word,—a crater perpetually in eruption. But I have said enough to show that this artist is one of the most wonderful men who has lived since 1830, that climacteric period of art.

XV.

ST. ISAAC'S.

THE first object that fixes the attention of the traveller, who, sailing up the Gulf of Finland, draws near St. Petersburg, is the dome of St. Isaac's, resting like a golden mitre above the city's silhouette. If the sky is clear and there is sunshine, the effect is like enchantment; but this first impression is a true one, and we shall do well to accept it. The church of St. Isaac's does indeed stand pre-eminent among the religious edifices which adorn the capital of All the Russias. Of modern construction, and but recently consecrated, we may regard it as the supreme effort of the architecture of the present day. Few temples have seen so short a period of time elapse between the laying of their corner-stone and their completion. The idea of the architect, a Frenchman, M. A. Ricard de Montferrand, has been followed first to last without modification or revision other than that introduced by himself during the erection of the work. He has had the rare good fortune to finish the edifice which he began, a building whose importance would seem to have justified it in absorbing more than one artist-life.

An all-powerful will which nothing—not even material obstacles—could resist, and which shrank from no sacrifice in the pursuit of its ends, had much to do with bringing to pass this prodigy of speed. Undertaken in 1819, under Alexander I., continued under Nicholas, completed under Alexander II., in 1858, St. Isaac's is a temple of faultless finish without and within, of absolute unity of style, bearing an exact date, and the name of its author. It is not, like most cathedrals, the slow product of time, a crystallization of the ages, where each epoch has, so to speak, secreted its stalactite, and in which too often the flow of religious faith, arrested or hindered, has not been able to permeate the whole. The symbolical derrick, which rises above so many unfinished temples in Europe, has never figured above the pediment of St. Isaac's. Uninterrupted labor in less than forty years has brought it to the point of perfection where it now is.

The aspect of St. Isaac's recalls, melted into one harmonious composition, St. Peter's at Rome, the Pantheon of Agrippa, St. Paul's in London, Ste. Geneviève in Paris, and the dome of the Invalides. In building a church with a cupola, M. de Montferrand of course made a careful study of edifices of this kind, and profited by the experience of his predecessors, without, however, losing his own originality. He selected for his dome that particular curve which was at once the most elegant and the most resistant, and, borrowing a grace from each system, he encircled it with a diadem of columns, and placed about it four bell-towers.

One would scarcely suspect, as he observes the regular simplicity of this plan, which the eye and the mind comprehend without hesitation, that St. Isaac's contains, within an apparently homogeneous construction, fragments of an earlier church which it was forced to absorb and utilize,—a church dedicated to the same patron saint, and rendered historically venerable by the names of Peter the Great, of Catherine II., and of Paul I., who all contributed more or less to its splendor, without, however, bringing it to perfection.

The plans submitted by M. de Montferrand to the Emperor Alexander I., had been adopted, and work had been commenced, when very serious doubts began to arise on two points: whether it would be possible, in uniting the new portions with the old, to secure foundations firm enough neither to settle nor be dislocated; and whether the cupola and its circle of columns could safely be raised, with their enormous weight, to so great height in air. Arguments against M. de Montferrand's projects were even publicly set forth in writing, and the activity with which the building had been carried forward suffered material abatement. However, they still kept at work in the quarries, cutting out the gigantic monoliths which were to support the pediments and the dome. At last, on the accession of the Emperor Nicholas, the plans, carefully revised, were decided to be feasible; work was resumed, and complete success has proved finally the wisdom of the decision.

It will not be possible for me to detail the ingenious methods by which the foundations of this enormous edifice were laid with security in the marshy soil, nor how the columns, each a monolith, were brought to the spot and raised to so great a height, although this work—all traces of which either are now hidden, or have ceased to exist—is not without great interest. The building itself, as it stands before us, is all with which I propose to deal.

The plan of the church of St. Isaac the Dalmatian— a saint of the Greek liturgy, by the way, and altogether distinct from the Old Testament patriarch—is a cross with arms of equal length, differing in this from the Latin cross, of which the foot is prolonged. The necessity of having the high altar in the eastern end of the church, and of preserving the iconostase already consecrated, joined to the not less inexorable necessity that the front portico, repeated exactly upon the farther side of the building, should look towards the river and the statue of Peter the Great, made it impossible to place the great door opposite to the sanctuary. The two entrances corresponding to the two principal colonnades are lateral in respect to the iconostase, opposite which a door opens upon the small octostylic portico, which has but one row of columns, this also being symmetrically repeated upon the side of the building corresponding. This arrangement, which the Greek ritual requires, architecture was forced to accept, and to harmonize, as best it might, with the aspect of a building which could not present to the river, from which it is separated by a broad square, anything less than its main frontage. For this reason, the arms of the gilded crosses surmounting the dome and the bell-towers are not parallel to the façades, but to the iconostase; so that the building has two frontages, one religious, the other architectural; and at the same time, this discordance, inevitable under the given conditions, has been so skilfully masked that it requires long and close scrutiny to detect it, while from the inside it is not to be perceived at all.

Standing at the corner of the boulevard of the Admiralty, St. Isaac's appears to you in all its magnificence, and from this point you can judge of the entire edifice. The main façade presents itself fully to the view, also one of the side colonnades; three of the four bell-towers are visible, and the dome is outlined against the sky, with its encircling columns, its golden coif, and its bold lantern, above which towers the emblem of our salvation.

At the first glance the effect is most satisfying. Whatever might be too severe, too serious, in a word, too classic, in the outline, is felicitously relieved by the richness and the color of materials the most beautiful that ever human devotion employed in the construction of a temple: gold, marble, bronze, granite. Without falling into any parti-colored effect, St. Isaac's borrows from these splendid materials a harmonious variety of tints, whose genuineness makes them the more enchanting; there is no paint there, nothing fictitious; nothing in all this magnificence utters a falsehood to God. The massive granite bears up the eternal bronze, indestructible marble clothes the walls, and pure gold shines from crosses, dome, and bell-towers, giving the building the oriental and Byzantine stamp of the Greek church.

St. Isaac's rests upon a granite foundation, which should have been higher, as it seems to me. Not that it is out of proportion with the building, but that, standing alone in the centre of a square lined with palaces and lofty houses, the church as seen from a distance would have been finer, if its base had been somewhat more elevated. This is the more true, from the fact that a long horizontal line tends to have a depression in the middle,—a fact which Greek art recognized in giving a slight slope to the architrave of the Parthenon on either side from the central point. A great square, however level it may really be, always seems a little concave in the centre. It is this optical illusion, not duly allowed for, which makes St. Isaac's, in spite of the real harmony of its proportions, seem to stand too low. This disadvantage, which, after all, is not very serious, might be remedied by sloping the ground a little from the base of the cathedral, to the extremities of the square.

The approach to each of the four porticos corresponding to the arms of the Greek cross, is by three colossal granite stairs, calculated for a giant's footsteps, built without care or pity for human limbs; on the three sides where there are entrances, however, these colossal steps are cut away opposite the doors, and the space filled by nine of reasonable dimensions. The fourth does not present this arrangement; there is no door into the building on this side, as the iconostase is at this end of the church, and the granite staircase, worthy of the temples of Karnak, reigns unbroken, save where on each side, in the angle near the wall, the steps for a narrow space are again divided by threes, so that access can be had, if desired, to the floor of the portico.

All this base of Finland granite, reddish specked with gray, is cut, polished, and put together with Egyptian accuracy, and will bear unwearied for countless ages the massive edifice which rests upon it.

The portico which looks towards the Neva is, as are all the others, octostyle, that is, composed of a row of eight columns, which are of the Corinthian order, monoliths, with base and capital of bronze. In the rear of these, two groups of similar columns, four in each, support the coffers of the ceiling and the roof of the triangular pediment, whose architrave rests upon the first row; in all, sixteen columns forming a most superb and imposing peristyle. The portico of the corresponding façade repeats this in every point. The other two, likewise octostylic, have but a single row of columns, of the same order and the same materials. They were added to the original plan while the building was in process of erection, and fulfil admirably the intention with which they were added: to give ornament to the sides of the church, which were somewhat too bare at first.

Standing among the columns, you are astonished at the great size of the shafts, which, seen from a distance, appear remarkable rather by reason of their elegance than their dimensions. These huge monoliths are not less than seven feet in diameter and fifty-six feet in height. Seen close at hand, they are like towers, circled with bronze and crowned with a brazen vegetation. There are forty-eight of these in the four porticos, not to speak of the pillars of the cupola, which are, it is true, only thirty feet in height. After Pompey's Pillar, and the Column of Alexander in St. Petersburg, these are the largest single stones that the hand of man has cut, rounded, and polished. Whichever way the light strikes, a ray, blue as the flash of steel, runs quivering along their surface smoother than a mirror, and by its perfect line, which no seam interrupts, proves to the doubting mind that the monstrous block is indeed but a single stone.

It is impossible to imagine what an idea of strength, power, and eternal duration is expressed in their mute language by these giant columns, springing upward with one impulse and bearing upon their Atlantean heads this weight of pediments and statues, which is for them so light a burden. They are like the very ribs of the earth, and it would seem they must endure as long as the earth itself.

The hundred and four monoliths employed in the construction of St. Isaac's, come from quarries situated in two small islands in the Gulf of Finland, between Viborng and Friedrichham. Everybody knows that Finland is one of the richest countries in the world in granite. Some cosmic cataclysm, anterior to all history, doubtless accumulated there in enormous masses this beautiful material, indestructible as nature.

To continue our linear sketch. On each side of the projection formed by the colonnade, opens in the marble wall a magnificent window with ornate bronze cornice supported by two granite colonnettes, the bases and capitals of these being also of bronze, and the window having a balcony with a balustrade; denticulated cornices, surmounted by attics, mark the principal architectural divisions of the building, and, jutting out, cast favoring shadows. In each angle is a fluted Corinthian pilaster, above which stands an angel with wide-spread wings.

Two quadrangular campaniles, springing from the grand line of the building at each corner of the pediment, repeat the *motifs* of the great windows: granite columns, bronze capitals, balcony with balustrade, triangular pediment; and show, through their semi-circular bays, the bells hung without wood-work, by means of a peculiar mechanism. A round, gilded roof, surmounted by a cross, the foot fixed in a crescent, coifs these bell-towers, the light strikes through them, and when the sun shines full upon the bells, strange, harmonious vibrations escape into the air. It is needless for me to say that these two bell-towers are reproduced identically upon the other side; indeed, from the place where we stand we can see shining the cupola of the third. Only the fourth is concealed from view by the mass of the dome.

At the two corners of the façade, kneeling angels hang garlands upon candelabra of antique form. Upon the acroteria of the pediment are groups and separate figures representing the apostles.

All this population of statues gives life to the silhouette

of the building, and interrupts, with the happiest possible effect, its horizontal lines.

Thus we have a fair, general notion of the masses of what may be called the first story of the church. Let us now examine the dome, which, from the square platform formed by the roof, springs boldly towards heaven.

A circular base, or socle, divided into three mouldings, retreating one above the other, serves as the foundation for the dome, and also the plinth for the twenty-four monoliths of granite, thirty feet high, with bases and capitals of bronze, which surround the main mass of the dome with a rotunda of columns, an aërial diadem through which plays and glitters the sunlight. In the spaces between the columns are pierced twelve windows, and upon the capitals rests a circular cornice surmounted by a balustrade cut by twenty-four pedestals, whereon stand, with wings vibrating, as it were, as many angels, bearing in their hands the instruments of the Passion, or attributes of the celestial hierarchy.

Above this angel-crown, which rests upon the brow of the cathedral, the dome still rises. There are twenty-four windows placed between the same number of pilasters, and from the cornice upward curves the immense cupola, dazzling with gold, and striated with nervures falling back to the perpendicular of the columns. An octagonal lantern, entirely gilded, and flanked by colonnettes, surmounts the cupola, and above this a colossal cross, cast in open-work,—*cléché*, to use the heraldic term, —stands victoriously implanted in the crescent.

There are in architecture as in music certain well-balanced rhythms whose harmonious symmetry charms eye and ear, without giving the slightest inquietude ; the mind foresees with pleasure the return of the *motif* at the place marked out for it in advance. St. Isaac's produces this effect ; it unfolds itself like a beautiful phrase of religious music, keeping the promise of its pure and classic theme, never deceiving the eye by a discordant note. The red columns are like choirs of equal number chanting the same melody upon all four sides of the building. The Greek acanthus spreads its green *fioriture* of bronze over all the capitals. Bandelets of granite stretch above the friezes like the lines of the musical scale, between which the statues correspond with one another by contrasts or resemblances of attitude which recall the required inversions of a fugue; and the great dome lifts up into the sky the supreme note of all, from among the four bell-towers, which serve as its accompaniment.

Doubtless the *motif* is simple, like all which are derived from Greek and Roman antiquity; but how splendid the execution! What a symphony of marble, of granite, bronze, and gold!

The classic austerity of the plan adopted by the architect of St. Isaac's forbade him to employ upon the exterior of this temple of severest outline, any of that fanciful ornamentation wherein the caprice of the chisel disports itself,—those garlands, those clusters of foliage, those groups of attributes mingled with figures of children and little genii,—ornaments often not very consistent with the character of an edifice, and useful only to mask vacant spaces. With the exception of the acanthi and the few rare decorations required by the order of architecture, St. Isaac's is adorned only with its statuary,—bas-reliefs, groups, and single figures in bronze;— this is all. Magnificent sobriety!

Retaining the same position at the corner of the boulevard of the Admiralty, I will now describe the bas-reliefs and statues as seen from this point, with the intention of making later the circuit of the building.

The bas-relief of the northern pediment—the one, that is, which looks towards the Neva—represents the Resurrection of Christ; it is the work of M. Lemaire, the author of the pediment of the Madeleine in Paris. It is grand and highly ornamental, filling well its place. The risen Christ springs from the tomb, the labarum in his hand, in the attitude of ascension; and, placed in the very centre of the triangle, the figure has the opportunity to be represented standing at its full height. On the left of this radiant vision, an angel, seated, repels, with a gesture of command, the Roman soldiers on guard at the tomb, whose attitudes are expressive of surprise, fear, and also of the desire to oppose the predicted miracle; on the right two angels, standing, welcome with reassuring kindness the holy women who have come to weep and scatter perfumes upon the tomb of Jesus. The Magdalen has sunk upon her knees; overwhelmed with grief, she has not yet perceived the miracle; Mary and Martha, bringing vases of spikenard and myrrh, are watching ascend in glory the radiant body to which they came to bring the honors due to the dead, and towards which one of the angels directs their attention with uplifted fingers. The group is well disposed in pyramidal form, and the bent postures, which the lessening height of the pediment requires, explain themselves naturally. The relief of the figures, according to their places, is calculated so as to produce firm shadows and decided contours, which do not embarrass the eye; a felicitous union of the raised figure and the flat surface produces all the effect of perspective that can be required from a bas-relief without destroying the great architectural lines.

Below the pediment, on a marble tablet set in the granite frieze, is inscribed a legend, in the old Slavic character, which is the sacred text of the Greek church. This inscription, in letters of gilded bronze, is this sentence: "Lord, in Thy strength the Czar shall rejoice."

Upon pedestals at the three angles of the pediment are placed the evangelist St. John and the two apostles St. Peter and St. Paul. The evangelist, who occupies the central position, is seated with the symbolic eagle at his side; he holds a pen in the right hand; and in the left, a roll of papyrus. The two apostles are identified, the one by the keys, the other by a great sword upon which he leans.

Beneath the peristyle, above the principal door, a bas-relief of bronze, semi-circular in the upper part, like the vaulted space in which it is framed, represents the Christ on the Cross, between two thieves. At the foot of the tree of suffering, the holy women are lamenting, sinking upon the ground in an agony of grief; in one corner, Roman soldiers are throwing dice for the possession of the vesture of the Divine Sufferer; in the other, awakened by his last cry, the dead arise, and lift up the stones from off their sepulchres. In the semi-circles over the two side-doors are seen, at the left, the Bearing of the Cross; at the right, the Descent into the Tomb. The Crucifixion is by M. Vitali; the other two bas-reliefs by Baron Klodt.

The great bronze door has also bas-reliefs disposed as follows: in the lintel, the Triumphal Entry of Christ into Jerusalem; in the left leaf of the door, the Ecce Homo; in the right, the Flagellation; beneath, in the oblong panels, two saints in sacerdotal dress, St. Nicholas and St. Isaac, each occupying a niche whose semi-circular top forms a shell; in the lower panels, two little kneeling angels bearing a Greek cross with inscriptions.

The drama of the Passion, with all its phases, is thus unfolded beneath the portico, the apotheosis shining gloriously upon the pediment.

We will now pass around to the eastern portico, whose great bas-relief is also by M. Lemaire, and represents an event in the life of St. Isaac himself. The story is that, as the Emperor Valens was departing from Constantinople to go against the Goths, St. Isaac, who lived in a cave just outside the city, stopped him on his way, and predicted to him that he would not succeed in his enterprise, inasmuch as he had incurred the divine displeasure by the support which he had rendered to the Arians. The offended Emperor caused the saint to be loaded with chains and dragged away to prison, with the assurance that if his prophecy proved false, he should die; but that if events made it good, his liberty should be restored to him. The Emperor, however, was himself killed upon the expedition, and the saint received his liberty and great rewards at the hands of the succeeding Emperor, Theodosius.

In the bas-relief, Valens is represented mounted upon a horse who rears half-way, affrighted by the obstacle of the saint standing in the middle of the road. An equestrian statue is at all times a difficult matter, and but few exist which are perfectly satisfactory. In bas-relief, the difficulty is even greater, but M. Lemaire has very skilfully vanquished it. This horse, executed with truthfulness, but without too minute detail, as suits statuary used in connection with architecture, carries the rider well, whose figure, thus elevated, produces a fine effect, and dominates, in a simple and natural manner, the groups around him. The saint has just uttered his prediction, and already soldiers are beginning to execute the emperor's orders. They lay fetters upon his outstretched arms, which supplicate and threaten. This two-fold action of the figure could scarcely have been better expressed. Behind Valens, his warriors crowd upon one another, drawing out their swords, grasping their bucklers, putting on their armor,—all expressing the idea of an army going upon an expedition. Behind St. Isaac is concealed an army more powerful with Heaven, of unhappy ones, of the poor, of women who hold their nurslings to their breasts. The composition has breadth and fidelity and action, and the restraint imposed by the shape of the pediment does not impair the effect of the remoter groups.

Upon the acroteria are three statues: on the pedestal at the top, St. Luke the evangelist, with his ox lying beside him, is represented painting the first portrait of the Virgin, which is the sacred type of the Byzantine pictures; at the sides, St. Simeon with his saw, St. James with a book.

The Slavonic inscription signifies literally: "Upon

Thee, O Lord, do we rest, and we shall have no fear for eternity."

As the iconostase is situated at this end of the building, there is no door on this side, and consequently no bas-relief under the colonnade, which is decorated only with Corinthian pilasters.

The southern pediment was entrusted to M. Vitali. It represents the Adoration of the Magi, a subject which the great masters of painting have rendered almost impossible upon canvas, and which the modern sculptor rarely attempts, on account of the multiplicity of figures it requires, although the simple-minded Gothic imagemakers did not shrink from it in their patiently wrought triptychs. This is a composition of great magnificence, of an affluence a little too facile, perhaps, but seductive to the eye.

The Virgin, wrapped in her veil, which, by an ingenious idea of the sculptor, parts like the curtains of a tabernacle, offers to the adoration of the Magi, who are bowed or prostrated before her in attitudes of oriental respect, the infant, the future Redeemer of the world, of whose divinity she already feels a prescience; this miraculous birth preceded by angelic visitants,—these kings hastening from the depths of Asia, guided by a star, to kneel before a manger, with their golden vases, and their boxes of perfumes,—all this troubles the heart of the holy Mother Ever Virgin; she almost is afraid of this child who is a God! Meanwhile, St. Joseph, leaning against a rock, takes but a slight part in what is going on, accepting with submissive faith, but without clearly understanding them, all these strange events.

In the train of Gaspar, Melchior, and Balthasar are stately personages,—officers, bearers of gifts, and slaves, who fill both ends of the composition. Behind them have crept in, with timid curiosity, adoring at a distance, shepherds clad in goat-skins. In the space between one group and another, an ox puts out his honest head with its shining muzzle. But why is the ass omitted? He should be pulling his bit of straw from the manger, and he, too, with warm breath, should caress this future Saviour of the world, who has just been born in a stable. Art has no right to be more proud than the Divinity Himself. Jesus did not despise the humble beast; it was seated upon a she-ass that he made his entry into Jerusalem.

Following the invariable rhythm of the decoration, three statues figure upon the acroteria of this façade: at the summit, St. Matthew, writing from the angel's dictation; at the two ends, St. Andrew with his cross in the form of an X, St. Philip, with his book and crosier.

The inscription of the frieze is this sentence: "My House shall be called the House of Prayer."

Entering beneath the peristyle, we find the arrangement of the northern portico repeated.

Over the main door is a great galvano-plastic bas-relief, representing the Adoration of the Shepherds. This is a more familiar repetition of the Adoration of the Magi, described above. The central group is nearly the same, though the Virgin turns with more sympathetic *abandon* toward the shepherds, who are bringing to the new-born child their rustic offerings, than towards the Magian kings laying rich presents at his feet. She does not play the queen, but makes herself gentle towards these humble, simple, poor ones, who give the best they have. She presents her child to them in all confidence, unfolding his wrappings that she may show them how strong he is, and the shepherds, bending over, or with one knee on the ground, admire and adore. full of faith in the words of the angel. They crowd around: one woman has a basket of fruit upon her shoulder; a child brings a pair of doves; and over all, angels are hovering about the star which has designated the stable at Bethlehem.

Over the lateral doors are bas-reliefs by M. Laganovski: the Angel announcing the Birth of Christ to the Shepherds, and the Massacre of the Innocents. Upon the lintel of the great bronze door is the Presentation in the Temple; upon the leaves of the door, the Flight into Egypt, and the Child Jesus among the Doctors; below, a warrior-saint and an angel, St. Alexander Newski and St. Michael; still lower, two little angels bearing crosses.

This portico contains in its decoration the whole poem of the nativity and childhood of Christ, as the other contained the drama of the Passion.

In the pediment of the eastern side we have seen St. Isaac, persecuted by the Emperor Valens; upon the west we find his triumph, if such a word may accord with the humility of a saint.

The Emperor Theodosius the Great returns victorious from a war against the barbarians, and at the Gilded Gate, St. Isaac, gloriously delivered from his prison, presents himself in his poor hermit's frock, girt with a chaplet of beads, holding in the left hand a double-armed cross, and raising the right in benediction above the Emperor's head. Theodosius bends in an attitude of devotion, and his arm thrown around the Empress Flavilla involves her in his own movement, and seems to wish to associate her in the benediction of the saint. The intention is charming and very happily rendered. August resemblances may be remarked in the majestic heads of the Emperor and Empress. At the feet of the laurel-crowned Theodosius is seen the eagle, and emblems of victory. At our right, warriors whose attitude breathes the most lively fervor, bow the head and bend the knee, lowering before the cross the insignia of human authority. At a little distance a personage with scowling face and gesture of spite and fury is retreating, leaving the field to St. Isaac, whose influence has carried the day: this is Demophilos, chief of the Arians, who had helped to persuade Theodosius, and to gain the victory for heresy. Also is to be observed that woman of Edessa with her child, whose sudden appearance drove back the troops sent for the persecution of the

Christians. At the left, a lady of honor belonging to the court, attired in rich garments, is supporting a poor paralytic woman, symbolizing the reign of charity in this Christian court. A little child, who is at play in all the graceful suppleness of his age, contrasts finely with the rigid immobility of the paralytic. In the corner of the bas-relief, by a synchronism which idealized sculpture permits, figures the architect of the church, draped after the antique, and presenting a miniature model of the cathedral destined later to rise under the patronage of St. Isaac.

This beautiful composition, whose groups are so happily balanced, is the work of M. Vitali.

Under this portico, more simple than those of the north and south, there are no semi-circular bas-reliefs. It has but a single door, opening opposite the iconostase. This bronze door is divided like the others, and contains in bas-relief, in the lintel, the Sermon on the Mount; in the upper portion of the two leaves, the Resurrection of Lazarus, and Jesus healing a paralytic. St. Peter and St. Paul occupy the oblong panels, and below, angels bear up the symbol of redemption. The vine and the corn, symbols of the eucharist, are employed in the decoration of this door and of the others.

St. Mark, with the lion, which Venice bears in her coat-of-arms, is writing his gospel on the summit of the pediment, and the two extremes are adorned, the one by St. Thomas bearing the square, and extending the sceptical finger wherewith he desired to convince himself of the resurrection of Christ; the other by St. Bartholomew with the instruments of his martyrdom, the wooden horse and the knife.

Upon the tablet of the frieze is this inscription: "To the King of Kings."

Its archaic form renders the Slavonic character well adapted for inscriptions upon buildings. It is, in itself, an ornament. There are still other sentences under the peristyles, and above the doors, expressing religious or mystic ideas. I have translated only those which are most in sight.

The sculptures upon all the doors are modelled by M. Vitali, assisted by N. M. Salemann and Bonilli; to him also are due the figures of the evangelists and apostles standing on the pedestals above and at each end of the pediments. These figures are fifteen feet two inches in height. The angels kneeling near the candelabra are seventeen feet high, and the candelabra themselves twenty-two feet. These angels with their great wings spread wide are like mystic eagles who have swooped down from the heavenly heights upon the four corners of the building.

Also, as I have said, a crowd of angels rests upon the crown of the dome. They are so far away that the minute details of their aspect cannot be perfectly distinguished; but their elegant and graceful outlines strike the beholder even at the distance from which he sees them.

Thus, on the cornice surrounding the cupola, on the acroteria, and along the edge of the roof, we have, without counting the figures in high relief of the pediments, the bas-reliefs above the portals, and the saints and angels who stand in niches of the doors,—fifty-two statues, thrice the natural size, forming for St. Isaac's an eternal people of bronze in attitudes of great variety, and yet everywhere obedient, like an architectural chorus, to the cadences of a linear rhythm.

Before we enter the temple, of which I have now made a sketch as faithful as the insufficiency of words will permit, let me again say that it would be a great error to imagine, though its outlines are thus pure, noble, and severe, its ornamentation infrequent and sober, and its style austerely classic, that it has, in its perfect regularity, anything of the cold, monotonous, and slightly wearisome effect of what—for want of a more correct expression—we call classic architecture. The gold of its cupolas, the rich variety of its materials preserve it from this disadvantage; and the climate gives it color with plays of light and unexpected effects, so that it is no longer Roman, but perfectly and wondrously Russian. The fairies of the North hover about this grave and solemn edifice, and nationalize it completely, yet without depriving it of its stately, classic grandeur.

Winter, in Russia, has a poetry all its own; its rigors are compensated by beauties, by effects and aspects which are most picturesque. The snow ices with silver these golden cupolas, sharpens with its gleaming line the outlines of pediment and entablature, lays white touches amid the brazen acanthus leaves, puts here and there a luminous point on the salient part of a statue, changes with magic transformations the entire tone of the coloring. Thus seen, St. Isaac has a truly local originality. It is superb with color, whether, all brightened with white touches, it stands relieved against a curtain of gray cloud, or whether its profile is cut, clear and fine, upon one of those skies of rose and turquoise which shine over St. Petersburg when the air is dry and cold, and the snow creaks under foot, like powder of glass. Sometimes after a thaw comes an icy north wind congealing in a night, over the whole surface, the sweat of marbles and granites. Then a net-work of pearls, finer, more round than drops of dew upon plants, envelopes the giant columns of the peristyle; the reddish granite assumes the most delicate rose-color, with something on its surface like the velvet down of a peach, or the bloom of a plum; it is transformed into a substance unknown, like those precious stones of which is built the heavenly Jerusalem. The crystallized vapor covers all the building with a diamond dust, emitting flashes and sparkles, wherever the sunshine touches it; a cathedral all of gems, you would say, in the City of God.

Each hour of the day has its own mirage. If you look at St. Isaac's in the morning from the quay of the Neva, it has the burning color of amethyst and of topaz in the midst of an aureole of milky and roseate splendors.

The heavy white fogs which surge about its base, detach it from the earth, and it seems floating in an archipelago of vapor. At evening, in a peculiar incidence of light, from the corner of the little Morskaïa, with its windows traversed by the rays of the setting sun, it seems all ablaze, as if on fire within, the windows so flame out from the dark walls. Sometimes in foggy weather, when the sky is low, clouds come down upon the cupola, and coif it like a mountain-top. It was wonderful, as once I saw it, when the lantern and the upper half of the dome had disappeared under a bank of vapor. The cloud cutting with its fleecy zone the gilded hemisphere of the lofty tower, gave the cathedral a prodigious elevation. It seemed a Christian Babel rising upward to seek—not now with vain boast to brave—Him without whom no construction endures.

Even the night, which in other climates casts its impenetrable crape over all buildings, cannot entirely conceal St. Isaac's. Its cupola remains visible beneath the black dais of the sky with pale golden tints like a vast half-luminous ball. No blackness of darkness, not even in the gloomiest December midnight, can prevail against it. Always, it can be seen above the city; the dwellings of man fade away in shadow and in sleep, but the dwelling of God shines, and seems to watch.

When the darkness is not so extreme, and the gleaming starlight, and the vague shining of the Milky Way allow the phantoms of objects to be discerned, the great masses of the cathedral are grandly outlined, and assume a mysterious solemnity. Its columns, polished as a mirror, are faintly sketched by some unexpected shining here and there, and along the summit of the building, statues half-seen, confusedly suggest celestial sentinels placed on duty about the sacred edifice. Whatever light there is scattered through the sky, concentrates itself upon one point in the dome with such intensity, that the nocturnal passer-by would take this solitary golden spangle for a lighted lamp. An effect even more magical is sometimes produced: luminous touches flame at the extremity of each one of the nervures which cut the dome, and encircle it with a sparkling crown, a starry diadem placed above the temple's golden tiara. An age having more faith and less science than our own would call it a miracle, so dazzling and so inexplicable does this effect appear.

When the moon is at its full and shines free from clouds, at about midnight, in the opaline light, St. Isaac's assumes ashen, silvery, bluish, violet tints of unimaginable delicacy; the roseate shades of the granite pass into hortensia; the bronze draperies of the statues grow white as linen vestments; the gilded coifs of the bell-towers have the reflections, the transparencies, and the faint white tints of amber; and the threads of snow along the cornices flash here and there like spangles. The planet, in the depth of this Northern sky, blue and cold as steel, sees reflected its silver face in the golden mirror of the dome, and the light that shines therefrom suggests the electrum of the ancients,—gold and silver melted into one.

Sometimes those fairies of the North, whose presence makes amends for the length of her icy nights, unfold their splendors above the cathedral. From behind the sombre silhouette of the vast edifice, the Aurora Borealis displays its polar pyrotechnics. The bouquet of fusees, effluvia, irradiations and phosphorescent bands, unfolds itself with a radiance by turns silvery, pearly, opalescent, rose-color,—extinguishing the stars, and making this ever-luminous cupola seem black, save the one brilliant point, the golden lamp of the sanctuary which nothing can eclipse.

I have sought to paint St. Isaac's in the days and nights of winter. The summer is no less rich in novel and admirable effects.

In those immense days which are scarcely interrupted by an hour of diaphanous night,—at once the twilight of evening and of dawn,—St. Isaac's, flooded with light, stands revealed in all the stately clearness befitting a classic temple. All illusions have disappeared, and the superb reality is distinctly seen; even when the transparent shadow wraps the city, the sun still shines upon the colossal dome. From the horizon where it dips to emerge almost immediately, its rays always reach the gilded cupola. In the same way in the mountains, the highest peaks yet flame in the sunset, when the lower summits and the valleys have been for a long time hidden under the mists of evening. There, however, the light at last steals away from the crimsoned *aiguille* and seems to return, reluctant, into heaven; while here, the shining splendor never deserts the dome. Though all the rest should fade away in the firmament, one star would remain upon St. Isaac's forever.

Having now given, as far as in me lies, an idea of the exterior of the cathedral under its different aspects, I will endeavor to describe the interior, which is not less magnificent.

The usual entrance is on the southern side of the building, but let us try to find open the western door, which is opposite the iconostase, for this gives the finest effect. As you enter, you are overpowered with amazement, the colossal grandeur of the architecture, the profusion of the rarest marbles, the brilliancy of the gilding, the color in the frescos, the polished pavement like a mirror in which all objects are reflected, unite in an effect absolutely dazzling, especially if your attention is directed, as it must be, towards the side where stands the iconostase,—iconostase, a marvellous edifice, a temple within a temple, a façade of gold, malachite and lapis-lazuli, with doors of solid silver; but which is after all, only the veil of the sanctuary. Thither the eye turns invincibly, whether the open doors reveal in dazzling transparency the colossal Christ painted on glass, or, whether, closed, they only show the crimson curtain whose color seems dyed in the Divine blood.

The interior plan of the edifice is marked by a simplicity which the eye and the mind comprehend at once: three naves, terminating at the three doors of the iconostase, cut transversely by the nave which represents, within the building, the arms of the cross externally indicated by the projection of the porticos; at the point of intersection, the cupola; and at the angles, four lesser domes completing the symmetry, and marking the architectural rhythm. Upon a substratum of marble rest the fluted columns and pilasters of the Corinthian order, with bases and capitals of bronze, which decorate the interior of the edifice. They are surmounted by an attic cut by pilasters, forming panels which contain frescos. Upon this attic rest the archivolts, whose panels are also adorned with religious subjects.

The walls in the spaces between the columns and pilasters, from sub-structure to cornice, are lined with white marble, whereon are outlined panels and compartments of the green marble of Genoa, of griotte, of yellow Sienna marble, of variegated jaspers, of red Finland porphyries—in a word, everything beautiful which the richest quarries could supply. Recessed niches supported by consoles contain paintings, and agreeably interrupt the monotony of the level surface. The metallic ornaments of the panels are in gilded galvanoplastic bronze, and are detached with vigorous projections from the marble ceilings of the recesses. The ninety-six columns and pilasters are from the quarries of Tvidi, which furnish a beautiful marble veined with gray and red. The white marbles come from the quarries of Seravezza which Michel Angelo was wont to prefer to those of Carrara. To say this is to say all— for what a connoisseur in marble must he have been who designed St. Peter's and the tomb of the Medici!

Having given in a few lines this general idea of the church we will come to the dome which opens, over the visitor's head, its gulf firmly hung in air, where iron, bronze, brick, granite, and marble combine their almost infinite power of resistance in accordance with the best calculated mathematical laws. From the pavement to the top of the lantern is 296 ft. 8 in. The length of the building is 288 ft. 8 in., its breadth interiorly 149 ft. 8 in. I am not disposed to give undue prominence to figures, but here they are necessary to show the real magnitude of the edifice, and to help the reader to understand the relative proportions of the details.

Far up the lantern a colossal Dove spreads its white wings surrounded by golden rays, at an immense height. Lower, curves a demi-cupola with golden palm-leaves upon an azure field; then comes the great spheric vault of the dome, bordered around its upper orifice by a cornice whose frieze is decorated with garlands and angel-heads, and at its base, resting upon the entablature of twelve fluted Corinthian pilasters which separate the windows, also twelve in number. A false balustrade, serving as a transition from architecture to painting crowns this entablature, and, lighted by a vast sky, is spread out a grand composition representing the Triumph of the Virgin.

This painting, as well as all the rest of the decoration of the dome was entrusted to M. Bruloff, known at Paris by his picture "The Last Day of Pompeii," which figured at one of the expositions. M. Bruloff deserved the honor; but a condition of illness terminated by premature death, prevented him from executing this important commission. He was able only to make the cartoons, and though his idea and his directions were religiously carried out, it is impossible not to regret the eye, the hand, and the genius of the master himself in these paintings, whose design is certainly admirably adapted to their destination. Doubtless he would have been able to give them all that they lack; the master's touch, color, fire, whatever must be added in the execution to the best conceived work, and which even equal talent realizing the thought of another can never possibly supply.

To put some order into my description, let us imagine

ourselves facing the iconostase: we shall thus have before us the group which is the centre and in a sense the most important part of the whole composition. The Virgin in the midst of a halo sits enthroned upon a golden seat; her eyes cast down, her hands clasped modestly upon her breast, she seems, even in the skies, to submit to this triumph rather than accept it, but she is the handmaid of the Lord, *ancilla Domini*, and she resigns herself to the apotheosis.

On either side of the throne stand St. John the Baptist, the Fore-runner, and St. John the beloved disciple of Christ, the latter distinguished by the eagle.

Above the throne hover little angels with lilies, symbolic of purity. Tall angels with wide-spread wings, placed at intervals in the boldest postures of fore-shortening, support the banks of cloud on which stand these groups which I will describe: going from the spectator's left, and making the circuit of the cupola till we complete the cycle of the composition. One of these angels bears the long sword, the attribute of St. Paul, who kneels above him upon a cloud near St. Peter, with his head turned toward the Virgin; cherubs are opening the book of the Epistles and are playing with the golden keys of Paradise.

Upon the cloud which floats above the balustrade, we observe next to St. Peter and St. Paul, an old man with white beard in the dress of a Byzantine monk; it is St. Isaac the Dalmatian, the patron saint of the Cathedral. Near him is St. Alexander Newski, clad in cuirass and crimson mantle; angels hold flags behind him, and the image of the Christ upon a golden disk indicates the services rendered to religion by this warrior saint.

The next group is composed of three holy women kneeling: Anna, the mother of the Virgin, Elizabeth, the mother of the Fore-runner, and Catherine, who is sumptuously attired with mantle of ermine and brocaded dress, and a crown on her head;—not that she belongs to a royal or princely house, but because she unites the triple crown of virginity, martyrdom, and learning, for which reason her original name of Dorothea is changed into Catherine, whose Syriac root *Cethar* means crown. This luxury, therefore, is entirely allegorical. The angel who stands beneath this cloud bears a fragment of a wheel with teeth bent backward, the instrument of St. Catherine's martyrdom.

Separated by a little interval from the group just described, a third cloud bears up St. Alexis "the man in God," clad in a monk's garment, and the Emperor Constantine, with golden cuirass and crimson drapery; at his side an angel holds the axe tied in a bundle of rods; another angel standing behind him, bears an antique sword in its scabbard, the insignia of command.

The last group as we return to the throne of the Virgin, represents St. Nicholas bishop of Myre and patron saint of Russia,—clad in a dalmatic and a green stole covered with golden crosses,—kneeling in adoration before the Mother of God; he is surrounded by angels holding banners and sacred books.

The reader will have noticed that these figures are all the patron saints of Russia and of the imperial family. The mystic idea of this immense composition which is not less than 228 ft. in circuit, is the triumph of the Church, symbolized by the Virgin.

The arrangement of this painting suggests slightly that of the dome of Ste. Genevieve by Baron Gros. I do not mention it as any reproach to M. Bruloff; such resemblances are inevitable in religious subjects whose leading features must be determined in advance. Conforming to the intention of the architect with more fidelity than some others of the artists employed in the decoration of St. Isaac's have done, M. Bruloff, or those who have executed his plans, have held to light, dull tones, avoiding the high color and heavy shadow which is always harmful in mural painting, disturbing as it does the great outlines of the architecture.

These paintings, and in fact all which ornament the

cathedral, even in the case of their having gold backgrounds, do not attempt to reproduce those formal and rigid canonical outlines which belong to Byzantine art. M. de Montferrand judged wisely that the church of which he was the architect, borrowing as it does its forms from the pure Greek or Roman style, the artists charged with its paintings should seek their inspiration from that great Italian school which has ever shown itself wisest and most expert in decorating edifices built in this style. Hence the paintings of St. Isaac's are not at all archaic, contradicting in this the customs of the Russian church, which has always chosen to conform to certain models fixed from the earliest existence of the Greek church, and preserved as a matter of tradition by the religious painters of Mt. Athos.

Twelve great angels, gilded, serving as caryatides, support consoles on which rest the bases of the pilasters which decorate the interior of the dome, and separate the windows from each other. They measure twenty-one feet in height, and are executed by the galvano-plastic process in four pieces, the sutures being invisible. Thus it was possible to make them so light that despite their size, they were not too great a weight upon the cupola. This crowd of golden angels, standing as they do in a flood of light, and glittering at a thousand points with the brilliancy of the precious metal produce a very splendid effect. The figures are disposed according to a certain definite architectural regularity, but with a variety of attributes and motion which relieves them from monotonous uniformity. Diverse attributes, such as books, palms, crosses, balances, crowns, trumpets, give cause for slightly varied attitudes, and designate the celestial functions of these shining figures.

The space left vacant between the angels is filled with apostles and prophets in sitting postures, each having the attribute by which he is identified. All these figures, broadly draped and of noble style, are relieved against a background of pale golden light, nearly unvaried throughout. The general tone is light, resembling the fresco as nearly as possible.

The four evangelists, of colossal size, occupy the pendentives. For these figures the artist has made choice of those proud and impetuous attitudes, in which the painter of the Sistine chapel takes delight. The pendentives, by their peculiar shape, require the composition to be forcibly adapted to them, and the restraint imposed by the frame often helps the inspiration. These Evangelists are most expressive figures.

By the winged lion we recognize St. Mark, who in one hand holds his gospel, and with the other, lifted, seems to preach or bestow a benediction. A circlet of gold shines about his head, and broad blue drapery enfolds his knees.

St. John, clad in a green tunic and a red mantle, is writing upon a long strip of papyrus unrolled by two angels. At his side, the mystic eagle flaps his wings and darts from his eyes the lightnings of the Apocalypse.

Leaning against his ox, St. Luke regards attentively the portrait of the Virgin, the work of his own pencil, which angels are presenting to him. A labarum floats above his aureole-crowned head and drapery of orange-red falls about him in heavy folds.

Beside St. Matthew stands his companion angel. The saint, in violet tunic and yellow mantle, has in his hand a book. In the sombre sky which serves as a background to this as well as to the other figures, are, hovering cherubs, and a single star sparkles.

In the tops of the pendentives are framed four pictures representing scenes in the Passion of Christ. In one, Judas, going in advance of the soldiers who carry lanterns and torches gives the perfidious kiss which points out his master. In another, Christ, standing between two soldiers armed with knotted cords, is scourged. The third shows us the Just One, to whom the Jewish people preferred Barabbas, led away from the judgment-seat, while Pontius Pilate washes his hands of that blood which is to leave upon them an eternal stain. The fourth picture represents what the Italians call the *spasimo*, the fainting of the Victim under the weight of the cross, upon the way to Calvary. The Virgin, the holy women, and St. John attend the Divine Sufferer, in attitudes of unspeakable woe.

The attic of the transverse nave represents the arm of the Greek cross; at the right, as we face the iconostase, is the Sermon on the Mount, of M. Pietro Bassine. Upon the plateau of a hillock, overhung by trees, Christ, seated, is preaching, surrounded by his disciples; the crowd press about him to listen; paralytics have climbed up thither upon their crutches; the sick are brought upon their beds, eager to hear the Divine words; the blind come groping; women listen with all their hearts, while in a corner Pharisees are talking and disputing; the arrangement is beautiful, and the well distributed groups leave to the central figure its due importance.

The two lateral paintings have for their subjects the parables of the Sower and the Good Samaritan. In the former Jesus is walking in the fields with his disciples: he points out to them the Sower casting abroad his seed, and the birds of the air flying about his head. In the latter, the Good Samaritan, dismounting from his horse, pours oil upon the wounds of the young man abandoned by the roadside, to whose complaint the Pharisee had refused to listen. The first of these pictures is by M. Nikotine; the second, by M. Sasonoff. In the vaulted roof, in a panel surrounded by rich ornaments, cherubs are holding up a book against a background of the sky.

Facing the Sermon on the Mount, at the opposite end of the nave, in the attic, is developed a great painting by M. Pluchart, the Multiplication of the Loaves. Jesus occupies the centre, and his disciples are distributing to the hungry crowd the miraculous loaves which are constantly renewed, symbolizing the bread of the Eucharist, whereby are nourished all the generations of mankind; upon the two side walls are, the Return of the Prodigal Son, and the Laborer of the Eleventh Hour, whom the stewards would drive away, but whom the Master receives; cherubim bearing a sacred chalice are represented in the vaulted ceiling.

The central nave from the transept to the door is decorated by M. Bruni. In the great panel at its extremity, Jehovah, enthroned upon a cloud and surrounded by archangels, angels, and cherubim in a circle symbolizing eternity, seems to sit content with creation and to bestow upon it his benediction. At his word, the infinite has been stirred to its very depths, and from nothing has arisen everything.

With its trees, and flowers, and animals, the terrestrial Paradise glows upon the attic of this nave. The first human pair are living in peace amid the animal races, whom sin and death, its consequence, shall later render inimical. As yet, the lion does not tear the gazelle, the tiger does not spring upon the horse, the elephant seems ignorant of his own strength, and all respect upon the brow of the guests of Eden, the image of God.

In the vault delighted angels are represented, admiring the sun and moon, those great lamps just set in heaven.

The panel of the attic has for its subject the Deluge. The waters poured forth in cataracts by the abyss and by the skies, have covered the young world, so soon perverted and causing God to regret its creation. A few peaks, which the flood will soon cover, alone emerge from the shoreless sea. The last remnant of the condemned race are clinging desperately to the mountain summits. In the distance, amid the rain which falls in torrents, floats the ark of Noah, bearing within it all that is to survive of the old creation.

To the Deluge, upon the other wall, corresponds The Sacrifice of Noah. From a primitive altar made of a fragment of rock rises in the serene air to Heaven the bluish smoke of the accepted sacrifice; the patriarch, standing, with his giant figure of the antediluvian, towers above his sons and their wives, prostrated upon the ground around him.

In the back-ground, upon a curtain of vanishing clouds the rainbow bends its colored bow, sign of the promise that the waters shall not again cover the earth, sheltered henceforth, until the Last Judgment.

Further on, the Vision of Ezekiel covers a great space of the vault. Standing upon a fragment of rock, under a sky lit by red flames, in the midst of a valley of Jehosophat whose dead population are awakening to life like the grain in the furrow, the prophet gazes upon the frightful scene which unrolls before him: at the call of the angel's trumpet, the phantoms arise in their shrouds; skeletons drag themselves along with fleshless fingers, and adjust their scattered bones; the dead look forth from their sepulchres, filled with horror and remorse. These larvæ, who were the inhabitants of the earth, seem to beg for mercy, and to regret the night of the tomb, save a few righteous ones full of hope in the Divine goodness, and not alarmed by the awful gesture of the prophet.

There is great power in imagination, and a magisterial vigor of style in this painting, which is of great size; the study of the Sistine frescos is apparent in it. Its coloring is strong and sober, and of that historic tone, the noble garment of thought, which modern artists are so disposed to abandon for a fatiguing brilliancy of effect and a trivial fidelity of detail, out of place in great decorative painting.

At the end of the same nave, in the vault of the iconostase, M. Bruni has painted the Last Judgment, of which Ezekiel's Vision is but the prophecy. A colossal Christ, twice, or possibly three times the size of the other figures, is standing before the cloud-built steps of His throne; I highly approve of this Byzantine fashion of making the divine and principal figure predominate in this visible manner; it strikes at once the cultured and the uncultured imagination, the former by the ideal, the latter by the material side. The ages are at an end; time is no longer, all is now eternal,—reward and chastisement. Overthrown by the angel's breath, the old skeleton falls to dust; his scythe broken. Death, in his turn, is dead.

At the right of the figure of Christ, are thronging upward crowds of the blessed, with pure and slender forms,—long, chaste drapery,—faces radiant with beauty, love, and ecstacy, and are fraternally received by the angels. At His left, repulsed by stern and pitiless angels with flaming swords and strong wings, whirl downwards, in the impetuosity of their fall, those accursed groups wherein are recognized with their hideous shapes all the evil tendencies which drag man into the abyss: Envy, whose locks scourge the meagre temples like knotted serpents,—Avarice, sordid, angular, and contracted,—Impiety, casting toward the sky its look of powerless menace;—all these guilty ones, weighed down by their sins, plunge into the gulf, where crisped hands of demons whose bodies are not visible, await them to tear them with their eternal tortures; these hands, knotty and clawlike, resembling the iron combs of executioners, are highly poetic, and produce the most tragic horror. It is an idea worthy of Michel Angelo or Dante. These hands, which I saw upon the cartoon, I sought vainly in the fresco. The projection of the cornice and the curve of the sombre vault in this corner probably prevent them from being seen.

By these rapid descriptions, necessarily subordinated to the general survey of the church, it will be seen how important a share M. Bruni had in the decoration of St. Isaac's. It is to be desired that we should have engravings or photographs of the works of this remarkable artist, who certainly has not had the celebrity he deserves. These compositions, with their great number of figures three or four times the natural size, cover immense surfaces, and there are few modern painters who have had occasion to execute anything comparable to them. Nor are the labors of this artist limited here; in the sanctuary itself are several pictures of his which I shall mention later.

In the two ends of the transversal nave, whose centre is occupied by M. Bruni's Last Judgment, are paintings which have not sufficient light to be fairly seen. They are as follows: The Resurrection of Lazarus; Mary at the feet of Christ; Jesus healing the Man possessed of Devils; the Marriage at Cana; Christ saving St. Peter upon the Sea; these are all by M. Scheboniëf, and occupy one half the nave. The other side has the following: Jesus raising the Widow's Son and Jesus Christ calling the Children, by M. Scheboniëf; the Healing of the Paralytic; the Repentant Woman; and the Restoring of Sight to the Blind, by M. Alexrieff.

Another transversal nave—for the church which presents three in its length, has five in its breadth—contains the following paintings by different artists: Joseph receiving his Brethren in Egypt; Jacob on his Death-bed, surrounded by his Sons; the Sacrifice of Aaron; the Arrival of Joshua in the Promised Land; and the Fleece found by Gideon. These upon one side; the other contains: the Passage of the Red Sea; Moses saved from the River; the Burning Bush; Moses and Aaron before Pharaoh; Miriam praising God; Jehovah delivering the Tables of the Law to Moses; and Moses dictating his last Commands.

At each extremity of the lateral naves at the right and left of the door rises a cupola. In the first, M. Riss has represented, in the vault, the apotheosis of Saint Fevronius, surrounded by angels bearing palms, and also instruments of torture, torches, faggots, and swords; in the pendentives, upon a gold background imitating mosaic, the prophets Hosea, Joel, Haggai, and Zachariah: in the recesses of the arches, historic and religious subjects, among others Ménine and Poyarsky, names at which every Russian heart thrills with patriotism. I may be permitted to devote a few lines to this picture, of which merely to announce the subject is not sufficient, as it would be in pictures whose themes are drawn from the Holy Scriptures, and hence familar to all Christian readers, whatever be the communion to which they belong.

The kniaz Poyarsky, and the mujik Ménine have resolved to save the country, menaced by a Polish invasion. They are advancing at the head of their troops. The noblesse and the people act together, in the persons of these two heroes, who, wishing to place their enterprise under the protection of God, cause to be borne before them by the clergy, the sacred picture of Our Lady of Kazan, on which falls, in sign of Divine approval, a celestial radiance. As the procession passes, men, women, children, old people, men of every age and station, fall prostrate upon the snow. In the background are palisades, and the crenellated wall of the Kremlin with its towers.

The second recess shows us Dmitri-Douskoï, kneeling at the door of a convent, and receiving the benediction of Saint Sergius of Rodonej, who is coming forth surrounded by his monks, before the departure of the hero to his victorious encounter with the Tartar hordes under Mimaï.

The third painting has for its subject Ivan III. showing to St. Peter the metropolitan, the plan of the Cathedral of the Assumption at Moscow. The holy personage appears to approve of them, and to invoke the blessing of Heaven upon the pious founder.

A council of apostles, upon whom descends the Holy Spirit, fills the fourth vault.

In the cupola corresponding to this are the following paintings, all from the hand of M. Riss: in the top, the Apotheosis of St. Isaac the Dalmatian; upon the pendentives, Jonah, Nahum, Habakkuk, Zephaniah. The recesses formed by the arches are filled with subjects relating to the introduction of Christianity into Russia: Proposal made to Vladimir to adopt the Christian faith; Baptism of Vladimir; Baptism of the Inhabitants of Kief; Announcement of the Adoption of Christianity by Vladimir. These cupolas are of the Ionic order.

All these paintings, skilfully composed, are, however, a little too much like historical pictures. The artist, fond of effect, has not been sufficiently mindful of the conditions of mural painting. Scenes which are framed in arches or in architectural divisions, require to be tranquillized rather than dramatized, and to resemble the polychromatic bas-relief. When he works in a church or in a palace, the painter, ought to be, first of all, a decorator, and to sacrifice his own personal preferences to the general effect of the building. His work ought to be so united therewith that it could not be detached. The great Italian masters in their frescos, which are so different from their pictures, have shown a thorough comprehension of this particular side of art.

I do not address this reproach especially to M. Riss; in different degrees it is merited by most of the artists employed in painting in St. Isaac's, who have not always made the sacrifices required by their peculiar works.

The piers against which the columns and pilasters rest are decorated as well as the walls with subjects executed by different artists, in niches, having consoles bearing inscriptions. In these niches are pictures by M. Neff, which are fine in color and sentiment, and may be ranked among the most satisfactory in the church. They are: the Ascension; Jesus Christ sending His Picture to Abgarus; the Lifting of the Cross; the Birth of the Virgin; the Presentation in the Temple; the Intercession of the Virgin, and the Descent of the Holy Spirit. Also, others by M. Steuben, and by M. Mussini, the subjects drawn from Scripture and from tradition.

All the paintings in St. Isaac's are in oils, distemper being unsuited to humid countries; besides this, its much-vaunted durability has failed to resist the action of two or three centuries, as is only too well proved by the more or less advanced state of deterioration in which we find those masterpieces which their authors believed sure of eternal preservation and unfading freshness. There remained encaustic painting; but its handling is difficult, unfamiliar, and infrequent. The wax, besides, assumes in highly wrought portions an objectionable lustre; and furthermore, too short a time has passed over attempts in this method of painting for us to have other than theoretic assurance of its durability. It was, then, with good reason that M. de Montferrand made choice of oil for the paintings of St. Isaac's.

We now come to the iconostase, that wall of sacred pictures set in gold, which conceals the arcana of the sanctuary. Those who have seen the gigantic screens in Spanish churches can form an idea of the importance bestowed by the Greek religion upon this part of the sacred edifice.

The architect has carried his iconostase to the height of the attics, so that it forms part of the architectural order and suits well the colossal proportions of the building, of which it fills the whole breadth, from one wall to the other. It is, as I have said, the façade of a temple within a temple!

Three steps of red prophyry form the base. A balustrade of white marble with gilded balusters ornamented with precious marbles, traces the line of demarcation between the priest and the worshippers. The finest marble of the Italian quarries serves as the original material of which the wall of the iconostase is composed, and this wall, though elsewhere it would be itself superb, is nearly concealed from sight by the splendid ornaments which cover it.

Eight columns of malachite, of the Corinthian order, fluted, with bases and capitals of gilded bronze, and two pilasters, compose the façade and support the attic. The tone of the malachite with its metallic lustre, its green, coppery shades, strange and charming to the eye, its polish perfect like that of a gem, surprises by its beauty and magnificence. At first sight you hesitate to believe that it is real, for we know that malachite is used only for tables, vases, caskets, bracelets, and other personal ornaments, while these columns and pilasters are forty-two feet in height. Sawn in the block by circular saws invented for the purpose, the plating of malachite is fitted over a copper drum with such perfection that you can scarcely believe that it is merely a plating, while within the copper an iron cylinder, cast solid, bears up the weight of the superposed attic.

The iconostase is pierced by three doors; that in the centre gives access to the sanctuary; the two others, to the chapels of St. Catherine and Saint Alexander Newsky. The order is thus distributed: in the corner a pilaster, and one column; then the door of a chapel; then three columns and the principal door; three more columns, chapel door, a column, and a pilaster.

These columns and pilasters divide the wall into spaces forming frames which are filled with pictures upon gold backgrounds imitating mosaics, and to be replaced by veritable mosaics as soon as the latter are completed. Between the base and cornice there are two stories of frames separated by a secondary cornice which the columns interrupt, and which rests at the middle door upon two colonnettes of lapis-lazuli, and, at the doors of the chapels, upon pilasters of white statuary marble. Above is an attic, cut by pilasters, and decorated with porphyry, jasper, agate, malachite, and other precious materials found in Russia, and also with ornaments of gilded bronze of a richness and splendor surpassed by no church-screens in Italy or Spain. The pilasters parallel to the columns also mark off compartments containing paintings on gold backgrounds.

A fourth story, like a pediment, rises above the line of the attic, and terminates in a great golden group of angels in adoration before the cross, by Vitali; one angel kneeling alone on either side. In the midst of the pediment, a painting, by M. Givago, represents Christ in the garden, accepting the bitter cup in that sad watch when all His dearest disciples had fallen asleep.

Immediately under this, two great angels in full relief, holding sacred chalices, their wings silvery and palpitating, their tunics puffed out by the air, accompanied by little angels in a lower relief, which recedes insensibly into the wall, are placed at either side of a panel of greater size, representing the Last Supper, partly in painting, partly in bas-relief. The figures are painted; the background, which is gilded, represents, with skilfully retreating distances the hall wherein took place the paschal love-feast. This painting is also by M. Givago.

Above the arch of the door, which is decorated by a semi-circular inscription in Slavonic characters, rises a group thus disposed: in the centre, the Christ,—"priest forever after the order of Melchisedek,"—throned upon a richly decorated seat. He holds in one hand the round world, represented by a globe of lapis-lazuli; and with the other makes the gesture of benediction. An aureole surrounds his head; his garments are golden. Behind his throne is a crowd of angels; at his feet lie the winged lion and the symbolic ox. At his right kneels the Holy Virgin; at his left, St. John the Precursor.

This group which cuts away the cornice presents a remarkable peculiarity: the figures are statues with the exception of the head and hands, which are painted on a plate of silver or other metal, cut of suitable shape. This union of the Byzantine icon with sculpture produces an effect of remarkable power, and an attentive examination is required to discover that the under portions are not in relief. The gilded reliefs were modelled by M. Klodt; the flat surfaces painted by M. von Neff.

To this central subject are attached by an insensible transition patriarchs, apostles, kings, saints, martyrs, a crowd of the devout, who form the court and army of Christ, and whose groups fill the spaces of the archivolt.

These figures are merely painted on golden backgrounds.

The arches of the two side doors have for ornament the tables of the law, and a chalice surrounded by rays, in marble and gold, accompanied by little painted angels.

When the sacred door which occupies the centre of this immense façade of gold and silver, lapis-lazuli, malachite, jasper, porphyry, and agate, a giant jewel-box of all the wealth that human magnificence, deterred by no expense, can gather, closes mysteriously its leaves of silver-gilt, chiselled, sunk, wrought in waving patterns, and not less than thirty-five feet in height by fourteen in breadth, you can perceive amid the glitter, pictures, in frames of wrought leafage the most marvellous that ever surrounded work of pencil, representing the four Evangelists in half-length, and, in full length, the angel Gabriel and the Virgin Mary.

But when, during the service, the sacred door opens its broad leaves, a colossal Christ, forming the window opposite, at the back of the sanctuary, appears in gold and purple, raising his right hand in benediction, in an attitude where modern skill is united to the stately Byzantine tradition. There is nothing more beautiful and more splendid than this figure, revealed in strong light as in a sky upon which opens the arched doorway of the iconostase. The mysterious darkness which reigns in the church at certain hours augments still further the brilliancy and the transparency of this superb window, which was painted at Munich.

I have thus indicated the principal divisions; I will now describe the figures contained in them, beginning with that file of the first row which is at the right of the spectator as he stands facing the iconostase.

We have first the figure of Christ upon his throne of Byzantine architecture, holding the globe and extending his hand in benediction; then St. Isaac the Dalmatian, unrolling the plan of the cathedral. These two figures are executed in mosaic upon backgrounds of little cubes of crystal lined with ducat gold, with the same warm, rich effect so admired in the St. Sophia at Constantinople, and St. Mark's at Venice. A painting of precious stones must needs have a field of gold.

St. Nicolas, bishop of Myra, and patron saint of Russia, in brocade dalmatic, with lifted hand, and holding a book, occupies the third panel. St. Peter, separated from St. Nicolas by the door of the lateral chapel, terminates the row. All these figures are by M. von Neff.

Going from the group of Jesus Christ in His Glory surrounded by His Elect, the first figure upon the second row is St. Michael combating the Dragon; then follow, in one panel, St. Anne and St. Elizabeth. The last compartment contains Constantine the Great, and the Empress Helena clad in purple and gold. This row is by M. Theodore Bruloff.

In the attic, following the same order, are the prophet Isaiah, whose extended finger seems to pierce the mists of futurity; Jeremiah with the roll, wherein are inscribed his lamentations; David leaning upon his harp; Noah, designated by the rain-bow; finally Adam, the father of men, painted by M. Givago.

At the left of the sacred door, the Virgin, with her child upon her knees, comes first, corresponding with the Christ on the other side. This picture is already executed in mosaic, as well as the neighboring panel, representing St. Alexander Newsky in costume of war, with buckler and banner of the faith, whereon is represented the image of Christ. Next to St. Alexander Newsky stands St. Catherine, a crown on her head and a palm-branch in her hand, having at her side the wheel which designates the mode of her martyrdom; beyond the chapel is St Paul, who leans upon his sword. All this row is the work of M. von Neff.

In the second row are: St. Nicholas, in frock of drugget; St. Magdalen and the Czarina Alexandra in the same panel—the one indicated by the vase of perfume, the other by the crown, the sword, and palm; St. Vladimir and St. Olga, indicated by their imperial garments—all being painted by M. Theodore Bruloff.

In the third, the figures succeed one another in the following order: Daniel, with a lion lying near him; King Solomon, bearing a model of the Temple; Melchisedek, king of Salem, presenting the sacrificial bread; and lastly, the patriarch Abraham—all by M. Givago.

This rampart of figures, separated by columns of malachite, compartments of precious marbles, and richly ornamented cornices, produces, in the mysterious half-light that fills this part of the cathedral, a magnificent and imposing effect. Sometimes a ray of light causes backgrounds of yellow gold to glitter; a plating gleams, and cuts out sharply, as if it were a real figure, the saint who is depicted thereon; or, a net-work of light slips down the flutings of the malachite; a spangle clings here or there to a gilded capital; a wreath is lighted up and brought out sharply in relief. The painted heads of the golden group assume a strange life, and remind one of those miraculous pictures which are said to gaze at you, to speak, and shed tears. Sometimes the lighting up of candles throws unexpected radiance upon details hitherto in the dark, and suddenly brings out all their value. According to the hour of the day, the veil of the sanctuary darkens or grows brilliant, with warm, deep shadows, or with flashes of splendid light.

At the left of the iconostase, as you stand facing it, is the chapel consecrated to St. Catherine; on the right, that of Alexander Newsky, both of which are decorated with extreme richness, and in perfect harmony with the decoration of the main portion of the building. The iconostase in each is composed of white statuary marble, incrusted with malachite, and decorated with ornaments of gilded bronze, and bears upon its summit sculptured groups gilded,—that of St. Catherine's chapel representing Christ springing from the tomb amid the affrighted guards; that of St. Alexander's chapel representing Jesus upon Mount Tabor.

Above St. Catherine's chapel rises a cupola whose decoration is as follows: In the top the Assumption of the Virgin; the pendentives contain St. John of Damascus, St. Cyril of Jerusalem, St. Clement, and St. Ignatius. In the arches, the martyrdoms of St. Catherine, St. Dmitri, St. George, and St. Barbara's Renunciation of the World. These are all by M. Bassine.

In the chapel of St. Alexander Newsky, the dome represents in the ceiling Jehovah in the skies, surrounded by a circle of angels and seraphim. In the pendentives, St. Nicodemus, St. Joseph the husband of Mary, St. James the Less, and Joseph of Arimathea. The arches are filled by scenes from the life of St. Alexander Newsky. In one, he prays for his country; in a second, he is gaining a victory over the Swedes, his white horse rearing amid the *mêlée;* in the third, stretched upon his death-bed, he makes an edifying and Christian end, amid candles burning around him and priests reciting prayers; in the fourth, they are piously bearing his remains to their last resting-place upon a rich catafalque lying on a boat.

Upon the doors of these chapels are painted great figures of saints and prophets upon golden backgrounds, and in what I may call the modernized Byzantine style.

I come now to a description of the Holy of Holies, concealed from the eyes of the worshippers by the veil of gold and malachite, of lapis-lazuli and agate, which forms the iconostase. One rarely penetrates into this mysterious and sacred place, wherein are celebrated the secret rites of the Greek church. It is a sort of hall or choir, lighted by the painted window whence shines the colossal figure of Christ which is seen within when the doors of the sanctuary are opened. Its two side walls are formed by the inner surface of screens occupied by paintings representing a multitude of saintly figures.

The altar, of white statuary marble, is marked by the most noble simplicity. A model of the church of St. Isaac's in gilded silver and of great weight, represents the tabernacle. This model presents some details which are not found in the real structure. Thus the counter-forts which sustain the campaniles are adorned with great groups in relief, like those of the Arc de l'Etoile; and the attic, which is smooth in the real building, offers a suite of bas-reliefs, of which, it seems to me, the effect would have been very pleasing.

Having thus carefully and minutely described the exterior and interior of the church, I may now sketch with freer and more careless pencil some of the principal effects of light and shade within this immense edifice.

The light seems to be somewhat deficient in St. Isaac's, or at least to be very unequally diffused. The dome sheds a flood of light into the centre of the building, and the four great windows give sufficient for the cupolas in the four corners. But other portions remain in shadow, or at least receive light only at certain hours of the day and through fugitive incidence of rays. The fault was intentional, for nothing would have been more easy than to cut windows through a structure standing free on all four sides. M. de Montferrand desired this mysterious half-light, favorable to religious impressions, and to collected devotion. But he perhaps forgot that this obscurity which harmonizes with the Romance, the Byzantine, or the Gothic architectures, is less fortunate in an edifice of the classic style, made for light, all covered with costly marbles, gilded ornaments, and mural paintings, which ought to be seen, and which, his devotions ended, one desires to see. Many of these paintings were executed in great part by light of lamps, a fact which is itself a sort of condemnation of the position in which they are placed. It would have been easy, in my opinion, to conciliate everything, and to have, in turn, the light or shade needed, by having windows darkened by blinds, hangings, or opaque shades. Religion would have lost nothing, and art would have gained by this. If St. Petersburg has its long summer days, it has also its long winter nights, which encroach upon the day, and during which only the most sparing light filters through the sky.

However, it must be owned that striking effects result from these alternations of light and shade. When you look down the dark side naves into the chapels of St. Catherine and St. Alexander Newsky, whose iconostases of white marble, adorned with gilded bronze, incrusted with malachite and agate, set with paintings on gold backgrounds, each receive the light of a great side window, you are dazzled by the splendor of these façades, framed as they are in the sombre vaults. The great window on which is represented the Christ shines forth in the shadow with a marvellous intensity of color. The deadened light is in no way objectionable for the isolated figures whose outlines stand out distinctly upon a field of gold. The brilliancy of the metal detaches the figure clearly enough, but in compositions containing many groups, and on a natural background, this is not always the case. Many interesting details escape the eye, and even the glass. The Byzantine churches, or, to speak more exactly, the Greco-Russian churches, wherein reigns the religious mystery which M. de Montferrand has sought to obtain in St. Isaac's, contain no pictures properly so called; the walls are covered with decorative paintings, the figures in which are traced, without any attempt at effect or illusion, upon a uniform field of gold or of color, with conventional attitudes and invariable attributes, rendered by simple outlines and flat coloring, and clothing the edifice like a rich tapestry whose general tone contents the eye. I am well aware that M. de Montferrand recommended to the artists entrusted with the paintings in St. Isaac's, to work broadly and in a decorative manner; a counsel easier to give than to follow, with the style of architecture adopted.

Each artist has done his best, in accordance with his nature and the resources of his talent, in unconscious obedience to the modern character of the church, excepting in the iconostases, where the figures, isolated, or placed one beside another in golden panels, appear in strong relief, and assume those clear-cut contours which painting, destined to ornament a building, ought to possess.

The compositions of M. Bruni, of which, as they presented themselves in the description of the church, I have indicated the subjects and the arrangement, commend themselves to our approval by a grandeur of style, and a truly historic manner, formed by a profound and thoughtful study of the Italian masters. I refer with special emphasis to this merit, for we, like the rest of the world, are losing it. M. Ingres and his school are its last depositaries. A certain anecdotic point, a too minute care for effect and for detail, a fear lest undue severity might prevent success, take away from modern works that stamp of magisterial gravity which, in the past centuries, was possessed even by second-rate works. M. Bruni is faithful to the grand traditions; he has sought inspiration from the frescos of the Sistine and the Vatican, and unites to this inspiration, besides his own personal feeling, something of the profound and reflective manner peculiar to the German school. You can see that, if M. Bruni has gazed long upon Michel Angelo and Raphael, he has also cast a thoughtful glance at Overbeck, Cornelius, and Kaulbach, artists too much ignored in Paris, and whose works weigh more than is believed in the balance of the art of the present day. He meditates, he arranges, balances, and reasons out his compositions without that haste to begin to paint, which is to be detected in so many modern pictures otherwise full of merit. With M. Bruni, the execution is but a means of expressing the thought,—not an end in itself; he knows that when the subject is rendered upon the cartoon in a noble, grand, and characteristic way, the most important part of the work is done. Perhaps he neglects coloring more than he ought, and employs too large a proportion of those sober, neutral, deadened, *abstract* tints—so to speak—which a care to make the idea alone conspicuous leads a painter to select. I do not like, in historical painting, what is called illusion; it is not fitting that too coarse reality, a too material life, should confuse these serene pages whereon the image only, not the object itself, should be reproduced; and still it is well to guard a little, especially with a regard to the future, against the dull and gloomy surroundings which a study of the old frescos seems to recommend. The paintings in St. Isaac's executed by M. Bruni, are those most worthy of its character which the church contains; they have individuality and *maestria*. Although he succeeds well in figures which demand energy, and understands anatomy sufficiently to venture upon that violence of muscular action which some subjects require, M. Bruni possesses in addition, as a special gift, a power of exciting religious feeling, a grace and angelic suavity resembling the manner of Overbeck; in his figures of angels and cherubim and saints, there is an elegance, a distinction,—if one may use a word which has generally a more mundane application,—and a poetry, charming in the extreme.

M. von Neff has conceived of the work entrusted him, rather in the character of an artist working for a picture-gallery, than a man employed as a decorator of a public building; but it is impossible to be displeased with him for this. His paintings, placed much nearer the eye, in those niches of the walls and pilasters which serve as frames and give mural painting the look of a picture, do not demand the sacrifices, in the way of effect and of perspective, which are required by the attics, the vaults, and the cupolas. This artist has a warm and brilliant coloring, a skilful and accurate execution, which remind me of Peter von Hess, whose works I have seen in Munich. Jesus sending His Picture to

Abgarus, and the Empress Helena finding the True Cross, are remarkable pictures, and might be detached from their places without any loss of value. All the other paintings by M. von Neff in the niches of the pilasters bear the stamp of the master, and reveal a highly endowed artist, one who has a very correct feeling for color and clare-obscure. The isolated figures executed by him upon the iconostases, the heads and portions of the nude painted by him in the great gilded group over the sacred door, have a relief and a strength of tone that is truly marvellous. It would be difficult more successfully to unite painting to sculpture, and work of the pencil to that of the chisel.

The paintings of M. Bruni, for composition and style, and those of M. von Neff, for coloring and execution, seem to me most satisfactory in their kind.

M. Pietro Bassine, in his numerous works, has exhibited an affluence of ideas, a facility of execution, and that decorative skill which distinguishes the painters of the eighteenth century, to whom, in our day, public taste restores the esteem of which they were unjustly deprived by David and his school. We can now say, by way of eulogium, that an artist resembles Pietro de Cortona, Carlo Maratte, or Tiepolo. It is easy for M. Bassine to cover enormous spaces. He understands the more mechanical part of his work; his compositions "make a picture," a talent more rare than is supposed, and one which we are losing every day.

The sober, pure, and correct talent of M. Mussini is well known in Paris; in the niches of the pilasters, many compositions are due to him, and confirm his well-earned reputation. MM. Markoff, Zavialoff, Pinchart, Sazonoff, Theodore Bruloff, Nikitine, and Scheboniëf deserve praise for the manner in which they have achieved their tasks.

If I fail to express a decided opinion in relation to Charles Bruloff's dome, it is because his illness and death (as I said in describing the composition, whose excution is due to M. Bassine) prevented him from painting it himself, and thus impressing upon it the stamp of his own personality, one of the most powerful and remarkable that Russian art has ever produced. There was in Bruloff the material of a great painter, and, amid numerous faults, genius, which redeems everything. His head, which he took pleasure in reproducing many times, with the increasing pallor and emaciation of illness, is brilliant with it. Under that disordered fair hair, behind that forehead growing more wan every day, beneath which shone the eyes where life had made its last stand, surely there was artistic and poetic thought.

I will now sum up in a few words that long study of the Cathedral of St. Isaac. It is without doubt, whether one approve the style or not, the most important religious edifice erected within this century. It does honor to M. de Montferrand, who has brought it to completion in so short a time, and has been able to fall asleep in his tomb, saying, with more truth than many a conceited poet: *Exegi monumentum ære perennius*,—a satisfaction rarely granted to architects, whose plans are sometimes so long in coming to reality, and who can be present in the spirit only, at the inauguration of the temples they commenced.

Rapid as has been the construction of St. Isaac's, the time between the laying of its first and of its last stone has been long enough for many changes to take place in the minds of men. At the time when the plans of this cathedral were accepted, the classic taste reigned alone and unchallenged. The Greek or Roman style was the sole type of perfection. All that the genius of man had conceived in giving form to the ideal of a new religion went for nothing. The Romance, the Byzantine, the Gothic architecture seemed in bad taste, contrary to rule,—in a word, barbarous. A historic value was found therein, but certainly no person would have thought of taking it for a model. At most, they pardoned the Renaissance, because of its love for the antique, with which it mingled many exquisite originalities and charming caprices, blamed by severe critics. At last came the Romantic school, whose eager studies of the mediaeval period and the national origins of art, made men at last understand the beauties of those basilicas, those cathedrals and chapels, so long disdained as the work of believing, but ignorant, ages. A very complete, rational art, perfectly understanding itself, obedient to fixed rules, possessing a complicated and mysterious symbolism, was discovered in these buildings, as astonishing by their bulk as by the finish of their details, which had before been believed the chance-work of ignorant stone-cutters and masons. A reaction followed, which, like all reactions, soon became unreasonable. No merit at all could be recognized in modern edifices copied from the classic pattern, and there is doubtless more than one Russian who regrets that in this sumptuous temple, Saint Sophia at Constantinople was not imitated rather than the Roman Pantheon. Such an opinion may be formed and may be defended; perhaps even at the present day it would be the prevailing one. I should find nothing unreasonable in it myself if the construction of St. Isaac's were now about to commence; but when the plans for this church were drawn, no architect would have done otherwise than M. de Montferrand has done; any attempt in another direction would have been deemed insane.

For myself, all theories apart, I consider the classic style the most suitable for St. Isaac's, metropolis as it is of the Greek faith. The use of these forms, which are consecrated outside of time and fashion, and, inasmuch as they are eternal, can never become barbaric or superannuated, however long the building may endure, was wisest for a great edifice like this,—impressing upon it a stamp of universality. Known by all civilized peoples, the emotions excited by these forms must be admiration only, pure from all surprise or criticism; though another style might have been more local, picturesque, novel, it would have had the grave disadvantage of giving rise to diversities of opinion; it might even have seemed strange and fantastic,—an impression fatal to the desired effect. M. de Montferrand did not seek the curious—he sought the beautiful; and St. Isaac's is unquestionably the most beautiful of modern churches. Its architecture admirably suits St. Petersburg, the youngest and newest of European capitals.

Those who regret that St. Isaac's is not in the Byzantine style, produce upon me somewhat the same effect as do those who regret that St. Peter's at Rome is not in the Gothic style. These great temples, centres of a faith, should have nothing peculiar, temporary, local, about them; it is right that all the centuries, and the faithful from every land, should be able to kneel therein, amidst the opulence, the splendor, and the beauty!

XVI.

MOSCOW.

DELIGHTFUL as I found my life in St. Petersburg, I was still haunted with the desire to visit Moscow,—the real Russian capital, the great Muscovite city,—an undertaking which the railway renders easy.

Being now sufficiently acclimated not to dread a journey when the thermometer stands at —12°, when the opportunity of going to Moscow with an agreeable companion presented itself, I seized its forelock white with frost, and donned my full winter costume,—pelisse of marten, cap of beaver, furred boots coming above the knee. One sledge took my trunk, a second received my person assiduously wrapped, and here I am, in the immense railway station, waiting the hour of departure, which is set for noon, but the Russian railways do not pride themselves, as ours do, upon a chronometric punctuality. If some great personage is expected, the locomotive will moderate its ardor for some minutes, a quarter of an hour perhaps,—to give him time to arrive. Those who are going by the train are accompanied to the station by friends and relations, and the separation, when the bell strikes for the last time, never takes place without much shaking of hands, many embraces and tender words, often interrupted by tears. At times, even, the whole group take tickets, enter the carriage, and escort the departing one as far as the first station, to return by the next train. I like the custom; it seems to me a touching one; they desire to enjoy the society of their friends for yet a few moments longer, and to postpone, as long as they can, the sad moment of parting. In the faces of these mujiks—otherwise far from beautiful—a painter would have observed expressions pathetic by their simplicity. Mothers and wives, whose sons or husbands are going away—perhaps for years—in their deep and unfeigned grief, remind one of the holy women with reddened eyes and mouth contracted by suppressed sobs, that the mediæval artists represent along the way to Calvary. In divers countries have I seen inn-yards, when the diligence was leaving,—quays of embarkation,—railway-stations for departing trains, —but never, in any place, adieus so tender and so heart-breaking as those which I have witnessed in Russia.

The fitting up of railway-carriages in a country where the thermometer more than once in a winter goes down to thirty-five or forty degrees below zero, could not be expected to resemble that wherewith temperate climes are content. The hot-water tins, in use in the west of Europe, would soon contain only a block of ice, under the traveller's feet. The air rushing in through cracks around the doors and windows would introduce colds in the head, congestions, and rheumatisms. On Russian trains, many carriages united together and communicating by doors, which the travellers open or shut at will, form, so to speak, a suite of rooms, preceded by an ante-chamber and dressing-room, where the lesser articles of luggage may be placed. This ante-room opens upon a platform surrounded by a balustrade, which you reach by a stairway more convenient than the steps to our railway carriages.

Stoves, filled with wood, heat the compartment and maintain a temperature of 66° or 68°. The windows, listed with strips of felt, entirely exclude the cold air and retain the interior heat. You see, therefore, that a journey from St. Petersburg to Moscow, in the month of January, in a climate the mere mention of which makes a Parisian shudder and his teeth chatter in his head, has nothing really polar about it. You would be quite sure to suffer more in making the trip from Burgos to Valladolid, at the same time of year.

Around the sides of the first carriage runs a wide divan for the use of sleepy people and of those who are not afraid to cross their legs in Turkish fashion. I preferred the spring-seated arm-chairs with well-stuffed head-rests which are found in the second section, and installed myself comfortably in a corner one. Thus ensconsed, I seemed to myself to be, for the time, living in a house on wheels, rather than to be enduring the restraint of a public conveyance. I was at liberty to rise and walk about, to go anywhere in the compartment with the same amount of freedom enjoyed by the traveller on a steamboat,—a luxury of which one is deprived who is boxed up in a diligence, a post-chaise, or the railway carriage as it is still constructed in France.

My seat being selected, I left my travelling-bag to indicate and retain it, and, as the train was not ready to move, I walked a few steps along by the track, and the peculiar shape of the smoke-stack of the locomotive attracted my notice. It is coiffed with a vast funnel, which gives it a resemblance to those hooded chimneys that rise so picturesquely in profile above the red walls in Canaletto's Venetian pictures.

Russian locomotives are not coal-burners, like the French and those of the Western countries, but consume wood in all cases.

Logs of birch or pine are piled symmetrically upon the tender, and are renewed at stations where there are wood-yards. This makes the old peasants say that at the rate things are going in Holy Russia, they will soon be forced to pull down the log-huts to get wood to feed the stoves; but before all the forests are gone, or even all sufficiently near the railways, the explorations of engineers will have discovered some bed of anthracite or bituminous coal. This virgin soil must conceal inexhaustible wealth.

At last, the train moves off. We leave at our right,

upon the old high-road, the arch of triumph of Moscow, stately and grand of outline, and we see fly past us the last houses of the city, ever more and more scattered, with their board fences, their wooden walls painted in the old Russian fashion, and their green roofs frosted with snow, for, as we leave the centre of the city behind us, the various buildings, which, in the fashionable quarters affect the styles of Berlin, Paris, and London, fall back into the national characteristics. St. Petersburg begins to disappear; but the golden cupola of St. Isaac's, the spire of the Admiralty, the pyramidal towers of the church of the Horse-Guards, the domes of starred azure and bulb-shaped tin belfries yet glitter upon the horizon, with an effect as of a Byzantine crown resting on a cushion of silver brocade. The houses of men seem to sink back into the earth, the houses of God to spring upward towards heaven.

While I was looking out, there began to appear upon the window-glass, as a result of the contrast between the cold air without and the heated air within, delicate arborizations of the color of quicksilver, which soon cross their branches, spread out in broad leaves, form a magic forest, and cover the pane so completely that the view is entirely cut off. There is certainly nothing more exquisite than these branches, arabesques, and filigrees of ice wrought with so delicate a touch by the hand of Winter. It is a bit of Northern poetry, and the imagination can discover Hyperborean mirages therein. However, after you have contemplated them for an hour, you become annoyed by this veil of white embroidery, through which one can neither see nor be seen. Your curiosity is exasperated at the idea that, behind this ground glass, a world of unknown objects is passing by, which will, perhaps, never come under your eyes again. In France, I should have lowered the glass without hesitation; in Russia, it would be perhaps a mortal imprudence so to do. Cold, the wild beast, forever lying in wait for his prey, would have stretched into the carriage his polar-bear's paw, and cuffed me, with all his claws unsheathed. In the open air, he is an enemy fierce, indeed, yet loyal and generous in his rough way; but beware of letting him within doors, for then it becomes a struggle for life; should but one of his arrows wound you in the side, it may be a long, hard struggle before you are a sound man again.

There was need, however, to do something about it; it would have been a great pity to be transported from St. Petersburg to Moscow in a box, with a milky square cut in it, through which nothing could be seen. I have not, thank Heaven! the temperament of the Englishman who had himself transported from London to Constantinople with a bandage over his eyes, removed only at the entrance of the Golden Horn, that he might enjoy suddenly, and without enfeebling transition, this splendid panorama, unrivalled in the world. Therefore, bringing my furred cap down to my eyebrows, raising the collar of my pelisse and fastening it close around me, drawing up my long boots, plunging my hands into gloves of which the thumb only is articulated—a real Samoyed costume—I made my way bravely to the platform in front of the railway carriage. An old soldier in military capote, and decorated with many medals, was there, looking out for the train, and seemed in no way inconvenienced by the temperature. A small gratification, in the shape of a silver ruble, which he did not solicit, but neither did refuse, made him obligingly turn his head towards another point of the horizon, while I lighted an excellent cigar obtained at Eliseïef's, and extracted from one of those boxes with glass sides, which exhibit the merchandise without the necessity of breaking the band which has been stamped at the custom-house.

I was soon compelled to throw away this pure Havana "*de la Vuelta de Abajo*," for though it burned at one end, it froze at the other. An agglutination of ice welded it to my lips, and every time I took it from my mouth, a bit of skin came off attached to the leaf of tobacco. To smoke in the open air with the thermometer at —12°, comes near being an impossibility; hence, conformity with the ukase prohibiting the out-of-door pipe or cigar is less difficult. In the present case, the scene unfolding before me was of interest enough to compensate for the small privation.

As far as the eye could see, a cold drapery of snow covered the land, leaving the undefined forms of all objects to be conjectured beneath its white folds, very much as a winding-sheet reveals the dead figure which it hides from sight. There are no longer roads, nor footpaths, nor rivers, nor any kind of demarcations. Only elevations and depressions, and those not very perceptible, in the universal whiteness. The beds of frozen streams are become only a kind of valley, tracing sinuosities through the snow, and often filled up by it. At remote intervals, clusters of rusty birch-trees, half-buried, emerge and show their naked heads. A few huts, built of logs, and loaded with snow, send up smoke, and are a stain upon the whiteness of this melancholy pall. Along the track you remark lines of brushwood planted in rows, destined to arrest in its horizontal course the white, icy dust that is moved along with frightful impetuosity by the snow-blow, that *khamsin* of the pole. It is impossible to imagine the strange, sad grandeur of this immense white landscape, offering the same aspect as does the full moon seen through a telescope. You seem to be in some planet that is dead, and is delivered over to eternal cold. The mind refuses to believe that this prodigious accumulation of snow will melt, and evaporate, or else return to the sea in the swollen currents of rivers; and that, some day, the spring will make these colorless plains green and flower-strewn. The low, overcast sky with its uniform gray, which is made yellowish by the white earth, adds to the melancholy of the landscape. A profound silence, broken only by the rumbling of the train over the rails, reigned in the solitude, for the snow deadens all sounds with its carpet of ermine. In all the wide waste there was not a person to be seen, not a trace of man or animal. The human being kept himself close behind the log-walls of his isba; the animal, deep in his lair. Only as we drew near stations, from some fold in the snow emerged sledges and kibitkas, the little dishevelled horses racing on the full gallop across country, without regard to the buried roads, and coming from some unseen village to meet the train. In our compartment there were some young men of rank going out hunting, clad for the occasion in touloupes, new and handsome, of light salmon-color, and ornamented with stitching in form of graceful arabesques. As I have before explained, the touloupe is a kind of caftan of sheepskin, the hair worn inwards, as are all furs in really cold countries. A button fastens it at the shoulder, a leather belt with plates of metal secures it around the waist. Add to this an Astrakan cap, boots of white felt, a hunting-knife at the belt, and you have a costume of truly Asiatic elegance. Although it is the mujik's costume, the noble does not hesitate to assume it under these circumstances, for there is nothing more convenient or better adapted to the climate. Furthermore, the difference between this touloupe, clean, supple, soft as a kid glove, and the soiled, greasy, shining touloupe of the mujik, is so great that no comparison between the two would be possible. These birch and pine woods that you perceive on the horizon as mere brown lines, harbor wolves and bears, and sometimes, it is said, the moose, a wild creature of the North, the pursuit of which is not without danger, and requires agile, strong, and courageous Nimrods.

A troïka, with its three superb horses, awaited our young gentlemen at one of the stations; and I watched them plunge into the depths of the country, with a rapidity which had no need to envy that of the locomotive, by a road quite concealed under the snow, but marked out from point to point by posts. At the pace at which they were going, I soon lost them from sight. They were to meet, at some chateau whose name has escaped me, comrades of the chase, and promised themselves to have better luck than La Fontaine's simpletons who sold the bear-skin before they had killed the bear. Their plan was to kill the bear, and to keep his skin for one of those rugs bordered with scarlet, and with the head stuffed, against which the traveller who is a novice never fails to stumble, in the drawing-rooms of St. Petersburg. By their tranquilly deliberate air, I judged well of their cynegetic prowess.

I do not mention, station after station, the localities through which runs the railway; it would be of no great use to the reader for me to tell him that the train stopped at this or at that place, whose name awakens in him no idea and no recollection, especially since the cities or towns of importance are sometimes quite remote from the road, and are betrayed only by the green bulbs and the copper cupolas of their churches. For the railway from St. Petersburg to Moscow follows inflexibly the straight line, and allows itself to be drawn aside by no pretext whatsoever; it does not pay the compliment of curve or elbow to Tver, the most considerable city upon the way, the place whence the Volga steam-boats start; it passes disdainfully by, at some distance, and to reach Tver you must take sledge or droschky, according to the time of year.

The stations, built on a uniform plan, are magnificent. In their architecture the red shades of brick and the white of stone are united in a way pleasing to the eye; but in seeing one you see all. I will describe that at which we stopped for dinner. This station has the peculiarity of being placed, not at the side of the road, but in the middle, like the church of Mary-le-bone in the Strand. The iron ribbon of the railway goes on both sides of it, and this is the place where the trains from Moscow and from St. Petersburg meet and pass each other. The two trains pour out upon the platforms at the right and left their passengers, who sit down together at dinner. The train from Moscow brings travellers from Archangel, Tobolsk, Kiatka, Irkoutsk; from the banks of the Amoor; from the shores of the Caspian; from Kazan, Tiflis, the Caucasus, the Crimea; from the depths of all the Russias, European and Asiatic; who shake hands in passing, with acquaintances from the West, brought by the St. Petersburg train. It is a cosmopolitan love-feast, where are spoken more languages than at the Tower of Babel. The dining-hall is lighted by wide, arched windows with double glass, on opposite sides of the room; a mild, greenhouse temperature prevails in it, and permits Bourbon-palms and tulip-trees and other tropical plants to expand their great, silky leaves. The luxury of rare plants which I have so much admired in St. Petersburg, still continues, and gives a holiday air to the inside of houses, refreshing the eye with green after the dazzling white of the snow. The table was splendidly laid, covered with silver and crystal, bristling with bottles of every form and of all vintages. The slender *quilles* of Rhine wine stood taller by a head than the long-corked bottles of Bordeaux, coiffed with metallic capsules, or the Champagne bottles with their helmets of lead paper; there were represented all the famous growths,—the Château d'Yquem, the Haut Barsac, the Château Lafitte, the Genau-Larose, the Veuve Cliquot, the Rœderer, the Moët, the Sternberg-Cabinet; also, all the celebrated English beers; a complete assortment of illustrious beverages, bedizened with gilt labels printed in high colors, with attractive designs and authentic coats-of-arms. It is in Russia that the best French wines are consumed; the purest juice of our vintages, the most precious drops from our wine-presses, run down these septentrional throats, which consider not the cost of that which they swallow. With the exception of a soup, the Russian chtchi, the *cuisine*, it is needless to say, was French, and I recall to mind a certain *chaud-froid de gélinottes*, which would not have been disowned by Robert, that famous officer of the kitchen, of whom Carême said, " In the *chaud-froid* he is sublime!" Waiters in black coats, white gloves, and white cravats circulated around the table, and served with quiet assiduity.

My appetite having been satisfied,—while the other travellers were draining glasses of every shape,—I examined the two private parlors at the extremity of the hall, reserved for persons of distinction, and the elegant little booths where were offered for sale satchels, Toula boots and slippers of morocco wrought with gold and silver thread, Circassian rugs embroidered with silk on a scarlet ground, braided belts made of gold thread, cases containing fork and spoon of platina with gold niello-work of exquisite design, models of the broken bell of the Kremlin, Russian crosses of wood carved with a patience truly Chinese and adorned with an infinity of microscopic figures; a thousand fascinating nothings, made to tempt the tourist, and lighten his viaticum by a few rubles, if he have not—like myself—strength to resist the lust of the eyes, and to be content with a look merely. After all, it is difficult, when you think of absent friends, not to load yourself with a store of these pretty trifles, which show, on the return home, that you did not forget;—and one generally ends by yielding to the temptation.

All the travellers from the different carriages being thus gathered in one hall for dinner, I had the opportunity to observe that, on a journey as well as in town, the women seem less sensitive to cold than do the men. For the most part, the former appear to be content with the satin pelisse lined with fur; they do not bury their heads in turned-up collars, nor load themselves with a mass of additional garments. Doubtless coquetry has something to do with it; what use in having a slender waist, a little foot,—and looking like a bundle? A pretty woman from Siberia attracted all eyes by an elegance which the journey had not in the slightest degree disarranged. You would have said that she had just stepped from her carriage to enter the opera. Two gypsies, attired with grotesque richness, struck me by the strangeness of the type, rendered yet more singular by the semi-barbarous costume. They laughed at compliments addressed to them by some young men, showing teeth savagely white, set in those brown gums, characteristic of the Bohemian race.

Emerging from this mild atmosphere, the cold, in spite of the pelisse which I had again laid upon my shoulders, seemed more stinging as night came on. And indeed the thermometer had fallen several degrees. The snow had assumed a greater intensity of white, and creaked under foot like powdered glass. Diamonded specks floated in the air and fell to the ground. It would have been imprudent to resume my post upon the platform. In so doing, I might have compromised the future of my nose! Besides, the landscape remained the same. White plains followed white plains; in Russia one must go over an immense distance before the horizon changes its aspect.

The veteran, with his breast-plate of medals, filled up the stove, and the temperature of the compartment, which had been somewhat lowered, went up very quickly; a mild warmth prevailed, and had it not been for the kind of swaying motion impressed by the traction of the locomotive, I could have believed myself in my own room. The lower-class carriages, fitted up with less comfort and luxury, are heated in the same manner. In Russia heat is dispensed to everybody. Lords and peasants are equal before the thermometer. The palace and the hovel mark the same degree; for this is a question of life or death.

Lying upon the divan, covered with my pelisse, my head resting on my travelling-bag, I lost no time in falling asleep in a state of perfect comfort, rocked by the regular vibration from the engine. When I awoke it was one o'clock in the morning, and the whim seized me to go outside and contemplate for a few minutes the nocturnal aspect of nature in this northern climate. The winter night is long and deep in these latitudes, but no darkness can quite conceal the white shining of the snow. Under the blackest sky you distinguish its livid pallor spread out like a pall beneath the vaulted roof of a tomb. Vague gleams, bluish, phosphorescent lights rise from it. It betrays objects hidden beneath it by the light on the relief, and sketches them as with a white crayon upon the black background of the darkness. This wan landscape, whose lines change their axis, and fold themselves back rapidly as the train flies along, has the strangest aspect. For a moment the moon, piercing the heavy clouds, threw its cold radiance across the icy plain; wherever the light fell the snow shone like silver, whilst the rest grew azure with bluish shadows, proving the truth of Goethe's observation in regard to the shadows upon snow, in his theory of colors. The melancholy is inconceivable of this immense, pale horizon which appears to reflect the moon and to send back her own light to her. It forms again around the train, always the same like the sea, and yet the locomotive fled at full speed, flinging out from its funnel crackling sheaves of red sparks; but it seemed to the discouraged eye that we should never get out of this white circle. The cold, increased by the displacement of the air, became intense, and penetrated to my very bones, notwithstanding the soft thickness of my furs; the breath crystallized upon my mustache,—an icy gag, as it were; my eyelashes caught together, and I felt, although I was standing, an invincible desire of sleep come over me; it was time to go inside. When there is no wind, the utmost rigor of cold can be endured, but the least breath sharpens its arrows, and gives an edge to its knife of steel. Ordinarily, in these low temperatures in which the mercury congeals, there is not the slightest wind, and you might traverse Siberia, a lighted taper in hand, without a flicker of the flame; but in the slightest current of air, you freeze, though you were wrapped in spoils won from the best-furred visitant of the pole.

It was one of the most agreeable sensations possible to find myself again in the benign atmosphere of my compartment, and to sink back into my corner, where I slept till daylight, with that peculiar feeling of pleasure that a man experiences when sheltered from severities of climate which are written in letters of ice upon the window-panes. The morning gray, as Shakespeare says (for Homer's rosy-fingered Aurora would have had chilblains in such a latitude), began, wrapped in her pelisse, to walk with boots of white felt across the snow. We were now nearing Moscow, whose dentated crown already was seen in the early morning light from the platform of the railway carriage.

Some few years ago, in the eyes of a Parisian, Moscow loomed vaguely, in the prodigiously remote distance, by the light of the fire which Rostopchin kindled, as by a sort of aurora borealis filling all the sky—its Byzantine crown of towers and odd-shaped belfries sharply relieved against a background of lurid smoke cut by flashes of flame. It was a city fabulously splendid and chimerically remote—a tiara of gems lying in a waste of snow, and the veterans of 1812 spoke of it with a kind of stupor, for, to them, the city had changed itself into a volcano. And really, before railways and steam-boats were invented, to reach Moscow was no trifling enterprise.

When I was a child, this city filled my imagination, and I used to stand in ecstasy, on the Quai Voltaire, before the windows of a dealer in engravings, where were exhibited great panoramic views of Moscow, tinted in imitation of water-color pictures, by a method then very much in use. These belfries shaped like onions; these cupolas surmounted with crosses in open-work; these painted houses; these figures with great beards and broad hats; these women coiffed with pivoïniks, and wearing short tunics belted just under the arms, seemed to me to belong to the lunar world, and the idea of ever making a journey thither did not occur to my mind as a possibility; furthermore, since Moscow had been burned, what interest could this heap of cinders present? It was long before I was willing to admit that the city had been rebuilt, and, indeed, that not all the ancient buildings had perished in the flames. Well, in less than a half hour I was to be able to judge whether the old engravings of the Quai Voltaire were or were not faithful!

At the station, a swarm of isvochtchiks were gathered, offering their sledges to the travellers, and seeking to decide their preference. I selected two. My companion and I entered one sledge, the other was laden with our trunks. According to the custom of the Russian driver, who never waits to know where you are going, the isvochtchiks who had taken charge of us incited their animals to a preliminary gallop, and dashed off in some direction. This kind of *fantasia* they never fail to execute.

The snow had fallen in much greater abundance in Moscow than in St. Petersburg, and the roadway, at whose edges it had been carefully heaped up with shovels, was higher by twenty inches than the level of the sidewalks. Over this solid layer smoothed, till it glittered, by the runners of the sledges, our frail equipages flew like the wind, and the horses' feet threw up against the dasher icy particles as hard as hailstones. The street through which we passed was bordered with public bathing-houses, vapor-baths, for the water-bath is but little in use in Russia.

If this people do not look as if they were clean, the fault is in appearance only, and is true of their winter garments, which it would be expensive to renew; but there is not a Parisian belle, all cold-cream, *poudre de riz*, and *lait virginal*, whose skin is cleaner than that of the mujik emerging from the warm bath. The poorest of them go thither at least once every week. These baths, taken in common, without distinction of sex, cost but a few kopecks. Of course there exist besides, for the rich, much more luxurious establishments, where are gathered all the refinements of the balneal art.

After a few moments of frantic speed, our drivers, judging that they had preserved a respectful silence as long as was needful, turned about and inquired whither we proposed to go. I indicated to them the Hôtel Chevrier, in the Street of the Old Newspapers. They resumed their course towards a goal now definitely fixed. On the way, I looked eagerly to the right and left, but without seeing anything extremely characteristic. Moscow is built in concentric zones; the exterior is the most modern and the least interesting. The Kremlin, which was formerly the entire city, represents the heart and the marrow.

Above houses which do not differ greatly from those of St. Petersburg, here and there I see the curve of cupolas of azure starred with gold, or bulbous belfries covered with tin; a church of *rococo* architecture shows a façade painted bright red, the effect oddly enhanced by the snow which lies on all the projecting portions; elsewhere, the eye is surprised by a chapel painted in Marie-Louise blue, frosted with silver by the touch of winter. The question of polychromatic architecture, so earnestly discussed in Paris, was settled long ago, without hesitation, in Russia; they gild their buildings, they silver them, they paint them of any color, without the slightest regard for sobriety or good taste—as the pseudo-classicists understand the word, for it is certain that the Greeks gave varied tints to their edifices and even to their statues. There is nothing more agreeable than this rich variety of coloring applied to that architecture which the West condemns to bleak grays, to neutral yellows, and to dirty whites.

The signs of the shops bring out, like ornaments of gold, the beautiful letters of the Russian alphabet with their Greek attitudes, so well suited, like the Cufic characters, to be employed in decorative friezes. The translation is made—for the use of strangers and of the illiterate—by a naïve representation of the objects contained in the shops.

We soon reached the hotel, whose great court-yard paved with wood exhibited, under sheds, the greatest variety of vehicles: sledges, troïkas, tarentasses, droschkys, kibitkas, post-chaises, coaches, landaus, *chars-à-bancs*, summer carriages and winter carriages; for in Russia no one walks, and if you send a servant out to buy cigars, he takes a sledge to go the hundred paces which separates the house from the tobacco-shop.

They gave us rooms adorned with mirrors, the walls hung with large-flowered paper, and the furniture sumptuous in the extreme, like the great hotels in Paris. Not the smallest vestige of local color, but, on the other hand, all the outfit of modern comfort. However romantic a man's tastes may be, he easily resigns himself to this, so great hold has civilization even upon characters the most rebellious towards its effeminacies; there was nothing Russian here, save the great green leather sofa, on which one can sleep so well, wrapped in his pelisse.

My heavy travelling garments hung up in the dressing-room, and my ablutions ended,—before making a dash at the city I thought it might be well to breakfast, in order not to be molested in my admirations by the pangs of hunger, and forced to return to my hotel from some absurdly remote quarter of the town. The repast was served to me in the centre of a glazed hall, arranged as a winter garden, and crowded with exotic plants. To be eating a beefsteak with potatoes *soufflées*, in Moscow, in a miniature virgin forest, is an odd enough sensation. The waiter, who stood ready to receive my orders a few steps from the table, although he wore a black coat and a white cravat, had the yellow complexion, projecting cheek-bones, and small, flattened nose which betrayed his Mongol descent and assured me that, for all his air of waiter of the Café Anglais, he could not have been born far from the confines of China.

As one cannot observe the minute details of a city while borne along in a sledge that is going like a flash, I resolved—at the risk of passing for a very ordinary seigneur, and drawing upon myself the contempt of the mujiks—to make my first expedition on foot, equipped with stout furred overshoes separating the soles of my boots from the icy sidewalk; and I soon arrived at the Kitaï Gorod, which is the business quarter of the city, upon the Krasnaïa, or Red Place,—the Beautiful Place, I ought rather to say, for in Russia the word is the same. One side of this square is occupied by the long façade of the Gostinoï Dvor, an immense bazaar, cut by streets, roofed with glass like our *passages*, and containing not less than six thousand shops. The encircling wall of the Kremlin, or Kreml, rises at the farther extremity with its peaked-roofed towers through which are cut entrances, and showing above its crenellated tops the cupolas, bell-towers, and spires of the convents and churches within. At the other corner, strange as the architecture of dreamland, rises, like a chimera, the impossible church of Vassili Blagennoi, which makes one doubt the witness of his eyes. There it stands with all the appearances of reality, and you ask yourself if this is not a mirage of the fancy, an edifice of clouds tinted by the sunset, liable at a breath of wind to change its shape or to vanish away. It is, without any doubt, the most original building in the world, reminding one of nothing he has ever seen before, and belonging to no style; a gigantic madrepore, you might say,—a colossal crystallization, an inverted grotto of stalactites. But it is useless to seek for comparisons to give an idea of something which has neither like nor prototype. Let me rather attempt to describe it, if indeed there exists a vocabulary to speak of a thing so unforeseen.

There is a legend about Vassili Blagennoi, which probably is not true, but which does not the less express with force and poetry the admiring stupor that this edifice, so singular and so independent of all architectural traditions, must have produced, in the semi-barbarous time in which it was erected. Ivan the Terrible ordered the construction of this church, by way of thank-offering for the taking of Kazan; and when it was finished, he found it so beautiful, admirable, and surprising, that he commanded the architect's eyes to be put out, that he might never build elsewhere others like it! According to a different version, the czar asked the architect—said to be an Italian, by the way—if he could construct a still more beautiful building; and, receiving an affirmative reply, ordered his head taken off, that Vassili Blagennoi might remain forever unrivalled. It is impossible to imagine a cruel act more flattering by reason of the jealousy which caused it; Ivan the Terrible must have been at heart a true artist, an impassioned *dilettante*. This ferocity, where art is concerned, displeases me less than does indifference. At least this is certain: from Vassili Blagennoi no second proof was ever struck off.

Imagine, upon a kind of platform isolated by sunken ground, the oddest, the most incoherent, the most amazing accumulation of cabins, cells, staircases projected upon the outside, arched galleries, unexpected recesses and equally unexpected salient portions, unsymmetrical porches, chapels in juxtaposition, windows cut through as if by accident, indescribable forms resulting from interior arrangement, as if the artist had begun at the heart of the building, and had done all his work from inside. From the roof of this edifice, which you would take for a Hindoo, Chinese, or Thibetan pagoda, springs a forest of bell towers in the strangest taste, and fanciful to an unapproachable extreme. The central one, the highest and most massive, presents three or four stories between the roof and the point where its spire begins.

First there are colonnettes and denticulated fillets; then, pilasters enclosing long, mullioned windows; finally, small arches superposed one upon another like scales; and, on the sides of the spire, crosiers indenting each angle; the whole terminated by a lantern surmounted by an inverted golden bulb, bearing the Russian cross upon its point. The others, less every way in size, assume shapes like minarets, and their fantastically carved turrets terminate in the odd expansion of their onion-shaped cupolas. Some are hammered into facets, others ribbed; these are cut diamond-wise, like the rind of the pineapple, those have spiral stripes; others are imbricated with scale-work, lozenged, figured in a honey-comb pattern; and all carry at their summits the cross, adorned with golden balls.

What adds still further to the fantastic effect of Vassili Blagennoi, is that it is painted from base to summit with the most incongruous colors, which, however, produce a harmonious whole delightful to the eye. Red, blue, apple-green, yellow bring out the important divisions of the architecture. Colonnettes, capitals, arches, ornaments are painted in different shades, giving them a very high relief. In the rare flat surfaces, divisions are simulated, panels containing pots of flowers, rosettes, ciphers, fanciful figures. The domes of the bell-towers are adorned with branching designs which suggest India shawls, and, placed as they are on the roofs of the church, they resemble sultans' kiosks. M. Hittorf, the apostle of polychromatic architecture, would behold in this church a brilliant confirmation of his theories.

That nothing might be wanting to the enchantment of the scene, particles of snow, caught by the projections of the roofs, the friezes, and the ornaments, adorn with silvery spangles the painted attire of Vassili Blagennoi, and sow with a thousand sparkling points this marvellous decoration.

Postponing to another day my visit to the Kremlin, I

at once entered the church of Vassili Blagennoi, whose odd exterior excited to the highest degree my curiosity to see whether the within fulfilled the promise of the without. The same fanciful taste had presided over the interior arrangement and decoration. A first, low-walled chapel, wherein flickered a few lamps, was like a cavern of gold; unexpected gleams flashed into the tawny shadows, and brought out like ghosts the rigid pictures of Greek saints. The mosaics of St. Mark's at Venice give an approximative idea of the wonderful richness of this effect. In the farther end the iconostase lifted itself up like a golden wall between the faithful and the arcana of the sanctuary, in a kind of half-darkness traversed by rays of light. Vassili Blagennoi does not present, as do other churches, one common interior composed of many naves communicating with each other and mutually intersecting at given points in accordance with the exigences of the ritual, whatever it may be, observed in each building. It is formed by a bundle of churches and chapels, tied together, so to speak, not individually independent. Each bell-tower has its own chapel, arranging itself as best it can in this mould. The chapel-roof is the inside of the spire, or is the bulb of the cupola. You fancy yourself inside an enormous helmet of some Tartar or Circassian giant. These vaults, furthermore, are magnificently painted and gilded within. It is the same with the walls, covered with figures intentionally and hieratically barbarous, after a pattern which the monks of Mount Athos have preserved from age to age, and which, in Russia, more than once deceives the inattentive observer in relation to the age of religious edifices. It is a strange sensation to find yourself in these mysterious sanctuaries, where personages well known to the Catholic faith, mingled with special saints of the Greek calendar, seemed, with their constrained, archaic, Byzantine aspect, to be awkwardly translated in gold by the childish devotion of some primitive tribe. These sacred figures, resembling idols, which look out at you through apertures in the precious metal of the iconostase, or stand up stiffly upon the gilded walls, opening their great, fixed eyes, raising their brown hands with fingers bent in a symbolic fashion, produce with their wild, extra-human, immutably traditional aspect, a religious impression which the works of a more advanced art could not occasion. These figures, amid the gleaming of gold and by the flickering light of lamps, readily assume a kind of phantom life, capable of impressing naïve imaginations, and inspiring in the declining daylight a certain sacred horror.

Narrow corridors, low-arched galleries where you touch the wall with each elbow and are forced to bend your head, wind about among these chapels, and give access from each to the others. There is nothing more whimsical than these passages; the architect seems to have taken pleasure in making a tangle of them. You go up and down, out-doors and in again; you go around outside a tower upon a cornice; you walk along in a wall by tortuous windings like the capillary tubes of madrepores or the roads that borers trace under the bark of wood. After so many turns and returns your head whirls, you are seized with dizziness, and you can almost imagine yourself the mollusk of some gigantic shell. I do not speak of the mysterious nooks, the inexplicable blind ways, the low doors that lead,—one knows not whither,—the obscure stairs going down into the depths; I should never end if I attempted fully to describe this building, wherein one walks as amid the architecture of dream-land.

The winter days are short in Russia, and already in the deepening shadows the lamps before the holy pictures were beginning to shine more brightly, as I emerged from Vassili Blagennoi, auguring well, from this specimen, of the picturesque wealth of Moscow. I had just been experiencing that rare sensation, the search for which drives the traveller to the ends of the earth. I had seen something that exists nowhere else. Therefore—I confess it—the bronze group of Minine and Poyarsky which stands near the Gostinoi Dvor and faces the Kremlin, affected me but little as a work of art; and yet the sculptor who composed this group, M. Martoss, does not lack talent. But in comparison with the wild license of Vassili Blagennoi, his work appeared to me too cold, too correct, too rationally academic. Minine was a butcher of Nijni Novgorod, who raised an army to drive out the Poles, at that time masters of Moscow, and gave the command of it to Prince Poyarsky. These two, the man of the people and the *grand seigneur*, delivered the Holy City from strangers, and on the pedestal, which is ornamented with bas-reliefs of bronze, is read this inscription: " To the mujik Minine, and to the prince Poyarsky, grateful Russia; in the year 1818."

In travelling I make it a rule, unless where time is too pressing, to stop short when the impression is vivid. There is a point at which the eye, saturated with forms and colors, denies itself to the absorption of new aspects. Nothing more can be received,—as when a vase is full to the brim. The anterior image remains, and is not effaced. In this condition you look, but you no longer see. The retina has not time to be sensitized for a new impression. This was my case in emerging from Vassili Blagennoi, and the Kremlin deserves a fresh look, a virgin eye. So, after casting a last glance at the extraordinary towers of the cathedral of Ivan the Terrible, I was about to call a sledge to return to my hotel, when I was arrested, upon the Krasnaïa, by a singular noise which caused me to lift my eyes to the sky.

Crows and ravens were sweeping through the air, croaking as they flew, sombre punctuation-marks upon the grayish sky. They were returning to their nests in the Kremlin, but this was only the advance-guard. Soon came denser battalions. From all points of the horizon, bands were flying hitherward, seemingly obeying the order of their chiefs and accomplishing a strategic march. The black swarms were not all at the same height, and seemed to arrange themselves in zones, actually darkening the air in their flight. Their number was augmented from moment to moment. There were cries and flapping of wings, to that degree that you could not have heard yourself speak; and ever new phalanxes arrived overhead, coming to increase the prodigious council of state. I had no idea there were so many crows and ravens in the world. Without exaggeration, they might have been counted by hundreds of thousands; even this figure seems too modest;—by millions, would come nearer the truth. It recalled to me Audubon's account of the passage of flocks of birds in America, which obscure the sun, throw a shadow on the earth like clouds, bend down the forests whereon they alight, and do not seem at all diminished by the immense massacres the sportsmen make among them. These innumerable bands, having effected a junction, whirled about over the Krasnaïa, rising, descending, describing circles, and making all the noise of a great storm. At last the winged multitude seemed to have formed a resolution, and every bird directed his flight towards his nest. In an instant the belfries, cupolas, roofs, towers, pinnacles, were wrapped in black whirlwinds and deafening cries. They fought with another fiercely for their places. The smallest hole, the narrowest cleft which might offer a shelter was the object of a desperate siege. By degrees, the tumult died away; each one had housed himself as best he could; not a croak was to be heard—not a raven was to be seen; and the sky, just now dotted all over with black specks, had resumed its livid gray in the twilight. You ask yourself wherewith can these myriads of evil birds be fed who could devour at one repast all the dead bodies of a defeat? and, above all, how, when the ground is covered for six months with its shroud of snow! The offal, the dead animals, and the carrion of a city could not surely suffice. Perhaps they eat each other, like rats in time of famine; but in that case their number would not be so immense, and they would finally disappear; whereas they are full of life and vigor and joyous turbulence. Their mode of alimentation remains not the less a mystery to me, and proves that the instinct of the irrational creature finds resources in nature, where the reason of the human being can see none.

My companion, who witnessed this spectacle with me,—but without astonishment, for it was not the first time that he had seen "the ravens of the Kremlin come home,"—said to me: "Since we are here upon the Krasnaï, and only a few steps from the best Russian restaurant in Moscow, let us not return to dinner at the hotel, where the repast they offer us will be pretentiously French. Your traveller's palate, well accustomed to exotic viands, will be tolerant of some local color, and you will admit that what is food for one man is food for another. Let us come in here; we shall have chtchi, caviare, roast pig, sterlets from the Volga, with salted cucumbers and horse-radish, accompanied by kwas (one should acquaint himself with everything) and iced champagne. Will that bill of fare suit you?"

Upon receiving an affirmative response, the friend who was kind enough to serve as my guide, conducted me to the restaurant at the end of the Gostinoi Dvor, just opposite the Kremlin. We ascended a well-heated staircase, and entered a vestibule which had the look of a fur-shop, where the servants relieved us of our pelisses, and hung them up against the wall, whence, in due season, they were safely restored to us,—as usual without check or number to indicate the ownership!

In the first hall we found the customary bar-room, with its bottles of kummel, of Vodka, brandy, and other liquors, and the caviare, herrings, anchovies, smoked beef, moose and reindeer tongues, cheese, and pickles. One of those Cremona organs, with play of trumpets and beating of drums, which the Italians carry about the streets on a little cart to which is harnessed a horse, was placed against the wall, and a mujik, turning a crank, amused us with an air from some fashionable opera. A succession of rooms — near whose ceilings hovered the bluish smoke of pipes and cigars — extended, to so great a distance that a second Cremona at the remote end was playing, without cacophony, a different air from the one performed by the first; thus we dined between Donizetti and Verdi.

That which gave this restaurant a characteristic physiognomy, was that the service, instead of being rendered by Tartars, travestied as waiters of the Three Brothers, was frankly committed to mujiks. Here, at least, we had the sensation of being in Russia. These mujiks, young and of good figure, the hair parted in the middle, the beard carefully combed, the throat bare, wearing the pink or white summer tunic belted at the waist, and the full blue trousers tucked into the boots, with all the freedom of a national costume — looked extremely well, and exhibited much natural elegance. They had, most of them, hair, of that light chestnut color which tradition attributes to the hair of Christ, and the features of two or three were distinguished by that Greek regularity which is found more frequently among the men in Russia than among the women. Thus costumed, in their attitude of respectful attention, they had the air of antique slaves on the threshold of a *triclinium*.

After dinner I smoked a few pipes of extremely strong Russian tobacco, and drank two or three glasses of excellent "caravan tea," listening the while absent-mindedly to the music from the Cremona organs athwart the vague murmur of conversation, and well content with having eaten "local color."

XVII.

THE KREMLIN.

WE naturally imagine the Kremlin blackened by time,—smoked to that sombre tint which pervades our ancient structures, and, as we think, contributes to their beauty in rendering them venerable. In France, we even carry this idea so far as to give a wash of soot and water to the restorations which, from time to time, we have occasion to make, in order to take away the crude whiteness of the stone and bring it into harmony with the older portions of the edifice. A very high civilization must have been obtained before this sentiment can be understood, and a value attached to the traces which centuries have left upon the epidermis of temples, palaces, and fortresses. Like all uncultured people, the Russians prefer what is new, or, at least, what seems so, and they believe that they manifest respect for their ancient buildings in renewing their painted dress as soon as it is in the least degree frayed or ravelled. They are the greatest whitewashers in the world. Nor do they stop short at the old Byzantine frescos which adorn the inside and even the exterior of their churches, but repaint them at once, as soon as the colors begin to grow dull, so that these pictures, solemnly antique and primitively barbaric as they seem, are often restorations of yesterday. It is not uncommon to see some ordinary house-painter perched aloft on a frail scaffolding, retouching a Madonna with all the tranquillity of a monk of Mount Athos, and filling up with fresh coloring, the old, unchanging contour. It is needful, therefore, to be extremely guarded in pronouncing upon the value of these paintings, which—if I may so speak—*have been* ancient, but are now altogether modern, notwithstanding their rigid outlines and hieratic savagery.

This little preamble has no other end than to prepare the reader for a picture in bright colors, instead of the wild, austere, and sombre one which he, with his western ideas, has dreamed of.

The Kremlin, always regarded as the Acropolis, the Holy Place, the Palladium, the very heart of Russia, had originally only the same protection which Athens had against the first Persian invasion; namely, a palisade of strong oaken posts. Dmitri Donskoi replaced this palisade by crenellated walls, and these, having become old and dilapidated, were rebuilt by the czar Ivan III. It is this wall which exists to-day, but often repaired and restored in many places. Coatings of roughcast, thickly laid on, hide the wounds which time has made and the black traces of the great fire of 1812, which indeed was able only with its tongue of flame to lick this exterior wall. The Kremlin has points of resemblance to the Alhambra. Like the Moorish fortress, it occupies the plateau of a hill, enclosing it with a wall flanked by towers; it contains royal abodes, churches, squares, and, amid the ancient buildings, a modern palace, as much out of place there as is the palace of Charles Fifth amid the delicate Saracenic architecture which it crushes with its ponderous mass. The tower of Ivan Veliki is not without resemblance to the Torre de la Vela; and from the Kremlin, as from the Alhambra, you enjoy a magnificent view, a picture whose enchantment the surprised eye retains forever. But do not push the comparison too far, lest it give way under the strain.

It is odd, but, seen from a distance, the Kremlin has perhaps something more oriental than the Alhambra itself, whose massive reddish towers in no wise betray the splendors within. Above the crenellated wall of the Kremlin, and between its towers with their ornamented roofs, seem to rise and fall like golden bubbles, the myriads of cupolas and bulbous bell-towers, with their metallic sheen, and flashing reflections of sunlight. The white wall—a silver basket—contains this bouquet of golden flowers, and you feel as if you had before your eyes one of those fairy cities which the imagination of the Arab story-teller builds in such lavish abundance,—an architectural crystallization from the Thousand and One Nights. And when winter has powdered with its diamond dust these edifices strange as a dream, you might fancy yourself transported to another planet, for nothing like this has ever before met your eye.

I entered the Kremlin by the Spasskoi gate, which opens upon the Krasnaïa. No entrance-way could be more romantic. It is pierced through an enormous square tower, before which is a kind of porch or outbuilding. The tower is three stories in height, each story retreating, and is surmounted by a spire resting upon open arches. The double-headed eagle, holding the globe in his claw, stands upon the point of this spire, which is octagonal, like the story it surmounts, ribbed at the angles, and gilded upon the flat surfaces. Each face of the second story bears an enormous dial, so that the tower shows the time of day towards each point of the horizon. Add, on ledges, here and there, a few touches of snow by way of effect, and you have some idea of the aspect of this, the principal tower, springing up in three jets from the denticulated wall which it interrupts.

The Spasskoi gate is the object of such veneration in Russia, by reason of some sacred picture or the legend of some miracle, concerning which I was not able to inform myself exactly, that no man may pass through it with covered head, were it the Autocrat himself. Any irreverence in this respect would be regarded as sacrilege, and might be dangerous. Therefore strangers are warned of the custom. You are not merely required to salute the sacred pictures at the entrance of the porch, before which lamps are burning perpetually, but to remain uncovered till you emerge from beneath the archway. Now it is not very agreeable to carry your fur cap in your hand, at a temperature of —24° all the way through a long passage down which draws a glacial wind. But one must conform to national usage, whether it be to take off your cap under the Spasskoi gate, or your boots at the threshold of the Solimanieh or the Saint Sophia. The true traveller will offer no objection, though he catch a frightful cold in the head.

Emerging from this archway, you find yourself upon the esplanade of the Kremlin, amid the most splendid mass of palaces, churches, and monasteries, of which it is possible to conceive. All this belongs to no known style of architecture. It is not Greek, it is not Byzantine, it is not Gothic, it is not Saracenic, it is not Chinese. It is Russian,—it is Muscovite. Never did architecture more free, more original, more careless of rules,—in a word, more romantic,—realize in visible forms its wildest caprices. Sometimes it seems to resemble the accidents of crystallization. Still, cupolas, bell-towers, with bulb of gold, are really the characteristics of this style, which seems to acknowledge no law, and by them it may be recognized at sight.

Below this esplanade, whereon are grouped the principal edifices of the Kremlin, creeps—following the slope of the ground, with many windings and turnings—the rampart, lined with a road all the way, and flanked with towers of an infinite variety of shapes, some round, other square; these, slender as minarets; those, massive as bastions; with retreating stories, square-sided roofs, open galleries, lanterns, spires, scale-work, ribs,—all conceivable methods of coiffing a tower. Battlements, cutting deep into the wall, notched at their summit like the cleft in an arrow, are alternately whole or pierced by an opening. I cannot speak of the value of this fortification from the strategic point of view,—but from the poetic, it fully satisfies the imagination, and gives the idea of a formidable citadel.

Between the rampart and the platform bordered by a balustrade, extend gardens, now powdered with snow, and a picturesque little church raises its bulbous bell-towers. Beyond, as far as the eye can see, unfolds a vast and marvellous panoramic view of Moscow, the crest of the wall, toothed like a saw, furnishing an admirable foreground and relief for the distant effects, which no art could improve.

The Moskwa, about as broad as the Seine, and sinuous like that river, surrounds with its curve all this side of the Kremlin, and from the esplanade you look down upon it lying far below, frozen solid, and resembling opaque glass, for the snow has been swept off from this portion of the river to make a trotting-course for horses in training for some approaching races upon the ice.

The quay, which is bordered with superb buildings of modern architecture, forms, with its solid, regular masonry, a kind of foundation of straight lines for the vast mass of houses and roofs which stretch away to the horizon line, raised by perspective, and by the height of the point of view.

A fine frost—let Méry shiver if he must!—having swept from the sky that great, monotonous cloud of yellowish gray which was drawn, the evening before, like a curtain along the darkened horizon, a measurably bright azure tinted the circular canvas of this panorama, and the increasing cold, by crystallizing the snow, renewed its whiteness. The pale sunlight—such as it is in Moscow in January, in those short, wintry days which suggest the nearness of the pole—slid obliquely across the city spread out fan-wise around the Kremlin, and grazed the snow-covered roofs, making them sparkle here and there like mica. Above these white roofs, resembling the foam-flakes of a congealed tempest, rose like rocks, or like ships, the loftier masses of the public buildings, temples, and monasteries. They say that Moscow contains more than three hundred churches or convents; I do not know if the figures are exact or purely hyperbolical, but it appears quite a reasonable statement, when, from the heights of the Kremlin, itself containing a great number of churches, chapels, and religious edifices, you look down upon the city which lies beneath you.

Nothing more beautiful, more rich, more splendid, more like fairy-land can be imagined than these cupolas surmounted by Greek crosses, these bell-towers shaped like bulbs, these six or eight sided spires, ribbed at the angles, cut out in open-work, curving, spreading out wide, rising sharply to a point, above the motionless tumult of snowy roofs. The gilded cupolas catch reflections of wondrous transparency, and the light on the salient point is concentred there into a star which shines like a lamp. Domes of silver or of tin seem to coif churches in the moon; farther on, there are casques of azure starred with gold, circular roofs made of plates of beaten copper imbricated like dragon-scales; or, perhaps, inverted onions, painted green and frosted here and there with snow; then, as the distance increases, details disappear even under the field-glass, and you distinguish only a sparkling crowd of domes, spires, towers, campaniles, of every imaginable shape—their silhouettes, a dark line against the bluish distance,—their relief indicated by one spangle of gold, of silver, of copper, of sapphire, or of emerald. To complete the picture, imagine upon the cold, bluish tints of the snow some faintly crimsoned streamers of light, pale roses of the polar sunset sown upon the ermine carpet of a Russian winter.

I stood there, insensible to cold, absorbed in mute contemplation, as in a kind of admiring stupor.

No other city gives this impression of absolute novelty, not even Venice, for which Canaletto, Guardi,

Bonington, Joyant, Wyld, Ziem, and the photographs, have long ago prepared us. Up to this time Moscow has rarely been visited by artists, and its peculiar aspects have been seldom reproduced. The rigorous Northern climate adds to the singularity of the scene by effects of snow, the wonderful coloring of its skies, and a quality of light differing from ours at home,— and makes up a special palette for the Russian painter, whose correctness is not readily understood outside the country.

Upon the esplanade of the Kremlin, with this panorama unfolded before your eyes, you feel that you are indeed in another land, and the Frenchman most in love with Paris does not regret the rivulet of the Rue de Bac.

The Kremlin contains within its walls a great number of churches, or cathedrals, as the Russians call them. So, too, upon its narrow plateau, had the Acropolis its multitude of temples. We will examine several of the churches of the Kremlin, but let us stop first at the tower of Ivan Veliki, an enormous octagon, having three retreating stories, of which the last, from above a zone of ornaments, becomes a round turret, and ends with a bulbous cupola, re-gilt with ducat-gold and surmounted by a Greek cross, its foot set in the conquered crescent. At every story, arches opening in the walls of the tower reveal the brazen sides of a bell. They are thirty-three in number, and among them is said to be the famous bell of Novgorod, whose stroke used to call the people to the tumultuous deliberations of the public square. One of these bells weighs not less than seventy tons; beside this metallic monster, the great bell of Notre Dame, of which Quasimodo was so proud, would seem nothing more than a hand-bell such as they ring at mass.

We obtain still further demonstration of their passion in Russia for colossal bells; close by the tower of Ivan Veliki, upon a base of granite, the astonished eye perceives a bell so enormous that it looks like a bronze tent, and the more because a great fissure forms in its side a kind of door by which a man may enter easily without lowering his head. It was cast by order of the Empress Anne, and ten thousand pounds of metal were put into the furnace. It was M. de Montferrand, the French architect of St. Isaac's, who had it lifted out of the ground, in which it had been half buried, either by the violence of a fall while they were originally setting it up, or in consequence of a fire or the breaking down of a building. Has a mass like this ever been hung? Has its iron tongue ever flung forth a sonorous tempest from that monstrous shell? History and legend are alike mute upon this point. Perhaps, like some ancient people who used to leave in their abandoned camps, bedsteads a dozen feet long, to make it seem that they belonged to a race of giants, the Russians have sought by this bell, disproportionate to all human use, to give remote posterity a gigantic idea of themselves, if, after many ages, this bell should be found, in the course of some excavation!

However this may be, the bell has beauty, like all things beyond ordinary dimensions. The grace of monstrous size, a grace wild and fierce, but real, is not lacking to it. Its sides sweep out in broad and mighty curves encircled by delicate ornaments. A globe surmounted by the cross crowns it; the eye is gratified by the purity of its contour, and even the very fracture itself opens like the mouth of some brazen cavern, mysterious and sombre. At the foot of the socle, like a door broken from its hinges, lies the fragment of metal corresponding with the aperture in the bell.

But enough of bells; let us enter one of the most ancient and characteristic cathedrals of the Kremlin, the first one built of stone, the Cathedral of the Assumption, —in Russian, the Ouspenskossabor. This one before our eyes is not, it is true, the original edifice founded by Ivan Kalita. That, after a century and a half of existence, fell to ruins, and was presently rebuilt by Ivan III. The existing church dates, then, only from the fifteenth century, despite its Byzantine air and its archaic aspect. I was surprised to learn that it is the work of Fioraventi, a Bolognese architect, whom the Russians call Aristotle, on account of his great knowledge. The idea which would be naturally suggested to the mind, is of some Greek architect called from Constantinople, his head still full of Saint Sophia and the Greco-Oriental types of architecture. The Assumption is nearly a square building, and its great walls spring upward with a wonderful pride. Four enormous pillars, as large as towers, mighty as the columns of Karnak, support the central dome placed upon a flat roof in the Asiatic style, and flanked by four lesser cupolas.

This arrangement, simple as it is, produces an imposing effect, and, without an appearance of heaviness, these massive pillars give a firm base and extraordinary stability to the inside of the building.

The interior of the church is completely covered with Byzantine paintings upon gold backgrounds. The pillars themselves are adorned with figures, rising in zones one above another, like the columns of temples or of Egyptian palaces. There is nothing more singular than this style of decoration where myriads of figures surround you,—a mute crowd, ascending and descending along the walls, marching in files, a Christian Panathenaia,—standing alone in an attitude of hieratic stiffness,—bending over in pendentives, vaults, and cupolas,—draping the temple with a human tapestry, motionless, yet ever seeming astir with life. Light, falling sparingly and at rare intervals, adds still further to the mysterious and disquieting effect. The tall, wild-looking saints of the Greek calendar assume, in this tawny and golden darkness, a really formidable appearance of life; they look at you fixedly, and they seem to threaten with their hands extended in benediction.

Militant archangels, knightly saints, with courtly and

soldierly bearing, are seen in their shining armor amid the dark-hued frocks of monkish saints and anchorites. They have that proud air, that remnant of the antique contour, which distinguishes the figures of Panselinos, the Byzantine master, from the work of whose pupil, the monk of Aghia Lavra, Papety has made such fine drawings. The interior of Saint Mark's at Venice, with its look of a gilded cavern, gives an idea of the Cathedral of the Assumption; but the interior of the Muscovite church springs upward with one impulse toward the sky, while the vault of St. Mark's is crushed mysteriously downwards like a crypt.

The iconostase, a lofty wall of gilded silver, which looks like the façade of some golden palace, is absolutely dazzling with fabulous magnificence. Through apertures in the goldsmith's work appear the brown heads and hands of Madonnas, and of male and female saints. Their aureoles in relief, catching the light, sparkle with the facets of the precious stones set in their rays, and flame like real glories; to those pictures which are regarded with special veneration, are fastened breast-plates, collars, and bracelets, starred with diamonds, sapphires, rubies, emeralds, amethysts, pearls, turquoises; the madness of pious luxury seems here to have reached its height.

What a fine *motif* of decoration is supplied by the iconostase, a veil of gold and precious stones, drawn between the belief of the faithful and the mysteries of the Holy Sacrifice! The Russians turn it to marvellously good account; and it must be owned that in sumptuous display, the Greek is not inferior to the Catholic religion, although it be so in the domain of pure art.

In a shrine of inestimable price, in the Cathedral of the Assumption, is preserved the vesture of our Lord. Two other reliquaries, dazzling with gems, contain, one, a piece of the Virgin's dress, the other, a nail from the true cross. The Virgin of Vladimir, painted by St. Luke's hand,—a sacred picture, regarded by the Russians as a palladium,—whose exhibition made the fierce hordes of Timour draw back and flee, is adorned with a solitaire, valued at more than a hundred thousand francs, and the mass of goldsmith's work which frames the picture cost two or three times that sum. Doubtless this luxury must seem slightly barbaric to a refined taste, fonder of beauty than of opulence: but it is not to be denied that these accumulations of gold, these diamonds and pearls, produce a religious and splendid effect. These madonnas—whose jewels are more costly than those of queens and empresses—are most imposing to the simple-minded worshipper. In this half-obscurity, by the vague light of lamps, they assume a supernatural radiance. Their diamond crowns scintillate like crowns of stars.

From the centre of the vaulted roof depends an immense chandelier of massive silver, of beautiful workmanship and of circular form, which takes the place of an ancient chandelier of great weight, carried off during the French invasion. Forty-six branches are attached to it.

In the Cathedral of the Assumption the consecration of the emperor takes place. The staging built up for the occasion stands in the space enclosed by the four great pillars which support the cupola, and faces the iconostase.

The tombs of the metropolitans of Moscow are ranged along the lateral walls. They are of oblong form, and, seen there in the shadow, they make one think of trunks packed and ready for the grand voyage of eternity.

The cathedral of the Holy Archangels, of which the façade is turned obliquely towards the Church of the Assumption, and is but a few steps from it, presents no essential difference of plan. We find always the same bulbous cupolas, massive pillars, an iconostase glittering with gold, and the Byzantine paintings clothing the whole interior of the building as with a sacred tapestry. Only here the paintings are not upon gold backgrounds, and have the look of frescos, rather than of mosaics. They represent the scenes of the Last Judgment, and also portraits, with fierce and haughty mien, of the ancient czars.

Here, too, are their tombs, covered with cashmeres and other rich stuffs, like the tombs of the Sultans at Constantinople. All is sober, simple, and severe. Death here is not made beautiful by the delicate blossoms of Gothic art, which in other lands cluster so luxuriantly about the tomb. No kneeling Angels, no theological Virtues, no weeping emblematic figures, no saints in niches of open-work, no fanciful scrolls entwined around heraldic devices, no knights clad in armor, the head upon a marble cushion, the feet upon a sleeping lion: only the corpse in its funeral coffer covered by a mortuary pall. Doubtless art loses by this, but the religious impression is enhanced.

In the Cathedral of the Annunciation, built against the palace of the czars, they call your attention to a very rare and curious painting, which represents the angel Gabriel appearing to the Virgin Mary to announce to her that she shall be the mother of the Lord. The interview occurs near a well, like that between Jesus and the Samaritan woman. According to the tradition of the Greek church, it is later,—after her humble acquiescence in the will of God,—that she is visited in her own dwelling by the Holy Spirit.

This scene, painted upon one of the exterior walls, is protected by a sort of awning against the inclemency of the seasons. To give an idea of the interior richness of the church, a single detail will suffice. The pavement is made of agates brought from Greece.

At the side of the new palace, and but a few steps from these churches, is a strange edifice, belonging to no known architectural style, Asiatic or Tartar in its aspect,—which, for a secular building, is much what Vassili Blagennoi is for a religious one,—that is to say, the perfectly realized chimera of a sumptuous, barbaric, fantastic imagination. It was built under Ivan III., by the architect Aleviso. From its roof spring up with graceful and picturesque irregularity, the golden-coiffed turrets of the chapels and oratories which are contained within it. An exterior staircase, from whose top the emperor shows himself to the people after his coronation, gives access to the building, and by its ornamented projection produces a truly original architectural incident. It is, at Moscow, what the Giants' Staircase is at Venice, and is called the Red Staircase (Krasnoi-Kriltosi).

The interior of this palace, the residence of the ancient czars, seems to defy description; you would say that its halls and apartments have been excavated successively and without fixed plan, in some enormous block of stone, —in such an odd, confusing, complicated fashion are they entangled among themselves,—level and direction changing at the caprice of an unbridled fancy. You walk through them as in a dream,—now stopped by a grating which opens mysteriously; now forced to follow a narrow, dark passage-way where your shoulders almost touch the walls; again, finding no other road than the notched border of a cornice, whence you can see the plates of copper of the roof, and the bulbs of the bell-towers;— ascending, going down, no longer knowing where you are; from time to time seeing through golden trellis-work, the gleam of a lamp upon some iconostase; and emerging, after all this in-door journey, into some hall of wild ornamentation and savage splendor, where it surprises you not to find the Grand Kniaz of Tartary seated, cross-legged, upon his mat of black felt!

Such is, for example, the hall they call the Gilded Chamber, which occupies the whole interior of the Granovitaïa Palata—the Facet Palace—so called, doubtless, because of its exterior cut in diamond-shaped blocks. This building adjoins the old palace of the czars. The golden vaults of this hall are supported upon a central pillar by means of elliptic arches, which are prevented from spreading by thick bars of gilded iron which cross them from side to side. Here and there are a few paintings, dark-colored stains upon the yellow splendor of the background. Around the arches are legends in the magnificent old Slavonic character. No decoration could be imagined at once richer, more mysterious, more sombre, more dazzling, than this of the gilded chamber. Shakespearian romanticism would delight to place here the *dénouement* of a drama.

Certain vaulted halls of the old palace are so low that a man a little below the medium height can scarcely stand upright in them. Here it was that, in an atmosphere heated to excess, the women, crouched in oriental fashion upon piles of cushions, used to pass the long hours of the Russian winter, looking out through the little windows to see the snow sparkle upon the gilded cupolas, and the ravens describe wide spirals around the belfries.

These apartments, with their parti-colored decorations whose palm-leaves, foliage, and flowers recall cashmere patterns, seem like Asiatic harems transported into a polar climate. The true Muscovite taste, falsified later by a misconceived imitation of Western art, appears here in all its primitive originality, and with its sharp barbaric flavor. I have often remarked that the progress of civilization seems to deprive nations of a feeling for architecture and for ornament. The ancient edifices of the Kremlin prove yet once more, how true is this seemingly paradoxical assertion. A fancy absolutely inexhaustible presides over the decoration of these mysterious chambers, where gold and green and blue and red mingle with rare felicity, and produce charming effects. This architecture, utterly careless of symmetrical correspondences, rises like a mass of soap-bubbles blown upon a plate through a tube of straw. Each little cell takes its place, and makes its own arrangement of angles and facets; and the whole glitters with all the tints of the rainbow. This comparison, puerile and grotesque as it seems, expresses, better than any other, the method of aggregation of these palaces,—so fantastic, and yet real.

It is in this style that I could have wished the new palace; but it is, however, a vast edifice of modern construction which might elsewhere, perhaps, have some beauty, but which, in the midst of the old Kremlin, is most incongruous. Classic architecture, with its grand, cold outlines, is more wearisomely solemn than ever amid these grotesque, high-colored palaces, and this tumultuous crowd of churches, darting towards heaven a gilded forest of cupolas, domes, pyramidal towers, and bulbous belfries. You might believe yourself, at sight of this Muscovite architecture, in some chimerical Asiatic city,—you could easily take the cathedrals for mosques, the belfries for minarets; but the rational façade of the new palace would bring you back to the very heart of the West and of civilization: a sad thing for a romantic savage like myself!

We enter the new palace by a stately flight of stairs, closed at the top by a magnificent grating of polished iron, which is opened a little way to admit the visitor. You then find yourself beneath the lofty vault of a domed hall, where sentinels, never relieved of their duty, are on guard: four figures, clad from head to foot in antique and curious Slavonic armor. These knights are really grand; they actually seem to be alive; you feel as if a heart were beating under their coats of mail. These mediaeval suits of armor set up in this way always cause me an involuntary shiver, so faithfully do they preserve the external semblance of the man who is gone forever!

From this rotunda two galleries lead, which contain inestimable treasures: the store-house of the Kaliph Haroun-al-Raschid, the wells of Aboul-Kasem, the Green Vaults at Dresden, all together, could present no such accumulation of wonders; and here historic value is added to that merely material. In these galleries scintillate and flash, and dart forth prismatic rays, diamonds and sapphires, rubies, emeralds, all those precious stones that avaricious nature hides deep in her mines, are here to be seen in as lavish abundance as though they were but glass. They are in constellations upon the crowns; they tip with light the points of the sceptres; they run down in dazzling rain over the insignia of empire, forming arabesques and ciphers till they almost conceal the gold of their setting. The eye is dazzled, and the reason scarcely dares conjecture the sums which this magnificence must represent. To essay to describe this prodigious jewel-box were folly. A book would not suffice for it. We must be content with a description of a few of the most remarkable pieces. One of the most ancient crowns is that of Vladimir Monomaque. It was a present from the Emperor Alexis Comnenes, and was brought from Constantinople to Kief by a Greek embassy in 1116. Besides its value as a historic memento, it is a work of exquisite taste. Upon a foundation of gold filigree work are set pearls and precious stones, arranged with an admirable understanding of ornamentation. The crowns of Kazan and of Astrakan, of oriental style, one sown with turquoises, the other surmounted by an enormous uncut emerald, are jewels to drive a modern goldsmith to despair! The Siberian crown is made of cloth of gold; like all the rest, it has a Greek cross upon its summit, and, like them, is starred with diamonds, pearls, and sapphires. The golden sceptre of Vladimir Monomaque, about three feet long, contains two hundred and sixty-eight diamonds, three hundred and sixty rubies, and fifteen emeralds. The enamel which covers the rest of the surface represents religious subjects treated in the Byzantine style. This also was a present from the Emperor Alexis Comnenes, as well as the reliquary in the shape of a cross, containing a fragment of stone from the tomb of Christ and a bit of wood from the cross. A golden casket rough with gems contains this treasure. A curious jewel is the chain of the first of the Romanoffs, of which every link bears engraved, following a prayer, one of the titles of the czar. There are ninety-nine! It is impossible to speak particularly of the thrones, the globes, sceptres, and crowns of different reigns; but I observed that, though the value remains as great, the purity of taste and beauty of workmanship diminish, as we approach the modern epoch.

Another thing not less wonderful, but more accessible to description, is the hall devoted to gold and silver plate. Around pillars are arranged circular credence-tables, rising in many stages like a dresser supporting a world of vases, tankards, flagons, mugs, goblets, jugs, decanters, pitchers, ladles, tiny casks, cups, beer-mugs, tumblers, pints, flasks, gourds, amphoræ,—everything relating to *Beuverie*, as says Master Rabelais, in his Pantagruelic language! Behind these vessels of gold and silver, gleam platters of gold and of gilded silver, as large as those off which Victor Hugo's Burgraves were served with oxen roasted whole. Each jar is coiffed with its nimbus. And what jars! Some of them are as much as three or four feet in height, and could only be lifted by the hand of a Titan. What enormous expense of imagination in this variety of plate! All forms capable of containing any beverage—wine, hydromel, beer, kwas, brandy—seem to be represented here. And how rich, fantastic, grotesque, the taste shown in the ornamentation of these vases of gold, of silver-gilt, and of silver! Sometimes there are bacchanals, with merry, chubby faces dancing around the vessel's paunch; now, leafage with animals and hunting-scenes appearing through it; at other times, dragons curling round the ears, or antique medallions set into the sides of a jug; a Roman triumph defiling by, with its trumpets and standards; Hebrews in the costumes of Dutchmen bearing the bunch of grapes from the Promised Land; some mythological nudity contemplated by Satyrs through the tufted arabesques. In accordance with the artist's whim, the vases take on the form of animals; spread out wide in bears; run up tall and slim in storks; flap great wings as eagles; puff themselves out in frogs; or throw back horns of stags. Farther on, I noticed a comf t-box shaped like a ship with swelling sails and carved poop, the dainties within to be taken out through the hatchways. Every possible whim of goldsmith's work is to be found realized upon this wondrous sideboard.

The hall of armor contains treasures to weary the pen of the most intrepid nomenclator. Circassian casques and coats of mail inscribed with verses from the Koran; bucklers with bosses of filigree; cimetars and *kandjars* with nephrite handles and scabbards set with gems; all those Eastern weapons, which are jewels as well as arms, gleam amid Western weapons of a simplicity the most severe. At sight of all this gathered magnificence, your head whirls, and you cry for mercy to the guide, too civil or too exact, who will not wrong you of a single piece!

I was especially delighted with the Capitulary Halls, consecrated to the different orders of Russian knighthood. The St. George, St. Alexander, St. Andrew, and St. Catherine occupy each a vast hall, wherein the themes of ornamentation are derived from portions of their coats-of-arms. The heraldic art is eminently decorative, and its application to public buildings always produces a good effect.

One may imagine without detailed description the sumptuous elegance with which the state apartments are furnished.

Everything richest that modern luxury can furnish is here; and amid all the splendor, not the very faintest suggestion of the charming Muscovite taste. It was, perhaps, inevitable, considering the style of the building. But I must own I was indeed surprised, in the last room of the suite, to find myself face to face with a pale phantom of white marble clad as for apotheosis, who fixed upon me his great, motionless eyes, and bent, with meditative air, his Roman Cæsar's head;—Napoleon, in Moscow, in the palace of the czars,—this was something I should never have expected to see!

XVIII.

TROÏTZA.

WHEN you have a few leisure days in Moscow, after the principal curiosities have been seen, there is an excursion which will undoubtedly be proposed to you, and which you must accept with eagerness. It is a visit to the convent of Troïtza. The journey well repays you; no man ever regretted having made it.

So it was decided that I should go to Troïtza, and the Russian friend who had graciously undertaken to be my guide, busied himself in preparations for our departure. He engaged a kibitka, and sent forward a relay of horses to await us on the road; for, by starting early, the distance can be accomplished in a half-day, and one arrives early enough to get a general idea of the buildings, and the location. It was enjoined upon me to rise at three o'clock in the morning.

A habit of travelling gives the faculty of waking at the precise minute, without need of persistently tintinnabulating alarm-clock. So I was on foot and ready, having fortified myself with a slice of meat and a glass of very hot tea (in Moscow, a most excellent beverage), when the kibitka drew up before the hotel door.

In trying to see through the double windows what sort of weather it was, I made the observation that the thermometer within doors registered 66° above zero, and the thermometer without, 37° below. A little wind, which had cooled itself upon the ice-fields of the pole, had been blowing through the night, and had brought on this glacial relapse.

Thirty-seven degrees below zero is certainly enough to give a shiver to the least sensitive natures; happily I had already undergone all the rigors of a Russian winter and had grown accustomed to these temperatures, made for white bears and the reindeer. Still, as I was to remain nearly all day in the open air, I attired myself accordingly: two shirts, two waistcoats, two pairs of trousers, enough to clothe from head to foot a second mortal; upon my feet, woollen socks, and boots of white felt enclosed in other furred boots coming above the knee; on my head, a cap of beaver's back, warmly wadded; for gloves, Samoyed mittens, the thumb alone articulated; and outside of all an enormous fur pelisse, the collar raised in the back as high as the top of the head, in order to defend the nape of the neck, and fastening in front with hooks, in order to defend the face. In addition, a long strip of knitted wool, wound five or six times around my torso, like a string tied with many knots around a bundle, to prevent any hiatus in the pelisse through which the air might effect an entrance. Thus arrayed, I resembled an ambulatory sentry-box, and, in the warm air of my room, these superposed garments seemed immensely heavy, and quite overwhelmed me with their weight; no sooner did I find myself in the outside air, than they appeared as light as a suit of Chinese grass-cloth.

The kibitka was waiting, and the impatient horses were holding down their heads, shaking their long manes, and biting at the snow. A few words of description concerning my vehicle: the kibitka is a sort of box, which resembles a cabin quite as much as a carriage, placed upon the frame of a sledge. It has a door and a window, which you must not think of closing, for the vapor of the breath condensed upon the glass, would change to ice, and you would find yourself thus deprived of air, and plunged into a kind of white darkness.

We arranged ourselves as best we could within the

kibitka, packed like sardines in a box; for, though there were only three of us, the quantity of garments with which we were loaded made us take up the room of six; as an additional precaution, they threw over our knees travelling-rugs and a bear-skin, and we set off.

It was perhaps four in the morning. In the blue-black sky the stars throbbed with vivid scintillation and that keen light which indicates intensity of cold; the snow, under the steel runners of the kibitka, emitted a sound like that made by a diamond scratching on glass. Furthermore, there was not a breath of air stirring, you would have said that the very wind was congealed. It would have been possible to walk with a lighted candle in the hand, without the flame's flickering! It is extraordinary how wind adds to the severity of the temperature: it changes inert cold to active cold, and converts particles of ice into the steel points of arrows! It was, in a word, what at Moscow, towards the end of January, would be called " fine weather."

The Russian coachman delights in going fast, and it is a taste which his horses share with him. It is needful to moderate rather than excite them. They always start off at full speed, and a person who is not accustomed to this vertiginous rapidity would be sure to think that the team was running away. Ours did not prove derelict in this respect, and galloped madly through the silent and solitary streets of Moscow, faintly lighted by reflections from the snow, in default of the dying light of frozen street-lamps. Houses, churches, public buildings went by rapidly on the right and left, with their sombre outlines oddly broken or relieved by white touches, for no darkness can quite extinguish the silvery shining of the snow. Sometimes, cupolas of chapels, seen for an instant in passing, had the effect of helmets of giants, rising over the rampart of a fancied fortress; the silence was broken only by the night-watch, who walked with regular step, letting their iron-shod staves drag behind them on the pavement, in testimony to their fidelity.

At the pace we were going, extensive as is the city of Moscow, we were soon outside its limits, and to the street succeeded the road. The houses disappeared, and, on either side, the country stretched away, vague and white under the nocturnal sky. There is a strange and odd sensation in thus traversing at full speed this colorless, limitless landscape, wrapped in its monotonous whiteness, resembling a lunar plain, men and beasts asleep around you, and not another sound to be heard besides the tramp of horses and the cut of the runners upon the snow. You might believe yourself in an uninhabited globe.

As we thus galloped along, our conversation happened —by one of those secret transitions which Edgar Poe's August Dupin so well knew how to explain, and which sometimes elicit remarks that seem abrupt even to rudeness, to the auditor who has not the secret of them—upon whom? upon what? You would guess in vain a thousand times—upon Robinson Crusoe! What circumstance could possibly have called up in my brain the idea of Robinson on the road from Moscow to Troïtza, between five and six in the morning, with the thermometer at 35° below zero, not at all suggestive of the climate of that island of Juan-Fernandez, in which Defoe's hero passed so many long and solitary years! A peasant's isba, built of logs, outlined for an instant at the roadside, awakened in me a confused recollection of the house made of trunks of trees which Robinson Crusoe constructed at the entrance of his grotto; this fugitive idea, however, was just disappearing without becoming attached in any perceptible way to the present situation, when the *snow*, at which I was unconsciously looking, imperiously recalled the image of Robinson, at that moment vanishing away in the cloud of idle reveries. Towards the end of the book, after his deliverance and return to civilized life, Robinson Crusoe made long journeys, and, traversing with his little caravan the *snow*-covered plains of Siberia, is attacked by a troop of wolves, who put his flesh in as much danger as did formerly the anthropophagi who landed upon his land.

Thus the idea of Robinson Crusoe came to me, in accordance with a logical sequence, secret but easily deduced by an attentive mind. Thence to pass to a possible apparition of wolves upon the road was inevitable. So the conversation turned of itself towards this subject, somewhat exciting in the midst of a vast snowy solitude, spotted here and there with russet patches indicating forests of pine and birch. Most shocking stories of travellers assailed and devoured by wolves were related; and at last, by way of climax, I repeated a legend which Balzac once told me with that enormous gravity with which he always uttered a joke. It was the story of a Lithuanian seigneur and his wife, going from their chateau to another, where a ball was to be given. Lying in ambush at the edge of a road, a pack of wolves awaited the carriage. The horses, pushed to the utmost by the coachman, and by the terror which these fearful beasts inspired, broke into a mad gallop, followed by all the pack, whose eyes gleamed like burning coals in the moving shadow of the carriage. The seigneur and the lady, more dead than alive, crouched each in a corner, motionless with terror, fancied that they heard confusedly behind them, groans and panting breath, and snapping jaws; at last the chateau is reached, and the gate, closing after them, cuts a few wolves in two! The coachman stopped under the *marquise*, and, as no one got down to open the carriage-door, they went to look, and there were the skeletons of the two lackeys, picked perfectly clean, still standing and holding on to the carriage in the correct position. *Voilà des domestiques bien dressés*, Balzac added, *et comme on n'en trouve plus en France!*

We had our laugh, but, for all that, nobody could be

sure but that one wolf, or many—famished as they are at this time in the winter—might take a fancy to give us chase. We had no weapons, and our only safety would have been the speed of our horses or the neighborhood of some farm-house. This would have been no joke; but, as I said, we had our laugh, and laughing drives anxiety away; besides, daylight was beginning to appear,—daylight, which scatters chimeras, and sends wild beasts to their lair. It is needless to add that we did not see the tail of even the smallest wolf!

The night had been radiant with stars, but, towards morning, fogs had arisen from the horizon, and the Muscovite Aurora came forth, pallid and black about the eyes, in the wan light. Perhaps she had a red nose, but Homer's epithet, "the rosy fingered," applied to the Greek Aurora, would not have been suited to her at all. However, her light sufficed to show, in all its extent, the landscape,—melancholy, yet not without grandeur,—which spread out around us.

It may be suggested that my descriptions resemble one another; but monotony is a characteristic of the Russian landscape, at least so far I am familiar with it. It consists of immense plains, slightly undulating, where you find no other mountains than the hillocks on which are built the Kremlins of Moscow and of Nijni-Novgorod, not higher than Montmartre. The snow, covering this ill-defined landscape for four or five months of the year, adds yet more to the uniformity of its aspect, by filling up hollows in the ground and beds of watercourses, together with the valleys which they excavate. All that you see for hundreds of leagues is an endless white covering, slightly raised here and there by inequalities in the concealed soil, and, according to the obliquity of the sun's rays, streaked at times with rosy lights and bluish shadows. When, however, the sky has its ordinary tint—that is to say, a leaden gray—the general color is a lustreless white, or, more correctly, a dead white. At distances more or less remote from each other, lines of reddish brushwood, half emerging from the snow, cut the broad, white expanse. Scattered birches and pines fleck the landscape with dark spots here and there; and posts, like those for telegraph-wires, mark out the road, often buried by driving snow-storms. Along the wayside, log-houses, the chinks stuffed with moss, the rafters of the roof crossing each other and making on top a kind of X, bring their sharp peaks into line, and on the edge of the horizon is sketched the low outline of some distant village, over-topped by a church with its bulbous cupolas. Not a living thing, save flocks of crows and rooks, and some-times a mujik on his sledge drawn by shaggy little horses, hauling wood or some other necessary supplies, to a dwelling far in the country. Such is the picture reproduced to satiety, and which renews itself around you as you advance, like the horizon at sea, ever renewed yet the same, as the vessel moves forward. Any picturesque effect is rare, and yet one never tires in looking out into this vast expanse, which inspires a vague melancholy, like all things that are great, silent, and solitary. Sometimes, in spite of the velocity of the horses, you feel as if you must be standing still.

We reached the relay, whose Russian name I forget. It was a wooden house with a court-yard full of télégas and sledges, poor-looking vehicles. In the low hall, mujiks in greasy touloupes, the beard blonde, the face red, and lighted by eyes of a polar blue, were grouped around a copper urn, drinking tea, while others lay asleep upon benches near the stove. A few, still more susceptible to cold, were lying upon the stove itself.

They conducted us into quite a high room, the walls and ceiling all of plank, like a pine box seen from within. It was lighted by a small double window, and had no other ornament than a picture of the Virgin, whose aureole and garments of stamped metal gleamed in the light of the lamp which was burning before it. These mysteriously embrowned faces, seen through apertures in their gold or silver shell, have much character, and command veneration more than paintings preferable from an artistic point of view could do. There is no hovel so poor that it does not possess one of these sacred pictures, before which no one passes without uncovering the head, and before which they often kneel in adoration.

A soft, hothouse temperature reigned in this room and rendered it comfortable, poorly furnished though it was. We laid aside our pelisses and heavy wrappings, and, with provisions which we had brought with us from Moscow, together with "caravan tea" steeped in the samovar of the tavern, we made our breakfast. After which, resuming our heavy armor against the arrows of Winter, we installed ourselves once more in our kibitka, ready to brave gayly the severities of the cold.

As you draw near Troïtza, dwelling-houses become more numerous. You feel that you are approaching something of importance. Troïtza is, indeed, the goal of long pilgrimages. They come thither from all the provinces of the empire, for Saint Sergius, the founder of this celebrated convent, is one of the most venerated saints of the Greek calendar. The road which leads from Moscow to Troïtza goes on to Yaroslaf, and in summer it presents, I was told, a most animated scene; it passes through Ostankina, where there is a Tartar camp, through the village of Rostopchin, and through Alexevskoï, which, a few years since, still preserved the ruins of the chateau of the Emperor Alexis; and when winter has not covered all things with its mantle of snow, you remark, all about you, tasteful country-houses. The pilgrims, clad in their armiaks, and wearing shoes made of the linden-bark—when they do not go barefoot, as a matter of devotion,—walk along the sandy road, making short day's journeys. Families travel in kibitkas, with mattresses, pillows, cooking-utensils, and the indispensable samovar,—like migratory tribes. But at the time of our excursion the road was perfectly solitary.

Before reaching Troïtza, the level of the ground sinks a little, hollowed out, probably, by some water-course now frozen and covered with snow. Beyond this ravine, upon a broad plateau, stands picturesquely the Convent of St. Sergius, with its look of a fortress.

It is an immense quadrilateral, surrounded by solid ramparts along whose tops runs a covered gallery, pierced by barbacans, which provides shelter for the defenders of the stronghold; for so this convent, which has been many times attacked, may suitably be called. Great towers, some square, some hexagonal, rise at the angles, and flank the walls at regular distances.

Some of these towers have a second tower springing from amidst a balustrade of belfries. The door leading into the interior of the convent is cut through a square tower, in front of which extends a broad, open space.

Above these ramparts rise, with graceful and picturesque irregularity, the roofs and cupolas of the buildings which compose the monastery. The immense refectory, whose walls are painted in raised diamond-shaped blocks, attracts the eye by its imposing mass, lightened by the belfry of an elegant chapel. Near it are the five bulbous domes of the Church of the Assumption, surmounted by the Greek cross; a little farther on, overtopping all the rest, the high, many-colored Trinity tower carries its stories up with turrets, and lifts far towards the sky its cross ornamented with chains. Other towers, belfries, and roofs are outlined confusedly above the belt of the walls, but it is impossible to locate them accurately in a description. There is nothing more charming than these gilded spires and cupolas, with touches of silvery snow here and there upon them, springing from a mass of buildings painted in brilliant colors. It gives the effect of an oriental city.

Across the square is a great hostelry, more like a caravansary than an inn, planned for the reception of pilgrims and travellers. Here we put up our carriage, and, before going to visit the monastery, made choice of rooms and ordered dinner. The accommodations would not compare favorably with those of the Grand Hotel, or Meurice's; but after all, it was quite comfortable for the place; a spring-like temperature prevailed in the apartments, and the larder seemed to be well stocked. The lamentations of tourists in regard to the filth and vermin of Russian inns surprise me.

Near the convent gate were little shops containing various small wares and a variety of those curiosities which travellers love to carry away as souvenirs. There were children's toys of primitive simplicity, colored with amusingly bad taste; dainty slippers of white felt, bordered with pink or blue, wherewith Andalusian feet could scarce be shod; furred mittens, Circassian belts, spoons and forks of platina niello-work, models of the broken bell at Moscow, chaplets, enamelled medallions of Saint Sergius, crosses of metal or wood, containing a crowd of microscopic figures of Byzantine style, and legends in the Slavonic character; loaves of fine bread from the convent bakery, bearing stamped on their crust scenes from the Old or the New Testament,—not to mention the heaps of apples for which the Russians have so great a liking. A few mujiks, purple with cold, kept these small shops, for here the women, without being subjected to the compulsory seclusion of the East, scarcely mingle at all in out-door life; you seldom see them in the streets. Business is carried on by men, and the shop-woman is a type unknown in Russia. This remaining apart is a remnant of the ancient Asiatic modesty.

Upon the entrance-tower are painted many episodes in the life of Saint Sergius, the great local saint. Like St. Roche and St. Anthony, St. Sergius has his favorite animal. It is not a dog, nor a pig, but a bear,—a wild beast well suited to figure in the legend of a Russian saint! When the venerable anchorite was living in his wilderness, a bear prowled about the hermitage, with intentions evidently hostile. One morning, upon opening his door, the saint found the bear standing up and growling, with paws outstretched, ready to bestow an accolade that was anything but fraternal. Sergius raised his hand and bestowed his benediction upon the animal, who fell back upon his fore-paws, licked the feet of the saint, and followed him about with the docility of the most gentle dog. The saint and the bear thenceforth kept house together with the utmost harmony.

After a glance at these pictures, which, if not ancient, have all the effect of antiquity, we made our way into the interior of the convent, which resembles the inside of a fortress; and such, indeed, is Troïtza, having sustained many sieges.

A few lines of historic detail in regard to this monastery will be necessary, perhaps, before passing to a description of the buildings and the wealth contained within its walls. St. Sergius lived in a cabin in the midst of a vast forest belonging to Gorodok, and there devoted himself to prayer, fasting, and all the austerities of hermit-life. Close by his cabin, he reared a church in honor of the Holy Trinity, and thus created a religious centre, to which gathered the faithful. Disciples full of fervor desired to remain with their master; to lodge them, Sergius built a convent which took the name of Troïtza, the Russian word for Trinity, in accordance with the designation of the church; and of this convent he was elected Superior. This occurred in 1338.

The care for his own salvation, and his devotion to heavenly things, did not prevent St. Sergius from taking an interest in the events of his time. The love of God in his heart did not extinguish the love for his native land. A patriotic saint he was, and, as such, is still the object of great veneration among the Russians. It was he who, in the time of the great Mongol invasion, excited Prince Dmitri to march against the fierce hordes of Mamai in the plains of the Don; and in order to unite religious enthusiasm with heroic ardor, two monks, designated by Sergius, accompanied the prince into battle. The enemy was repulsed, and Dmitri, in his gratitude, endowed the convent of Troïtza with great wealth, an example followed by princes and czars ever since, among others, by Ivan the Terrible, who was one of the most generous benefactors of the monastery.

In 1393, the Tartars attacked Moscow, and made raids about the environs in the Asiatic manner. Troïtza even then was too rich a prey not to excite their cupidity. The convent was attacked, pillaged, burned, reduced to a heap of ruins, and when—the devastating torrent past—Nikon returned to rebuild the monastery and bring back to it the fugitive monks, the body of St. Sergius was found under the ruins, in all the integrity of a miraculous preservation.

Troïtza, in times of invasion and trouble, has been an asylum for patriotism and a citadel to nationality. The Russians, in 1609, defended themselves here for sixteen months against the Poles, led by Hetman Sapicha. After many unsuccessful assaults, the enemy was compelled to raise the siege. Later, the convent of Saint Sergius afforded shelter to the young czars, John and Peter Alexeiovitch, fleeing from the revolt of the Strelitz. Peter I. also sought refuge here against these same Strelitz, and the gratitude of the illustrious fugitives enriched Troïza, on their accession to power, and made it a very storehouse of treasure. Since the sixteenth century Troïtza has never been pillaged, and the convent would have offered magnificent plunder to the French army, if they had pushed their advance so far, and if the burning of Moscow had not compelled them to retreat. Czars, princes, and boyards, whether through ostentation, or to obtain pardon from Heaven, have endowed Troïtza with the incalculable riches which it now contains. The sceptical Potemkin, none the less devout towards St. Sergius for that, offered sumptuous sacerdotal vestments. Beside its heaps of jewels, Troïtza possessed a hundred thousand serfs, and immense estates which Catherine II. secularized, after compensating the monastery by rich gifts. Formerly Troïtza lodged within its cells about three hundred monks; to-day there is scarcely more than one-third of that number, a scanty population for the vast solitudes of the immense convent.

Troïtza is almost a city : it includes nine churches,— nine cathedrals, as the Russians call them,—the palace of the czar, the residence of the archimandrite, the Capitulary Hall, the refectory, the treasure-rooms, the cells of the brethren, mortuary chapels, and offices of all kinds, in whose construction symmetry has not been at all considered, and which have risen at the desired moment in the suitable place, like plants growing in favorable soil. The appearance of it is strange, novel, and foreign. Nothing less resembles the picturesqueness of Catholic convents. The sadness of Gothic art with its frail columns, its pointed ogives, its open trefoils, its springing upward into the sky, inspires an entirely different order of ideas. Here, none of those long cloisters whose arches, enbrowned by time, frame some lonely little yard,—none of those old, austere walls, green with moss, washed out by rain, which keep the smoke and rust of centuries; none of those architectural caprices, variations upon a given theme, making a surprise out of the foreseen. The Greek confession, less picturesque in an artistic point of view, preserved the ancient Byzantine formulas, and fearlessly repeats itself, more mindful of orthodoxy than of good taste. It attains, however, immense effects of wealth and splendor, and its hieratic barbarism is very impressive to the untutored imagination.

Indeed, it is impossible for the most *blasé* tourist not to feel an admiring astonishment when he sees, at the end of the avenue of glittering frost-covered trees which opens before him as he emerges from the tower-porch, these churches painted in Marie-Louise blue, in bright red, in apple-green, with the white trimmings which the snow has added to them, rising oddly, with their golden or silver cupolas, from the midst of the many-colored buildings which surround them.

It was late in the afternoon when we entered the Trinity Cathedral, wherein stands the shrine of St. Sergius. The mysterious darkness enhanced the magnificence of the sanctuary. Along the walls, rows of pictured saints stood up dark against their gold backgrounds, and assumed a sort of strange, fierce life. It was like a procession of grave personages outlined darkly along the crest of a hill against a belt of sunset. In corners more obscure, the painted figures were like phantoms watching with their ghostly gaze all that went on within the church. Touched by some wandering ray, an aureole here and there shone like a star in a dark sky, or gave to some head of bearded saint the aspect of a John the Baptist's head upon the charger of Herodias. The iconostase, a gigantic façade of gold and precious stones, rose to the vaulted ceiling with its tawny gleams and prismatic scintillations. Near the iconostase, toward the right, a luminous centre attracted the eye; a great number of lamps helped to make in this corner a very conflagration of gold, and silver-gilt, and silver. It was the shrine of St. Sergius, the humble anchorite, who rests there in a sepulchre richer than that of any emperor. The tomb itself is of gilded silver, the canopy in solid silver, supported by four columns of the same metal, the gift of the Empress Anne.

Around this mass of precious metal, from which streamed floods of light, mujiks, pilgrims, the faithful of every class, in an admiring ecstasy, were praying, making signs of the cross, and performing all the religious duties of the Greek ritual. It was a picture worthy of Rembrandt. This dazzling tomb threw out splashes of flame upon the kneeling peasants, lighting up a head, making a beard gleam, bringing a profile into sharp relief, while the rest of the figure remained bathed in shadow, lost under the coarse thickness of the clothing. Some of these heads were magnificent, the faces illuminated with faith and fervor.

After having contemplated this spectacle so worthy of interest, I examined the iconostase in which is set the picture of St. Sergius, a picture regarded as miraculous, which was carried along by the Czar Alexis in his wars with Poland, and by the Czar Peter I. in his campaigns against Charles XII. It is impossible to form an idea of the wealth which faith and devotion, or remorse hoping to buy the pardon of Heaven, have accumulated in the course of ages upon this iconostase, a colossal jewel-box, a very mine of precious stones. The nimbi of certain sacred pictures are paved with diamonds; sapphires, rubies, emeralds, and topazes form mosaics on the golden robes of Madonnas; black and white pearls represent embroidery thereon; and when room fails, collars of massive gold, fastened at the two ends like the handles of a chest of drawers, are set thick with diamonds of an enormous size. One dare not guess their value; doubtless it surpasses many millions. Without question, one of Raphael's Madonnas, quite unadorned, is more beautiful than a Greek Mother of God with all her ornaments; but this lavish Byzantine and Asiatic prodigality produces its effect.

The Cathedral of the Assumption, which adjoins that of the Trinity, is built upon the same plan as the Assumption in the Kremlin, whose exterior and interior arrangements it repeats. Paintings which one might believe to be the work of the immediate pupils of Panselinos, the great Byzantine artist of the eleventh century, cover its walls and the enormous pillars which sustain the vault. You would have said the church was hung throughout with tapestry, for no relief interrupts the immense fresco divided by zones and compartments. The work of the chisel counts for nothing in the ornamentation of religious edifices consecrated to the Greek worship. The Eastern church, which employs so profusely the painted figure, seems to refuse the sculptured figure altogether. She seems to dread the statue as an idol, although she sometimes employs the bas-relief in the decoration of doors, crosses, and other objects appertaining to worship. I know of no detached statues in any Russian church except those which ornament the cathedral of St. Isaac.

This absence of all relief and all sculpture gives a strange and peculiar stamp to the churches of the Greek faith, which one does not appreciate at first, but comes at last fully to understand.

In this church are the tombs of Boris Godounof, his wife, and his two children, resembling in style and shapes the *turbés*, or Moslem tombs. Religious scruples banish from them the art which makes Gothic tombs such admirable structures.

St. Sergius, as founder and patron of the convent, well deserved to have a church in his honor on the spot where once stood his hermitage; and there is within the enclosure of Troïtza a St. Sergius' chapel, as rich, as highly ornamented, and as splendid as the sanctuaries of which I have been speaking. There is found the miraculous picture of the Virgin of Smolensk, surnamed "the guide" (*odighitria*). The walls are entirely covered with frescos, and through apertures cut in the gold of the iconostase, are seen the brown faces of Greek saints.

Meantime night had fully come on, and, however zealous one may be, the tourist's trade cannot be carried on in darkness. Hunger began to be urgent, and I returned to the inn, where the mild temperature of Russian houses awaited me. The dinner was passable. The inevitable cabbage-soup accompanied by balls of hashed meat, a young pig, and soudacs, a fish as peculiar to Russia as is the sterlet, composed the bill of fare, the whole enlivened by a mild white Crimean wine, a kind of "epileptic cocoa," which amused itself by counterfeiting champagne, but, after all, was not a disagreeable beverage.

After dinner, some glasses of tea and a few whiffs of an extremely strong tobacco that they smoke in pipes as small as those used by the Chinese, brought us along to bed-time.

My sleep, I confess, was not troubled by any of those nocturnal aggressors whose swarms transform the traveller's bed into a sanguinary battle-field. I am therefore deprived of the opportunity of placing on record at that point a malediction against vermin, and must reserve for another time the quotation from Heine: "*Un duel avec une punaise! fi! on la tue et elle vous empoisonne!*" To destroy this vile race, you need only to leave open your bedroom window, with the thermometer at —30°; it was winter when I visited Troïtza.

Early in the morning I was again at my tourist's work in the convent, and finished visiting the churches which I had not been able to see the evening before; of these it is useless to give a detailed description, for within, they repeat each other almost exactly, like a liturgic formula. Upon the exterior, in the case of some, the *rococo* style is most oddly joined to the Byzantine. To assign a true date to these edifices would be nearly impossible; that which seems ancient may have been painted but yesterday, and the traces of time disappear under incessantly renewed coats of paint.

We had a letter from an influential person in Moscow for the archimandrite, a handsome man with long hair and beard, and a most dignified face, whose features recalled the human-faced bulls of Nineveh. The archimandrite spoke no French, and sent for a nun who understood that language, bidding her in Russian accompany us in our visit to the Treasury and the other curiosities of the convent. This nun came in, kissed the hand of the archimandrite, and stood silently waiting till the custodian arrived with his keys. She had one of those faces which it is impossible to forget, and which emerge like a dream amid the trivialities of life. She was coiffed with that something resembling a bushel, like the diadem of certain Mithriac divinities, which is worn by the Russian clergy. From it descended long crape *barbes* with floating ends; they fell upon her ample black robe, of the same material of which lawyers' gowns are made. Her features, of ascetic pallor, where yellow, waxy tints had crept in under the delicate skin, were perfectly regular. Her eyes, surrounded by a broad, dark bruise, showed, when she raised the lids, the iris of a strange blue, and her whole person, though swallowed up and, as it were, lost in that floating sack of coarse black serge, betrayed the rarest distinction. She swept its folds after her down the corridors of the convent, with the same air with which she would have managed a train at some court ceremonial. Her ancient grace as a woman of the world, which she now strove to conceal under Christian humility, reappeared in spite of herself. At sight of her, the most prosaic imagination in the world could not have failed to weave a romance. What misfortune, what despair, what catastrophe of love could have brought her to this? She suggested the Duchess of Langeais in Balzac's *Histoire des Treize*, discovered by Montriveau in her Carmelite dress, buried in an Andalusian convent.

We reached the Treasury, and were shown, as the most precious object, a wooden goblet, and some rude sacerdotal vestments. The nun explained to me that this mean wooden vase was the pyx which St. Sergius had used in officiating at the altar, and that he had worn these coarse chasubles, thus making them inestimable relics. She spoke the purest French, absolutely free from accent, and as though it had been her mother-tongue. Whilst, with the most non-committal air in the world,—without scepticism and yet without credulity,—she was relating to me in historic fashion some marvellous legend—I have forgotten what—in relation to these relics, a faint smile parted her lips, and showed teeth finer than all the pearls of the treasure-house, dazzling enough to leave an ineffaceable memory, like those of Berenice, in Edgar Poe's novel.

These brilliant teeth brought youth back into the face discolored by grief and austerities. The nun, who had seemed at first thirty-six or thirty-eight, now appeared not more than twenty-five. It was but a momentary flash. She felt, with all a woman's sensitiveness, my respectful but eager admiration, and she resumed the lifeless air which suited her garments.

All the *armoires* were opened to us, and we were allowed to see the Bibles, the gospels, the liturgical books, with covers of silver gilt, incrusted with stones, onyx, sardonyx, agate, chrysoprase, aqua-marine, lapis-lazuli, malachite, turquoise,—with clasps of gold and silver in which were set antique cameos; the sacred chalices of gold with belts of diamonds; crosses paved with emeralds and rubies; sapphire rings; vases, and chandeliers of silver; dalmatics of brocade embroidered with flowers composed of gems, and with legends in old Slavonic written in pearls; enamelled censers; triptychs storied with countless figures; images of saints and madonnas; masses of precious metals, and heaps of uncut gems;—a very treasure of a Christianized Haroun-al-Raschid.

As I was just emerging, dazzled with wonders, my eyes fairly blinded and seeing black specks in the sunshine, the nun called my attention to a row of bashel-baskets on a shelf, which had escaped my notice and seemed to contain nothing of special account. She plunged her slender, patrician hand into one of them, she said: "These are pearls. There was no way of using these, and they have put them here. There are eight measures of them."

XIX.

BYZANTINE ART.

UNDERSTANDING by some remark of mine that I was not a stranger to art, the nun who had exhibited to me the convent treasures, thought that possibly the painting-rooms might interest me more than this accumulation of gold and diamonds and pearls, so she led me through broad corridors, interrupted by flights of stairs, to the halls where were at work the artist-monks and their pupils.

Byzantine art exists under conditions entirely peculiar, and it differs from everything which is understood by that word among the nations of Western Europe or those who accept the Latin faith. It is a hierarchical, sacerdotal, immutable art; nothing, or almost nothing, is left to the fancy or the invention of the artist. Its formulas are as fixed as dogmas. In this school, there is neither progress nor decay, nor epoch, so to speak. The fresco or picture finished twenty years ago cannot be distinguished from the painting which counts its centuries. Such as it was in the sixth, the ninth, or tenth century, such is now Byzantine art; and I employ this word in lack of a better, as we use the word Gothic, which everybody understands, though its meaning is not rigorously exact.

It is evident to any man who is familiar with paintings, that this art is derived from another source than is the Latin; that it has borrowed nothing from the Italian schools; that the Renaissance has never dawned upon it, and that Rome is not the metropolis where its ideal is enthroned. It lives from its own vitality, borrowing nothing, making no improvements, since at the first stroke it found its necessary form, open to criticism from an artistic point of view, but marvellously suited to the office which it fills. But,—do you ask,—what is the fountain-head of this tradition so carefully maintained? Whence is delivered this uniform instruction which has come down across the ages, undergoing no alteration from the varying media through which it has passed? To what masters do all these unknown artists yield obedience,—these artists whose pencils have covered the churches of the Greek confession with such a multitude of figures, that the enumeration of them— were it possible—would exceed the lists of the most formidable army?

A curious and learned introduction by M. Didron, prefixed to the Byzantine manuscript, entitled "The Guide to Painting," which has been translated by Dr. Paul Durand, replies to most of these questions. The compiler of this Guide to Painting was a certain Denys, a monk of Fourna d'Agrapha, a great admirer of the celebrated Manuel Panselinos of Thessalonica, who seems to be the Byzantine Raphael, and a few of whose frescos yet exist in the principal church of Kares, on Mount Athos. In a short preface, preceded by an invocation to "Mary, Mother of God and Ever-Virgin," Master Denys of Agrapha thus announced the aim of his work: "This art of painting, which, from infancy, I have studied so carefully at Thessalonica, I desire to propagate for the aid of those who, equally with myself, wish to devote themselves to it, and to explain to them in this work all the dimensions, the characteristics of the figures, and the colors of the flesh and of the ornaments with great accuracy. Besides, I have sought to explain the dimensions of all natural objects, the work peculiar to each subject, the different preparations of varnish, sizing, plaster, and gold, and the method of painting upon walls with the utmost perfection. I have thus indicated the whole series of the Old and New Testament subjects, the method of representing natural facts and the miracles of the Bible, and, at the same time, the Lord's parables, the legends, and the epigraphs suited to each prophet; the name and the character of countenance of the apostles and the principal saints; their martyrdom, and a part of their miracles according to the order in the calendar. I tell how churches are to be painted, and give other information necessary in the art of painting, as may be seen in the index. I have collected all these materials with much care and pains, aided by my scholar, Master Cyril of Chios, who has corrected the whole with great attention. Pray for us, then, all of you, that the Lord may deliver us from the fear of being condemned as unprofitable servants."

This manuscript, a real manual of Christian iconography and the art of picture-making, dates back, according to the monks of Mount Athos, to the tenth century. In reality it is not so old; scarcely does it belong so far back as the fifteenth. But that is of little consequence, for it unquestionably repeats ancient formulas and archaic methods. It still serves as guide, and, as M. Didron relates in his journey to the sacred mount, where he visited Father Macarios, the best Aghiorite painter after Father Joasaph, "This bible of his art was spread open in the midst of the painting-room, and two of the youngest students were reading aloud from it alternately, while the others painted and listened to the reading."

The traveller sought to buy this manuscript, of which the artist would at no price deprive himself, for without this book he could not have continued to paint; but he consented to let a copy of it be made. This manuscript contained the secret of Byzantine painting, and explained to the learned tourist,—who had recently been visiting the churches of Athens, Salamis, Triccala, Kalabach, Larisse, of the convent of the Météores, of Saint-Barlaam, of Saint Sophia, of Salonica, of Mistra, of Argos,—why he should have met everywhere the same profusion of painted decoration, everywhere the same arrangement, same costume, same age, same attitude of the sacred personages. "You would say," he exclaims, surprised at this uniformity, "that one single idea, animating at the same moment a hundred pencils, had created at a stroke all the paintings in Greece."

This exclamation might be uttered with equal justice in reference to the frescos which decorate nearly all the Russian churches. "The *atelier* in which all these are prepared," continues the traveller, "and where these Byzantine artists are trained, is Mount Athos: it is indeed the Italy of the Eastern Church. Mount Athos, that province of monks, contains twenty great monasteries, which are so many little cities: ten villages, two hundred and fifty isolated cells, and a hundred and fifty hermitages. The smallest of these monasteries include six churches or chapels; the largest, thirty-three; in all, two hundred and eighty. The villages, or skites, possess two hundred and twenty-five chapels and ten churches. Each cell also has its chapel, and each hermitage its oratory. At Karès, the capital of Athos, is the edifice which we should call the cathedral of the whole mountain, the Protaton, or metropolis, the Greek monks name it. On the summit of the eastern point of the promontory rises the isolated Church of the Transfiguration. Thus, in the whole circuit of Mount Athos, we may count nine hundred and thirty-five churches, chapels, and oratories. Almost all of these are painted in fresco and filled with pictures on wood. In the great convents the refectories are also for the most part lined with mural paintings."

This is certainly a rich museum of religious art. The student has no lack of subjects for study, and of models to reproduce, for, in this school, the artist's merit does not consist in invention, imagination, originality, but rather in copying with the utmost fidelity the sacred types which are set before him. The contours and proportions of every figure are determined in advance. Nature is never consulted; tradition indicates the color of the hair and beard, whether they shall be long or short, the tone of the drapery, the number, direction, and heaviness of the folds. For saints in long robes, there is invariably a break in the garment either below or above the knee. "In Greece," writes M. Didron, "the artist is a slave to the theologian. His work, which shall be copied by his successors, is itself a copy of the pictures his predecessors have painted. The Greek artist is as subservient to tradition as the animal is to instinct. He makes a figure in the same way that the swallow makes a nest, or the bee a cell. Nothing of it is his but the execution; the idea and the composition of the pictures belong to the Fathers, the Theologians,—in short, to the Orthodox church. Neither time nor place are anything in Greek art; the Morcote painter of the nineteenth century is the successor and copyist of the Venetian painter of the tenth, or the Athonite of the fifth and sixth. In the Transfiguration at Athens, the Hecatompyli at Mistra, or the Panagia of St. Luke, you find the saint John Chrysostom of the baptistery of St. Mark in Venice."

M. Didron had the good fortune to meet at Mount Athos, in the convent of Esphigmenon, the first one which he visited, a painter of Karès, the monk Joasaph, who was engaged in decorating with mural paintings the porch, or narthex, in front of the church. He was aided in his work by his brother, two pupils, one of whom was a deacon, and two apprentices. The subject which he was drawing upon the fresh plaster of the wall was a Christ, sending forth His disciples to preach the gospel and to baptize all the world;—a subject of importance containing twelve figures nearly the size of life. He sketched with rapidity and perfect accuracy, without other cartoon or model than his own memory; and while he was thus at work, his scholars filled in with the designated color the contours of the figures and the draperies, gilded the aureoles about the heads, or inscribed the text of legends which the master dictated whilst going on with his own work. The young apprentices were grinding and mixing colors. These frescos, the traveller assures us, executed so rapidly and without any subsequent correction, were much better than the pictures of our second and third rate religious painters; and as he expressed surprise at the talent and learning of Father Joasaph in finding for each personage, legends so appropriate and implying such vast erudition, the monk replied humbly that this was not so difficult as it seemed, and that with the aid of the Guide, and with a little practice, any one could do as much.

The lamented Papety exhibited in the *salon* of 1847 a charming little picture representing Greek monks decorating in fresco a chapel in the convent of Iviron, on Mount Athos. At that time I had not made my Russian journey, but even then this Néo-Byzantine art, of which I had the good fortune to see some isolated specimens, was extremely interesting to me, and Papety's picture, besides its merit as a work of art, excited my curiosity and gratified it also, showing me at their work these living artists, whose pictures seem to belong to the time of the Greek emperors. In a review of the exhibition, I spoke of the picture thus:

"They [the Greek monks] are both standing before the wall upon which they are at work, and which is curved like the inside of an oven. The outlines of the saints about to be colored are drawn in red on the fresh plaster, which is ready for the fresco. These drawings have an archaic stiffness suggestive of a long-past age. In the centre upon a stand are placed the artists' implements and colors. At the left is a trough containing mortar and marble dust, with the trowel for applying it."

This painter also sent to the exhibition some watercolors, representing the frescos of Manuel Panselinos copied from the convent church of Aghia-Lavra. They were Greek saints of grand and haughty aspect,—saints belonging to the warrior category.

And now I, too, was to see the work of artist-monks, like those of Mount Athos, religiously following the instructions of the Guide; a living Byzantine school, the Past working with the hands of the Present,—surely a rare and curious thing!

Five or six monks were painting busily in a large, well-lighted room with bare walls. One of them, a handsome man with black beard and sunburnt face, who was finishing a Madonna, was very impressive with his air of sacerdotal gravity, and the pious care which he bestowed upon his work. He reminded me of Ziégler's beautiful picture: "Saint Luke painting the portrait of the Virgin." Religious feeling possessed his mind far more than art; he painted as one might officiate in divine worship. His Mother of God might have been placed on the evangelist's own easel, so severely archaic was she, and so rigidly restrained within the prescribed limits. You might think her a Byzantine Empress, with such serious majesty she looked at you from the depths of her great, black, steadfast eyes. The portions which were to be concealed by the metallic plating—which is cut away to show the hands and face—were as carefully elaborated as if they had been destined to remain visible.

Other pictures, more or less advanced, representing Greek saints, and, among others, Saint Sergius, the convent's patron, were going on under the laborious hands of the artist-monks. These paintings, destined to serve as icons in chapels or in private dwellings, were upon panels covered with plaster of Paris in accordance with the methods recommended by Master Denys d'Agrapha, and having been a little smoked were in no way distinguishable from paintings of the fifteenth or of the twelfth century. There were the same stiff, constrained attitudes, the same hieratic gestures, the same regularity of folds, the same brown and tawny color in the flesh-tints,—all the teaching of Mount Athos. They were using white of egg, or distemper, afterwards coated with varnish. The aureoles and the ornaments destined to be gilded were slightly raised, the better to catch the light. The old masters of Salonica, could they have come back to the world, would have been well content with these students at Troïtza.

But at the present day no tradition can be maintained with entire fidelity. Among those who resolutely adhere to the old formulas, adepts from time to time are found with less rigid consciences. The new spirit, through some fissure, makes its way into the ancient mould. Those who desire to follow in the footsteps of the Athonite painters, and to preserve in the midst of our own epoch, the immutable Byzantine style, cannot help seeing modern pictures in which liberty of composition is allied to the study of nature. It is difficult to keep one's eyes shut always, and even at Troïtza the new spirit has found lodgement;—as in the metopes of the Parthenon two styles are distinguishable, one ancient, the other modern. Part of the monks conform to rule; a few, younger, have abandoned white of egg for oil, and—still maintaining their figures in the prescribed attitude and the immemorial costume—take the liberty of giving to the heads and hands tones more life-like, a color less conventional, introduce shading, and aim at relief. They make their women more humanly pretty, their men less theocratically fierce; they do not attach that forked beard which the Guide of Painting recommended, to the chins of their patriarchs or hermits. Their religious pictures approach in character the every-day profane painting, without having, in my opinion, its merits.

This more polished and pleasing method does not lack partisans; and examples of it may be seen in many of the modern Russians churches; for my own part, I greatly prefer the old school which is ideal, religious, and decorative, and has on its side the prestige of forms and colors remote from the commonplace reality. This symbolic fashion of presenting the idea by means of figures determined in advance, like a sacred writing whose character it is not permitted to alter, seems to me marvellously suited for the decoration of the sanctuary. Even with all its rigidity it would give scope for a great artist to assert himself by the boldness of the drawing, the grandeur of the style, and the nobleness of the contours.

It is my impression that this attempt to humanize Byzantine art will not succeed. There is in Russia a Romantic school in literature, fascinated, like the French Romantic school, with local color, who defend with learned theories and an enlightened criticism the old style of Mount Athos, for the sake of its antique and religious character, its profound conviction, and its absolute originality amidst the productions of Italian, Spanish, Flemish, or French art. A just notion of these polemics may be formed by recalling the impassioned pleas for Gothic architecture, and the diatribes against Greek, as applied to religious edifices, the parallels between Notre Dame and the Madeleine, which were the delight of our youth from 1830 to 1835. Every country has its era of false classic civilization, a kind of learned barbarism, in which it no longer understands its true beauty, disowns what is characteristic of itself, renounces its antiquities and its costumes, and, with a view to an insipid ideal regularity, demolishes its most admirable national buildings. The France of the eighteenth century, in other respects so grand, would willingly have razed its cathedrals to the ground as monuments of bad taste. The portal of Saint Gervais, by de Brosse, was sincerely preferred to the wondrous façades of the cathedrals of Strasburg, Chartres, and Rheims.

The nun seemed to regard these fresh-colored Madonnas not exactly with disdain, for, after all, they represented a sacred figure worthy of adoration, but with respect much less admiring. She delayed longer in front of those easels where paintings according to the ancient method were in process of elaboration. In spite of my own preferences for the old style, it must be admitted that some amateurs carry to an extreme their passion for ancient Byzantine pictures. By dint of seeking after the simple, the primitive, the sacred, the mythical, they arrive at an enthusiasm for smoky and worm-eaten panels whereon one may vaguely discern wild figures, of extravagant drawing and impossible color. Placed beside these images, the most barbaric Christ of Cimabue would seem a Vanloo or a Boucher. Some of these pictures date, as they assert, from the fifth or even the fourth century. I understand their being sought out as archaic curiosities, but that they should be admired as works of art I find it difficult to conceive. A few of these have been shown me in the course of my visit in Russia, but I confess I have not been able to discover in them the beauties which are so charming to their possessors. In a sanctuary they may be venerable, as ancient witnesses to the faith, but their place is not in a picture-gallery, unless it be a historic gallery.

Outside of this Byzantine art, whose Rome is upon Mount Athos, there has been no Russian painting properly so called. The few artists which Russia has produced do not constitute a school; they have studied in Italy, and there is nothing national about their pictures. The most celebrated and the best known in the west of Europe is Bruloff, whose enormous oil-painting, entitled The Last Day of Pompeii, produced a very considerable sensation in the *salon* of 1824. Bruloff, it will be remembered, is the same artist who designed the cartoons for the dome of St. Isaac's—a great apotheosis, in which he showed a thorough understanding of composition and perspective—in a style recalling somewhat the decorative painting of the latter part of the eighteenth century. The artist, who had a handsome pale face, romantic and Byronic, with a profusion of blonde hair, took pleasure in reproducing his own features, and I have seen many portraits of himself painted at different periods, representing him more or less wasted, but always with the same fatal beauty. These portraits, done with much spirit and freedom, seem to me the best of this artist's lesser works.

A name very popular in St. Petersburg is that of Ivanhoff, who, employed for many years upon a mysterious work of art, gave Russia the expectation and hope of a great painter. This, however, is a legend which I must take up at some other time, and which would carry me too far away from my present purpose.

Must we say that Russia will never have her place among schools of painting? I believe that she will have come to this when she shall have freed herself from the habit of imitating other nations, and when her painters, instead of going to copy Italian models, will be content to look round them and to seek inspiration from the natural scenery and the human types so varied and characteristic in this immense empire which begins at Russia and ends at China. My acquaintance with the groups of young artists who compose the Friday Society gives me cause to believe in a speedy realization of this hope.

Ever preceded by the nun, in her floating black garments, I next paid a visit to a laboratory perfectly fitted up, in which Nadar might have set himself to work as in his own quarters. To step from Mount Athos to the Boulevard des Capucines is a somewhat abrupt transition! To leave monks painting Panagias on gold backgrounds, and to find others coating glass plates with collodion, is one of those tricks which civilization plays you at moments when you are thinking least of her. The sight of a cannon turned upon me would not have caused me more surprise than did the brass tube of the camera accidentally directed my way. The evidence could not be denied. These monks of Troïtza, disciples of Saint Sergius, take views of their convent and make copies of their sacred pictures with perfect success. They possess the best instruments, they understand the latest methods, and their manipulations are carried on in a room whose windows are of yellow glass, a color which has the property of interrupting the rays of light. I bought a photograph of the monastery, which I still possess, and which has not faded overmuch.

In his book on Russia, M. de Custine complains that he was not admitted to see the library at Troïtza. They made no difficulty in my case, and I saw all of it that a traveller can, in a half-hour's visit,—the backs of books well-bound and well-arranged on shelves of bookcases. Besides theological works, Bibles, the writings of the Fathers, treatises on scholastic philosophy, commentaries, and books of liturgies in Latin, Greek, and Slavonic, I observed, in my rapid inspection, many French books of the last century and of the time of Louis Quatorze. Also I glanced into the immense hall of the refectory, terminated at one of its extremities by a very delicately wrought grating behind whose iron arabesques glittered the gold background of an iconostase, for the refectory adjoins a chapel, to the end that the soul may have its food as well as the body. My visit was finished, and the nun conducted me back to the archimandrite's apartments that I might take my leave of him.

Just before we entered, her old habits of society getting the better of the rules of the monastic life, she turned back and addressed to me a slight salutation, as a queen might have done from the steps of her throne, and her white teeth flashed for an instant in a faint, languid, and gracious smile. Then, with a change of expression as sudden as though she had lowered her veil, she resumed her lifeless face, her spectral look of renunciation of the world, and with phantom-like motion she knelt before the archimandrite, and piously kissed his hand, as if it were a patin or a relic. This done, she rose, and, like a dream, she vanished into the mysterious depths of the convent, leaving in my memory an ineffaceable trace of her brief presence.

There was nothing further to see in Troïtza, and we returned to the hostelry and bade the driver make ready the carriage. The horses being attached to the kibitka by a harness of ropes, the coachman seated upon a narrow box covered with sheepskin, ourselves warmly tucked in under our bear-skin, the bill paid, the *pourboires* given, there was nothing to do but to execute the *fantasia* of a departure *au galop*. A slight click of the mujik's tongue sent our team off at the pace of the wild horse of Mazeppa, and it was not till we reached the opposite side of the slope commanded by Troïtza, whence its domes and towers are yet seen, that the brave little animals resigned themselves to a reasonable gait. I shall have no occasion to describe the road from Troïtza to Moscow, having already described that from Moscow to Troïtza, the sole difference being that on the return objects presented themselves in inverse order.

The same evening I was again in Moscow, quite in the mood of attending a masked ball to be given that evening, tickets for which I found at the hotel. Before the door, notwithstanding the intensity of the cold, were standing sledges and carriages of various kinds whose lamps twinkled like frozen stars. A hot blaze of light leaped from the windows of the building in which the ball was going on, making with the blue radiance of the moon one of those contrasts desired for dioramas and stereoscopic views. Having crossed the vestibule, I entered an immense hall in the form of a parallelogram or of a playing-card, framed by great columns resting on a broad platform which rose like a terrace around the floor, and was united to it by flights of steps. This arrangement pleased me extremely, and it is worthy of imitation in our own halls destined for ball-rooms. It gives opportunity for those who do not take active part in the festivities to overlook the dancers without being in their way, and to enjoy at their ease the spectacle of the animated and moving crowd. It elevates and groups the figures in a more picturesque, showy, and scenic manner. There is nothing so disagreeable as a crowd all on a level. It is this which renders private balls so inferior in effects to those of the Opera, wreathed with their triple row of boxes filled with masks, and their troops of masked figures ascending and descending the stairs.

The decoration of the hall was extremely simple, but not the less elegant, rich, and pleasing. Everything was white,—walls, ceiling, and columns,—white, relieved by a few sober gold fillets upon the mouldings. The columns, covered with stucco and highly polished, personated marble well enough to deceive any one, and the light ran down them in long, glittering tears. Upon the cornices, rows of wax-candles outlined the entablature of the colonnade, and reinforced the chandeliers. The hall was so white that this amount of lighting had the effect of the most brilliant "daylight illumination."

Certainly, brilliant light and motion are elements of festivity, but that the fête may have its full *brio*, there must be also noise; noise, the breath and song of life! The crowd—though it was a crowd—was quiet; scarcely did a low murmur run like a shiver over the groups, making a faint, continuous bass to the fanfares of the orchestra. The Russians are silent at their pleasures, and one whose ears have been deafened by the triumphal bacchanals of Opera nights, is amazed at this phlegm and this taciturnity. Doubtless they are very much entertained within, but outwardly they have not that appearance.

There were dominos, a few masks, uniforms, black coats, and some Lesghine, Circassian, and Tartar costumes, worn by wasp-waisted young officers, but no characteristic dress which could be identified as peculiar to the country. Russia seems not yet to have produced its distinctive mask. As usual, the women were few in number, and it is they whom we look for at a ball. So far as I could judge, what we call the *demi-monde* was represented only by Frenchwomen exported from Mabille, by Germans and Swedes, some of them extremely beautiful. Possibly the Russian feminine element was mingled therein, but the stranger does not easily recognize it; I give my observation only for what it is worth.

Notwithstanding a few timid attempts at the *cancan*—of Parisian importation—the ball languished a little, and the metallic bursts of the music did not seem to warm it up very much. Everybody was on the watch for the gypsies, for the ball was to be interrupted by a concert, and when the Tzigani singers appeared on their platform, an immense sigh of satisfaction was heaved by every breast. At last there was to be some amusement! The real performance was about to begin! The Russians are passionately fond of the Tzigani, with their homesick, foreign singing which makes you dream of a free life amid primitive nature, outside of all restraint and all law, divine or human. This passion I share myself, and it drives me almost to madness. So I made good play with my elbows to reach a place near the platform where the musicians stood.

They were five or six haggard, wild-looking young girls, with that half-bewildered air which strong light causes to nocturnal, furtive, vagabond creatures of every race. They made one think of deer brought suddenly from a forest glade into a drawing-room. There was nothing remarkable about their costume; it seemed they had felt bound, in coming to sing at this ball, to lay aside their characteristic attire, and make a fashionable toilette. In consequence, their appearance was like that of ill-dressed maid-servants. But one quiver of the eyelashes, one black, untamed glance wandering vaguely over the audience, was enough to give back all their native character.

The music began. They were strange melodies of pensive sweetness or of wild gayety, broidered with infinite *fioritura*, like the singing of a bird that listens to himself, and grows wild with his own warbling,—sighs of regret over some brilliant past existence, with careless outbreaks of a free and joyous humor, which mocks at all things, even at its own lost happiness, if so be that liberty remains; choruses with stamping of the feet and outcries designed to accompany those nocturnal dances

which form upon the turf of forest glades what we call
"fairy rings;" something like a Weber, a Chopin, a
Liszt, in the savage state. At times the theme was borrowed
from some popular melody which has been the
rounds of all the pianos, but its commonplace character
vanished utterly under the runs and trills, the ornaments
and caprices; the originality of the variations made you
quite forget how trivial was the *motif*. Paganini's
marvellous fantasies upon the Carnival of Venice give
an idea of these delicate musical arabesques,—silk, gold,
and pearls embroidered upon the coarse material. A
gypsy man, a kind of clown with fierce aspect, brown
as an Indian, recalling the Bohemian types so characteristically
represented by Valerio in his ethnographic
water-color sketches, accompanied the singing with
chords from a great rebeck which he held between his
knees, playing in the manner of the oriental musicians;
another big fellow exerted himself upon the platform,
dancing, striking the floor with his feet, thrumming a
guitar while he marked the rhythm upon the wood of
the instrument with the palm of the hand, making
strange grimaces, and occasionally uttering an unexpected
cry. This was the joker, the buffoon, the merry-andrew
of the troupe.

It is impossible to describe the enthusiasm of the audience
immediately about the platform. They applauded
and called out to the singers, they kept time with their
heads, they repeated over the refrains. These songs,
with their mysterious extravagance, have the power of
an incantation; they make you dizzy and mad, and throw
you into the most incomprehensible moods. You listen,
and a mortal longing comes over you to disappear from
civilized life forever,—to go off and range the forests
accompanied by one of these sorceresses with cigar-colored
complexion and eyes like lighted coals. These
songs, whose seductive power is so like magic, are the
very voice of nature itself, noted and caught on the
wing in solitude. This is why they bring a profound

trouble to all upon whom weighs so heavily the complicated mechanism of human society.

Still under the spell of this melody, I walked dreamily amid the masked ball, my soul a thousand leagues away from it. I was thinking of a *gitana* of l'Albaycin, at Granada, who sang to me long since couplets to an air which much resembled one of those we had just heard, and I was seeking the words in some secret drawer of my brain, when I felt myself abruptly taken by the arm, and some one flung into my ear, with the small, shrill voice, falsetto like that of a hunchback, which dominos affect in beginning a conversation, these mystic words: *je te connais!* In Paris nothing could have been more natural. My face has been seen often enough at first performances, on boulevards, and in picture-galleries, for it to be as well known as though I were indeed a celebrity. But in Moscow, this affirmation at a masked ball seemed, to my modesty, a little hazardous.

The domino, on being requested to prove her assertion, whispered beneath the lace of her mask my name, very satisfactorily pronounced, with a pretty little Russian accent, which the disguised voice did not avail to conceal. A conversation began, and it was soon proved to me that, if the Moscow domino had never met me before this ball, she was at least perfectly familiar with my writings. It is difficult for an author, when a few verses of his poetry and a few lines of his prose are recited to him, at so great a distance from the Boulevard des Italiens, not to feel somewhat flattered as he inhales this incense, most fragrant of all to the nostrils of a literary man. In order to bring my *amour-propre* down to its proper level again, I was forced to remind myself that the Russians read a great deal, and that the most insignificant French authors have a more numerous public in St. Petersburg and Moscow than in Paris itself. However, to repay the compliment, I made an exertion to be gallant and to answer back quotations by madrigals, a difficult matter with a domino engulfed in a satin sack, the hood pulled down over the forehead, and the lace of the mask as long as the beard of a hermit! The only thing visible was a little hand, reasonably slender, and gloved severely in black. This was too much mystery by far: a man under these circumstances could be agreeable only at too great an expense of imagination. Besides this, I have a certain fault which prevents me from precipitating myself very ardently into masked ball adventures. Behind a disguise, I suppose ugliness more readily than beauty. This villanous bit of black silk, with its snub-nosed goat's profile, its narrow eyes, and its goat's beard, seems to me to be the model of the face beneath it, and I have great difficulty in separating the two. Women even whose unquestionable youth and notorious beauty are perfectly known to me, when masked, become objects of suspicion. Of course I speak only of the full mask. That little strip of black velvet, which our ancestors called *touret de nez*, and which great ladies wear out of doors, shows the mouth with its smile of pearls, the fine contours of cheek and chin, and by its intense black makes even fairer the rosy freshness of the complexion. It gives opportunity to conjecture a woman's beauty without quite revealing it. It is a coquettish reticence and not a disturbing mystery. At worst, you only risk a nose *à la* Roxelana, in place of the Greek nose of which you dream. One is easily consoled for this misfortune. But the close domino, when lifted at some propitious moment, may bring discoveries extremely embarrassing to a well-bred man. On this account, after two or three turns through the ball-room, I brought back the mysterious lady to the group which she designated to me. Thus terminated my adventure at the masked ball in Moscow.

"What! is that all?" says my reader. "You are concealing something through modesty. The domino, emerging furtively from the ball-room, doubtless indicated a mysterious carriage, and bade you enter it and seat yourself at her side. Then the lady tied her lace handkerchief about your eyes, saying that Love should be blind; and, after the carriage stopped, taking you by the hand, she led you down long corridors, till, the use of your eyes being restored to you, you found yourself in a superbly lighted boudoir. The lady had laid aside her mask, and freed herself from her domino, as the radiant butterfly throws off its dull-colored envelope; she smiled upon you, and seemed to enjoy your surprise. Tell us, was she *blonde* or *brune?* had she a little mark at the corner of her mouth, by which we may know her when we meet her in Paris, in society? We trust you sustained the honor of France in a foreign land, and that you showed yourself tender, gallant, witty, original, impassioned,—in fine, equal to the occasion. An adventure at a masked ball in Moscow! Nice title for a story, by which you have not profited; you—ordinarily so prolix when there are walls, landscapes, or pictures to be described!"

Truly,—though you should take me for a broken-down Don Juan, a Valmont who has retired from the world,—this is all that happened. The adventure ended there; and after a glass of tea mingled with Bordeaux wine, I returned to my sledge, which transported me in a few minutes to my hotel in the Street of the Old Newspapers.

The day had been well filled: in the morning, the convent; in the evening, the ball; the nun, the domino, Byzantine painting, and the Tzigani,—I deserved to sleep well!

On a journey you feel the value of time much more than in the every-day routine of life. For a few weeks, or months at most, you find yourself in a country whither it is possible you may never return; a thousand curious things which you will not see again solicit your attention. There is not a moment to be lost, and your eyes—like people eating lunch at a railway station and dreading the whistle for departure—devour double morsels. Every hour has its employ. The absence of business affairs, of regular occupations, of work, of annoyances, of visits to receive and repay, the isolation in an unfamiliar atmosphere, the constant use of a carriage, singularly lengthens out life, and yet, strange to say, the time does not appear short; three months on a journey are equal in duration to a year in one's accustomed residence. When you are at home, the days, in no way distinguished one from another, drop successively into the gulf of oblivion, and leave no trace behind them. In visiting a country which is new to you, unusual objects and unexpected acts mark the way all along in your memory, and, staking off the time, measure it, and make you appreciate its extent.

Apelles was wont to say: *Nulla dies sine linea;* (for lack of Greek, I quote the Latin—it must be owned these are not the very words of the painter of Campaspe.) The tourist should convert this sentence to his own use, and say, "No day without an expedition."

In accordance with this precept, the day after my visit to Troïtza, I went to see the Museum of Carriages and the Priests' Treasury at the Kremlin.

It is a curious exhibition, this, of antique and stately vehicles; coronation carriages, gala carriages, carriages for travelling and for country use, post-chaises, sledges, and other vehicles. Man, like nature, advances from the complicated to the simple, from the enormous to the proportionate, from sumptuousness to elegance. Carriage-making, like the fauna of primitive times, has had its mastodons and its mammoths. You stand amazed before the wondrous machines on wheels, with their tangled apparatus for suspension, their springs like a pair of tongs, their levers, their thick leather belting, their massive wheels, their twisted swans' necks, their driver's seats high as the forecastle of a ship, their body as large as a modern suite of rooms, their steps like a staircase, their outside perches for pages, their platforms for lackeys, their imperials crowned with balconies, with allegorical figures and plumes. It is a world in itself; and you ask how an engine like this can be set in motion; eight enormous Mecklenburg horses are scarcely enough. But if these carriages, considered in respect to locomotion, belong to a barbaric age, as works of art they are very marvels. Everything is carved, ornamented, wrought, with exquisite taste. Upon gilded backgrounds are spread out charming pictures, done by a master's hand, which, detached from their panels, would make a fine appearance in museums. They are all Loves, groups of attributes, bouquets of flowers, garlands, blazons, caprices of every kind. The windows are Venetian glass, the carpets are the softest and richest that Smyrna or Constantinople ever furnished, the hangings would be the despair of our modern looms: brocade, velvet, damask, brocatelle, cover the sides and the seats. The carriages of Catherine I. and Catherine II. contain toilette and card tables, and, as a characteristic detail, colored and gilded stoves of Saxon porcelain. The sledges for state occasions display also ingeniously grotesque shapes and ornaments charmingly fanciful. But the most curious thing is the collection of saddles for men and for women, and of harnesses of every description. Most of these came from the East, and were sent as presents to Czars and Czarinas, by Emperors of Constantinople, Grand Turks, and Persian Shahs. There is a frantic extravagance of gold and silver embroidery, completely covering the velvet or brocade on which it is wrought, with stars and suns made of precious stones. The bits, the headstalls, the curbs, are set with diamonds; and the bridles, of leather daintily quilted with gold thread or colored silk, are incrusted with uncut turquoises, rubies, emeralds, and sapphires. Like the Asiatic barbarian that I am, I confess this extravagant splendor of saddlery is more seductive to me than the modern English style; very fashionable, doubtless, but so meagre in appearance, so poor in material, and so sober in ornamentation.

A sight of these immense and sumptuous vehicles tells more of ancient court-life than all the memoirs of Dangeau and other chroniclers of the palace. It brings before the mind enormous ways of living which would be impossible at the present day, even with absolute power, for the prevalent simplicity of manners invades even the abodes of sovereigns. The gala-dress, the grand ceremonial costume is now but a masquerade, hastily laid aside as soon as the *fête* is over. Save on his coronation-day, the emperor never wears his crown. He wears a hat like the rest of the world, and when he goes out, it is in no gilded coach drawn by white horses with waving plumes. Once these magnificences were in daily use. Men lived familiarly amidst this pomp and splendor. Kings and the great had nothing, save death, in common with other men, and they moved across the dazzled earth like beings of a different race.

I was shown the Priests' Treasury, which is also in the Kremlin. This is the most prodigious accumulation of wealth that was ever dreamed of. There are to be seen ranged in *armoires*, whose doors open like the leaves of a shrine, tiaras, mitres, caps of metropolitans and archimandrites, mosaics of precious stones on brocade, dalmatics, copes, stoles, robes of cloth, of gold and silver, all flowered with embroidery and adorned with inscriptions done in pearls. At Troïtza it seemed that there were no more pearls in the world, that they were all gathered in the bushel-measures of the convent treasury; and here were quite as many more in the Treasury of the Priests! How many sacred chalices of silver, silver-gilt, chased gold, ornamented with niello-work, surrounded with belts of enamel, circled with precious stones; how many crosses, peopled by myriad microscopic figures; how many rings, crosiers, ornaments of fabulous splendor, lamps, flambeaux, books bound in plates of gold set with onyx, agate, lapis-lazuli, malachite,—have I not beheld behind their glass-doors, with that delight and that discouragement which the traveller feels in looking at something which he must describe in but a few lines, while he is conscious that it deserves a treatise in whose preparation he might spend an entire lifetime!

In the evening, I went to the theatre. It is large and splendid, and reminds me of the Odeon in Paris and the theatre at Bordeaux. This perfect regularity of arrangement touches me but little, and, for my part, I should prefer any little disorderly architectural caprice in the style of Vassili Blagennoi, for instance; but that would be less *civilized*, and would be called barbaric by people of good taste. It must, however, be admitted that, the type being what it is, the theatre at Moscow leaves nothing to be desired. Everything is on a grand scale,—stately, sumptuous. The painting of the audience-room, red and gold, gratifies the eye with its sober splendor, favorable to toilettes, and the imperial box, placed just opposite the stage, with its gilt staves, its double-headed eagles, its blazons and scrolls, produces a superb and imposing effect; it cuts two rows of boxes, and makes a pleasing interruption to the curving lines of the galleries. As in La Scala, San Carlo, and all the great Italian theatres, a broad passage-way surrounds the *parterre* and facilitates access, rendered also still more easy by an aisle through the centre of the house. Nowhere is space so parsimoniously economized as in Paris. The orchestra-chairs in the theatre at Moscow are admirable, but anywhere in the house you are well seated. The spectator is never sacrificed to the spectacle, as is too apt to be the case in Parisian theatres, and pleasure is not bought at the expense of torture. You have around you that full amount of space judged necessary by Stendhal for the best enjoyment of music without being molested by the influence of your neighbor. With that art of heating which the Russians possess in the highest degree, and which is with them a question of life or death, a mild, equal temperature is maintained everywhere, and one does not run the risk, if he open the door of his box part way, of receiving those *douches* of cold air which strike the shoulders so unpleasantly.

However, comfortable as it was, the theatre was not very well filled that evening. There were great empty spaces among the boxes, and almost whole rows of benches remained unoccupied, or presented rare groups of spectators scattered here and there. The crowd must needs be enormous to fill these immense theatres. In Russia, everything is on too large a scale, and seems made for a population to come. It was an evening of ballet, for ballet and opera alternate at Russian theatres, and are not combined as in Paris. The story of the performance that evening I do not remember. It was as disconnected as the Italian librettos, and only served to string together a succession of *pas* favorable to the talent of the actors. Although I have made programmes for ballets myself and understand the language of pantomime reasonably well, it was impossible for me to follow the thread of the action amid the *pas de trois*, the *pas de deux*, the *pas seuls*, and the evolutions of the *corps de ballet*, who manœuvred with admirable harmony and precision. What pleased me most was a kind of mazurka, performed by a dancer named Alexandroff, with a stately grace and elegance very remote from the disagreeable affectations of ordinary male dancers.

The traveller's life is made up of contrasts: the following day I went to visit the convent of Romanoff, a few miles distant from Moscow. This convent is celebrated for the excellent sacred music performed there. Like Troïtza, its exterior resembles a fortress. Within its walls are many chapels and buildings, and a cemetery, whose appearance in winter is particularly doleful. There is nothing sadder than these crosses embedded in snow, these funereal urns and columns emerging from the white covering which is spread like a second shroud above the dead. You cannot rid yourself of the idea that the hapless sleepers who lie beneath all this mass of snow must feel that they are very cold, and that they are buried more deeply in oblivion, for even their names are hidden by it, and the pious sentences wherein their souls are recommended to the prayers of the living.

Casting a melancholy glance at these half-covered tombs, whose desolation seemed yet further increased by a few black leaves of some evergreen trees, I entered the church. The iconostase, all gilt from top to bottom, specially attracted my attention by its prodigious height, greater than that of the tallest Spanish altar-screens. Service was going on, and, as I entered, I was surprised to hear sounds resembling the bass notes of our organs,— for I knew that the Greek ritual does not allow the use of these instruments. I was soon set right on this point, for, as I approached the iconostase, I perceived a group of singers, heavily bearded and dressed in black, like Russian priests. Instead of chanting with full voice as ours do, they sought for more subdued effects, and produced a kind of humming sound whose charm is more easily felt than described; imagine the noise which those great nocturnal moths make in flying, on a summer night; the note is grave, sweet, and yet penetrating. I think there were a dozen of them, distinguishable from the bassos by the way in which they swelled out their throats, and the sounds emerged from their mouths almost without one's being able to see them move their lips.

The imperial choir at St. Petersburg, and this in the convent of Romanoff, are the finest I have heard in the domain of religious music. We doubtless possess musical compositions more scientific and more beautiful, but the manner in which the plain-song is executed in Russia adds to it a mysterious grandeur and an inexpressible charm. It was, I was told, St. John Damascene who, in the eighth century, made a general reform in sacred music; it has been but little modified since that time, and they are the same chants, arranged for four voices by modern composers, which I heard. For a moment the Italian influence invaded Russian church-music; but it very soon ceased, and the emperor Alexander I. would suffer nothing but the ancient chants to be performed by his own choir.

Returning to the hotel, and yet vibrating from the celestial harmony, I found letters which recalled me to St. Petersburg; and with great regret, I bade adieu to Moscow,—Moscow, the true Russian city! crowned by the Kremlin with its hundred domes.

XX.

RETURN TO FRANCE.

ALREADY I had postponed for days, for weeks, even for months, the time of my departure for home. St. Petersburg had been a kind of icy Capua for my courage, where I had become enervated by the luxuries of a charming life, and it cost something, I am not ashamed to confess, to return to Paris to assume once more the collar of the daily newspaper which so long had rubbed my shoulders. To the charm of new scenes—to me always so great—had been added that of the most agreeable social relations. I had been petted, entertained, indulged, loved even,—I am foolish enough to believe,—and all this cannot be left without regret. Russian life, smooth, caressing, flattering, wrapped me about, and I found it hard to lay aside that soft pelisse. Yet it is impossible to remain at St. Petersburg forever! Letters from France arrived, each more urgent than the last, and the momentous day was irrevocably fixed.

I have said that I became a member of the *Vendrediens*, a society of young artists who meet every Friday at each other's houses, and pass the evening in executing in pencil, water-colors, or sepia, improvised compositions which are sold at Beggrow's, the Susse of St. Petersburg, and whose proceeds serve to aid some comrade in unfortunate circumstances. About midnight, a merry supper terminates the evening's work; the drawing materials are cleared away, and we attack macaroni,—that classic dish,—*salmis de gelinottes*, or some huge fish caught in the Neva through holes made in the ice. The entertainment is more or less sumptuous according to the financial condition of that *Vendredien* who receives the club on the given evening. But, be the beverage what it may,—Bordeaux wine, champagne, or only English ale, or even kwas,—none the less the supper is gay, cordial, and fraternal. Droll stories, studio jokes, agreeable nonsense, unexpected witticisms, flash on all sides like sky-rockets. Then they go off in groups, according as their homeward ways lie in the same direction, carrying on the conversation still, through the streets, silent, deserted, white with snow, in which no sound is heard save our bursts of laughter, the barking of some dog who is wakened as we go by, and the watchman dragging his iron-shod stick along the pavement.

The Friday which happened to be the evening before my departure, brought precisely my turn to entertain the company, and they assembled, to a man, at my lodgings in the Morskaïa street. Considering the solemnity of the occasion, Imbert, a celebrated *chef* from the Imperial household, consented to arrange the *menu* for the supper, and deigned even to put his own hand to it, in the preparation of a *chaud-froid de gélinottes*, the like of which I have never seen on any table. Imbert esteemed me by reason of a *risotto* I executed once in his presence, in accordance with the purest Milanese recipe, after we had been having some conversation on the subject of exotic *cuisines ;* he had pronounced it exquisite, and considered me no longer a *bourgeois ;* quite aside from any literary attainments, he regarded me as an artist! Never was approbation more flattering to me ; and he now made this *chaud-froid* for a palate he judged duly appreciative of its merit.

As usual, the evening began with work ; each man took his place at a desk prepared in advance under a shaded lamp. But the work made little progress ; everybody seemed preoccupied ; conversation kept all pencils suspended, and bistre and India ink dried in the cup between one touch and the next. For nearly seven months I had lived as a comrade with these young men, brilliant, sympathetic, lovers of the beautiful, and full of generous ideas. I was about to leave them. When people separate, who knows if ever they shall meet again!—especially when a great distance lies between, and your lives, which for a time have mingled, return into their wonted channels. A certain melancholy, therefore, hung over the *Vendrediens*, and the announcement of supper came opportunely to scatter it. The toasts drank to my prosperous journey brought back the lost gayety, and we were so long in draining the stirrup-cup, that they resolved to stay till morning and to accompany me *en masse* to the railway-station.

The season was advancing; the great breaking up had taken place in the Neva, and now only some floating ice was coming down to melt and disappear in the gulf which was open for the season. The roofs had lost their ermine covering, and in the streets the snow, changed into black paste, splashed up at every step. The damage done by the winter, which the white coating had long masked from sight, appeared full in view. The pavements were dislocated, the roadway broken up, and our droschky, rudely shaken out of one quagmire into another, gave us terrific blows in the back, and made us jump up like peas on a drum; for the bad condition of the roads by no means prevented the isvochtchiks from going as if the devil were carrying them off; if only the two front wheels follow them, they are satisfied, and care but little what becomes of the passenger.

We soon reached the railway-station, and there, finding that separation even then was coming too soon, the whole party entered the train and resoved to accompany me as far as Pskov, at that time the extent of the road. The habit of thus escorting friends or relatives who are going away seems to me peculiar to Russia, and it is a custom that pleases me. The bitterness of departure is softened by it, and solitude does not too rudely succeed to embraces and the grasp of friendly hands.

At Pskov, however, the parting must needs take place. The *Vendrediens* went back to St. Petersburg by the return train; this was my real departure; the true journey was now about to commence.

I was not returning to France alone; I had for my travelling companion a young man who had been living in the same house with me at St. Petersburg, and with whom I has speedily formed ties of friendship. Although a Frenchman, he knew—a rare thing!—almost all the northern languages: German, Swedish, Polish, and Russian, speaking them like his mother-tongue; he had travelled much in Russia, in all directions, in vehicles of every kind, and in all temperatures. In travelling he exhibited admirable self-control, could do without everything, and had an astonishing power of resisting fatigue, although he seemed of a delicate organization, and was accustomed to a life of the utmost comfort. Without him, it would have been impossible for me to have accomplished my homeward journey at that season of the year, and over roads so nearly impassable.

Our first care was to search out in Pskov a vehicle to hire or to buy, and, after much going and coming, nothing could be found but a queer-looking and dilapidated old droschky whose springs did not inspire much confidence. We bought it, but with the agreement that if it broke down before making forty versts, the seller should take it back, receiving a slight compensation for damages. My prudent friend was the person who suggested this clause, which proved useful, as we shall see.

Our trunks were fastened to the back of the frail vehicle; we seated ourselves upon the narrow box, and the driver lashed his horses to a gallop. It was truly the worst season of the year to travel in this country: the highway was but a road of mud, relatively a little more solid than the vast marsh of liquid mire which lay on both sides of it. At the right, at the left, and in front of us, the scene consisted of a sky splashed with muddy gray, resting on a horizon of black, wet lands; here and there the tangled, reddish heads of a few half submerged birches, a glimmer of pools of water, and now and then, a log-hut still retaining on its roof shreds of snow like strips left in tearing off wall-paper. Through the deceitful mildness of the temperature came, at the approach of evening, a breath of north-wind sharp enough to make us shiver under our furs. The breeze grew no warmer from sweeping over this *puree* of snow and ice; bands of crows punctuated the sky with black commas, and took their way, croaking as they flew, towards their nocturnal domiciles. It was not particularly cheerful, and if it had not been for my comrade's conversation, who described to me one of his Swedish journeys, I should have been plunged in melancholy.

Mujiks' carts, loaded with wood, were passing along the road, drawn by little horses muddy as spaniel-dogs and making a deluge of mud fly about them; but when they heard our bells, they drew respectfully to one side and let us go by. One of these mujiks had even the good manners to run after us with a trunk that had become detached, and whose fall we had not heard owing to the noise of our own wheels.

It was almost dark, and we were still a long way from the post-house; the horses went like the wind, knowing that their stables lay somewhere ahead; the poor droschky bounced upon its enfeebled springs and followed in diagonals the headlong team, its wheels not being able to revolve quickly enough in the thick mud. Suddenly it received a shock so violent, in going over a stone, that we had a narrow escape from being landed full in the mud. One of the springs had broken, the forward part of the carriage no longer held together. Our driver got off, and with a bit of rope mended the fractured vehicle as well as he could, so that we were able to arrive, in a lame condition, at the post-house. The droschky had not made fifteen versts. It was impossible to think of continuing our journey with such a "wooden shoe" as that. In the yard of the post-house there were no disposable vehicles, except télégas, and it was more than three hundred miles to the frontier.

To appreciate properly the horror of the situation, a brief description of the télega is necessary. This eminently primitive vehicle is composed of two planks placed lengthwise upon two axletrees, upon which four wheels are fastened. The planks are edged with a narrow rack; a double rope covered with a sheepskin goes across, attached at each end to the rack, and forms a kind of swing which serves for a seat. The driver stands upon a wooden cross-beam, or sits on a small plank. The trunks are heaped up at the back. To this machine are attached five little horses that a *fiacre* would disdain, so piteous is their mien in repose, and that the best race-horses could hardly keep up with, when once they are fairly launched. It is not a means of transportation suited to a sybarite; but at the break-neck pace we go, the télega is the only vehicle that can resist the roads, broken up by the thaw.

We held a council in the yard. My companion said to me: "Wait till I return. I will push on to the first relay, and will come back for you with a carriage,—if I find one."

"But why?" I asked, much surprised at this proposition.

"For this reason," said my friend, concealing a smile; "I have undertaken many a journey in a télega before this, with companions who seemed courageous and robust. They climbed bravely upon the seat, and, for the first hour, confined themselves to some grimaces and contortions, which they immediately suppressed. But soon, with broken back and aching knees, and brain shaken about in the skull like a dry nut in its shell, they began to swear, to groan, to bewail themselves, and to reproach me. Some of them wept, and implored me to put them on the ground, or to throw them into a ditch, preferring to die of hunger or cold upon the spot, or to be eaten by wolves, rather than longer to undergo such torture. Nobody ever went beyond thirty miles."

"You have too poor an opinion of me," I rejoined. "I am not an effeminate traveller. The galleys of Cordova, of which the bottom is only a netting of cordage,—the *tartanes* of Valencia, which resemble boxes in which billets are rolled about to round them, have not wrung one lamentation from me. I have travelled post in a cart, holding on with feet and hands to the rack. There is nothing about the télèga that can surprise me. If I complain, you may reply like Gantimozin to his companion on the gridiron: 'Am I on a bed of roses?'"

My brave reply seemed to convince him. They put horses to a télèga, heaped our luggage on it, and we were off.

"But dinner?" you say; "the Friday evening supper must be digested by this time, and a conscientious traveller owes to his readers the bill of fare of the slightest repast made upon the journey." I only took a glass of tea and a thin slice of black bread; for when you are making one of these unreasonable journeys, you should not eat, any more than does the postilion riding post.

I am not prepared to make the paradoxical assertion that the télèga is the easiest vehicle in the world. But in truth it seemed to me more tolerable than I expected, and I maintained myself without too much trouble upon the horizontal rope, which was somewhat improved by the sheepskin over it.

With the coming on of night the wind had grown piercing; the sky was now free from all vapors, and the stars shone, large and bright, in the sombre blue, as when the weather clears off cold after a storm.

Amid thaws, these returns of cold are not uncommon. The winter of the North retreats unwillingly towards the pole, and comes back now and then to fling a handful of snow into the face of spring. By midnight, the mud had completely hardened, the pools of water had frozen over, and the heaps of stiffened mire caused the téléga to jolt worse than before.

We reached the post-house, which could readily be identified by its white façade and the columns of its portico. All these relay-houses are alike, built, from one end of the empire to the other, upon a prescribed model. They took us off the téléga and our luggage with us, and placed us on another, which set off at the instant. We went at a headlong rate, and vague shapes, half seen through the darkness, fled past us in disorder on each side the road, like a routed army. It seemed that some unknown enemy was pursuing these phantoms. Hallucinations of the night began to molest my sleepy eyes, and dreams unconsciously were mingled with thoughts. I had not been in bed the whole previous night, and the imperious necessity of sleep made my head waver from one shoulder to the other. My companion bade me sit down in the bottom of the vehicle, and clasped my temples between his knees that I might not crack my skull against the rack. The most violent antics of the téléga, which sometimes, in sandy or swampy parts of the road, passed over logs laid transversely, did not awaken me, but made the design of my dream deviate, like an artist's, whose elbow one pushes as he is at work; the figure which began as the profile of an angel, ends, the mask of an imp.

My sleep lasted three quarters of an hour, and I awoke rested and fresh, as if I had slept in my bed.

There is an intoxicating delight in rapid motion. What joy to sweep like a whirlwind, with a noise of wheels and bells, through the vast silence of the night, while all men are asleep,—seen by the stars only, who wink their golden eyes and seem to point out to you your road. The consciousness of action, of motion, of going forward towards a goal, during hours ordinarily lost, inspires you with a queer sort of pride; you admire yourself, and think somewhat scornfully of the philistines who are snoring under their coverlets.

At the next relay the same ceremony; entrance with a grand flourish into a court-yard; ourselves decanted rapidly from one téléga to another; departure *au galop*.

"Well!" I said to my companion, when we had emerged from the post-house, and the postilion was sending his horses along the road at the very top of their speed, "I have not yet cried for mercy, and the téléga has been knocking us about for a very respectable number of miles. My arms still are fast at the shoulders, my legs are not put out of joint, and my dorsal vertebræ still support my head."

"I had no idea you were such a veteran. Now the worst is over, and I think I shall not be obliged to deposit you by the roadside, with a handkerchief tied to a pole to solicit for you the compassion of any coach or post-chaise that might chance to pass through these desert solitudes. But as you have slept, it is now your turn to watch; I propose to close my eyes for a few minutes. Don't forget, in order to keep up the pace, to hit the mujik in the back every now and then with your fist; he will pass it on to the horses in the form of a slap with the reins. Also call him 'Durak!' in a gruff voice; it can do no harm."

I acquitted myself conscientiously of the task thus laid upon me; but let me hasten to say,—that I may escape the accusation of cruelty in the eyes of philanthropists,—that the mujik was clad in a thick touloupe of sheepskin, whose wool deadened every shock from without. My blow was delivered upon a mattress.

When daylight came, I saw with surprise that snow had fallen over all the country lying before us. Nothing could have been more dismal than this snow, whose thin layer, like a shroud in rags, only half-covered the ugliness and poverty of the soil, broken up by the recent thaw. On the slope of rising ground where it lay in narrow strips, it vaguely suggested the columns of Turkish tombs in the cemetery of Eyoub or of Scutari, which have been thrown down or made to lean over in curious positions, by the sinking in of the ground.

After a time the wind began to take up clouds of fine pulverized snow, resembling sleet, which stung my eyes, and pierced with a million fine icy needles that part of my face which the necessity of respiration forced me to leave uncovered. It is impossible to imagine anything more disagreeable than this small, teasing torture, which was augmented by the speed of the téléga going against the wind. My mustache was soon set thick with white pearls, and bristling with stalactites, through which my breath came out vapory and bluish, as the smoke from a pipe. I felt chilled to the very marrow of my bones, for damp cold is far worse than dry, and I experienced that matutinal discomfort known of travellers, and those who have been having nocturnal adventures. *Franc compagnon* though one may be, the téléga for repose is not as good as a hammock, or even as that green leather sofa of which I have so often spoken!

A glass of very hot tea and a cigar, drank and smoked at the relay while they were putting in the horses, quite revived me again, and I went on bravely, much flattered by the compliments of my companion, who had never seen, he said, any Western man endure the téléga with so much heroism.

It is difficult to describe the country which we traversed, as it appears at this season of the year to the traveller whom imperious necessity compels to cross it. It is a region of slightly undulating plains of blackish coloring, staked off with posts, designed to mark out the road when it is buried under the snows of winter, which in summer suggest telegraphic poles out of employment. Along the horizon nothing is to be seen save forests of birch-trees, sometimes half-buried, and remote villages, lost amid the solitudes, betrayed only by their small, bulbous cupolas, painted light-green. At this moment, upon the sombre background of mud stiffened by the night's cold, the snow spread out here and there long strips like pieces of linen cloth which are unrolled upon the grass to whiten ; or—if this comparison seems too cheerful—like white braid sewn upon the rusty black of some funeral decoration of the poorest kind.

The pallid light, sifted through the immense grayish cloud which covered all the sky, was lost in vague glimmers, and gave neither light nor shade to any objects ; nothing had any relief, all things seeming mere outline filled up with flat color. In this ambiguous light everything appeared soiled, gray, washed-out, and wan, and the colorist would have taken no more pleasure than he who should have tried to sketch this vague, undefined, drowned landscape,—morose rather than melancholy. But one thing consoled me and saved me from yielding utterly to *ennui*, and that was—despite the regret I felt for St. Petersburg—the recollection that my nose was turned toward France ! Every jolt through this dismal wilderness brought me nearer home, and I was soon to see if, after seven months' absence, my Parisian friends remembered me yet. Furthermore, the exertion of making a difficult journey has something sustaining in it, and the satisfaction of triumphing over obstacles distracts one from the small discomforts of the detail. A man who has seen many lands does not count on finding " enchanting scenes " at every step ; he has become habituated to these blanks in nature, who, like the greatest poets, sometimes repeats herself, and sometimes nods. More than once you are tempted to say, like Fantasi, in Alfred de Musset's comedy : " What a failure that sunset is ! Nature is pitiable this evening. Just look at that valley, those four or five wretched clouds climbing up that mountain ! I used to make landscapes like that on the covers of my books when I was twelve years old ! "

We had long since left behind us Ostrov, Regitza, and other town or cities, upon which I, it will be readily believed, did not make, from the summit of my télega, any very minute observations. Had I remained longer in each place, I could but repeat descriptions already given, for they are all alike: everywhere, board fences, wooden houses with double windows through which you can perceive some house-plant, roofs painted green, and a church with five bell-towers, and a narthex colored by some painter on a Byzantine pattern.

Amidst this, the post-house stands distinct with its white façade, before which are grouped a few mujiks, in their oleaginous touloupes, and some yellow-haired children. As regards women, they are rarely seen.

It was growing late in the day, and we could not now be far from Dunaburg. We reached it by the last rays of a livid sunset, which gave no very cheerful aspect to this town, peopled for the most part with Polish Jews. It was such a sky as one sees in pictures representing plague-stricken cities, of a wan, grayish hue, full of unhealthy, green tints, like decomposed flesh. Beneath this sky, the black houses, soaked with rain or the melting snows, dilapidated by the winter, resembled heaps of wood or filth, half submerged by an inundation of mud. The streets were miry torrents. Water set free by the thaw ran down from every side, yellow, earthy, blackened, and carrying with it countless unnamable *débris*. Lakes of slime spread themselves out in open places, islets of filthy snow, which still resisted the west wind, rising here and there above the surface. In this unclean liquid—which might have called out a hymn in praise of Macadam—the wheels turned like the paddles of a steam-boat, throwing up splashes of mud against the walls and upon the rare passers-by, who wore boots worthy of oystermen. It came up to the very axle-trees. Happily, below this flood, there remained still a wooden pavement, which, though in poor condition by reason of being under water, still afforded solid ground at a certain depth, and saved us from disappearing bodily, ourselves, téléga, and horses, as in the *lises* of Mont Saint-Michel.

In the general spattering and splashing, our pelisses had become real celestial globes, with numberless constellations of mud not described by the astronomers, and, if it had been possible to appear filthy at Dunaburg, we were, as the phrase goes, not fit to be taken up with tongs.

The passage of isolated travellers is a rare thing at this period of the year. Few people have the courage to make the journey in a téléga, and the mail-wagon is the only other possible means of conveyance. But for this, it is necessary to set one's name down long in advance, and I had been obliged to leave in a hurry, like the soldier whose furlough had expired and who must rejoin his regiment at all risks, under penalty of being considered a deserter.

My companion held it as a principle that in journeys like this it was best to eat as little as possible, and his abstinence surpassed that of the Spaniard or the Arab. Nevertheless, when I represented to him that I was dying with a virile fury of hunger, not having applied myself to the satisfaction of "below the nose," as says Rabelais, since Friday night—and it was now Sunday evening—he kindly yielded to what he regarded as a weakness in me, and, leaving the téléga at the relay, set forth with me in search of a meal of some kind. Dunaburg goes to bed early; only a few scattered lights twinkled from the houses. To walk in such a sewer was not an easy operation, and it seemed to me that at every step an invisible boot-jack seized me by the heels. Finally we perceived a reddish glimmer coming from a kind of den that showed signs of being a tavern; the lamplight was mirrored in the liquid mud, making a net-work red as the blood that runs from under a slaughter-house. It was not appetizing, but at this point of hunger one cannot afford to be fastidious. We entered, not allowing ourselves to be repelled by the nauseous odor of the place, where a smoky lamp spluttered and burned with difficulty in the mephitic atmosphere.

The room was filled with strange-looking Jews clad in long, narrow surtouts, long as cassocks, shining with grease, concerning the original color of which it was impossible to say if it were black or purple, maroon or olive, but which at the present moment presented a tint that I shall designate thus: "filth intense." They wore odd-looking hats, with broad rims and enormous crowns, discolored, shapeless, in some places, the fur standing on end, in other places bald, old enough to be not picked up in the corner of a field by the hook of a bankrupt ragpicker. And the boots! Trodden down at the heel, out of shape, twisted in spirals, whitened by half-dried layers of mud, like feet of elephants that had long splashed through Indian jungles. Many of these Jews, the younger ones especially, had the hair parted on the forehead, and a long curl hanging behind the ear, a bit of dandyism which made a contrast to their horrible uncleanliness. It was no longer the handsome Oriental Jew, the heir of the patriarchs, possessed still of his Biblical rank, but the horrid Polish Jew, given over in the mud to all sorts of suspicious trades and sordid industries. And yet, there in the lamplight with their meagre faces, their sharp, restless eyes, their beards forked like a fish's tail, their shabby aspect, and their general tone of sour herring dried in the smoke, they recalled the pictures and the etchings of Rembrandt.

Custom did not seem to be very brisk in this establishment. In dark corners could be observed indeed a few individuals slowly drinking a glass of tea or of vodka; but of solid food, not a vestige. My companion, who understood and spoke both German and Polish, inquired of the master of the place if there were no way of procuring for me some kind of a meal. The question seemed to surprise him. It was the day following the Jewish Sabbath; nothing had been left over from last week, and, for some reason, the supply for the day had been devoured to the last crumb. However, he was touched by my famished appearance. His pantry was empty, the kitchen-fire was out; but next door, perhaps, bread could be obtained. He went to give orders, and in a few minutes I saw appear among this heap of human rags, a young girl bearing in triumph a sort of flat cake. She was a Jewess of marvellous beauty, the Rebecca of *Ivanhoe*, the Rachel of *La Juive*, a very sun, radiant as the alchemists' macrocosm, in the darkness of the gloomy room. Eleazar at the well would have given her Isaac's ring of betrothal. She was the purest type of her race that one ever dreamed of, a real flower of Bible times, blooming by some strange chance amid these vile surroundings. The Sulamite of Sir Hasirim was not more orientally bewildering. What gazelle eyes, what delicately aquiline nose, what beautiful lips, red as twice-dyed Syrian crimson, outlined upon the soft pallor of the skin! how exquisite the oval from brow to chin, made to be framed in the traditional bandelet!

She presented the bread to me, smiling like one of those daughters of the desert who incline their water-jars to the parched lips of the traveller; and, absorbed in looking at her, I never dreamed of accepting it. A faint color came into her cheek as she saw my admiration, and she set down the bread upon the corner of the table.

I sighed in my heart, as I remembered that the age for impassioned folly was over for me. My eyes all dazzled by the radiant apparition, I began to nibble my bread—which was at the same time underdone and burned—but which seemed to me as delicious as if it had come from the Viennese bakery in the Rue de Richelieu!

There was no further inducement to remain; the fair Jewess had gone away, making the smoky hall yet more gloomy by her departure. So, with a sigh, I returned to the téléga, saying to myself that it was not always jewel-cases of velvet that contained the richest pearls.

We soon reached the river Dwina, which we were to

cross. The shores are high, and the descent to the level of the water is made by plank slopes which are steep enough to remind one of "Russian mountains." Happily, postilions are skilful, and the little Ukraine horse is sure-footed. We came safe to the foot of the descent, where in the darkness we heard the waters boil and roar. There is neither bridge of boats nor ferry whereby to cross, but an arrangement of plank-covered rafts set end to end, and bound together by cables; thus constructed, the bridge yields better to the swollen waters, rising and falling with them. The passage, though without real danger, seems threatening enough. The river, greatly increased in volume by the melting snows, flowed full to the brim, and chafed against the obstacle which the rafts offered, stretching the cables to their utmost tension. Water and the night easily become terrifying and mysterious. Lights, which appeared I know not whence, moved about like phosphoric serpents; the foamy waves threw back strange sparkles which made the blackness more intense; we seemed to be floating upon a gulf, and it was with a sentiment of satisfaction that I felt myself again on land, borne along by the horses, who climbed the slope almost as rapidly as they had descended it on the other bank.

Imagine us resuming our headlong pace through the gray darkness, discerning nothing but vague shapes effaced from the memory as promptly as they pass before the eyes,—of which it is impossible to give any description. These undefined visions, which arise and vanish in the rapidity of our motion, are not without a charm; you seem to gallop athwart a dream. You seek to penetrate with your gaze the vague darkness, downy like sheets of wadding, in which every outline is blurred, every object only makes a stain of darker color.

I thought of the beautiful Jewish girl, whose face I strove to engrave upon my memory, going over it line by line before the sketch had become effaced, and I made an effort to remember how she was dressed, but without success. Her beauty had so dazzled me that I had seen nothing but her head. All the rest lay in shadow. The light was concentrated upon herself, and had she been clad in gold brocade wrought with pearls, I should have observed it no more than if it had been rags of calico.

With dawn the weather changed and went back decidedly to winter. The snow began to fall, but this time in large flakes; one layer succeeded another, and soon, as far as the eye could see, the country was all in white. Every moment we were forced to shake ourselves not to be covered in our télega, but it was labor lost; in a few minutes we were powdered anew like tartlets sugared by the pastry-cook. These silvery feathers flew past each other, caught together, arose, descended, blown by the wind. You would have said that countless down-beds were emptied from the aërial heights, and in this whiteness you could not see four paces before you. The little horses shook their dishevelled manes with vexation. The desire to get out of the storm lent them wings, and they galloped at the top of their speed towards the relay, in spite of the resistance offered to the wheels by the newly fallen snow.

I have a strange passion for the snow; nothing pleases me so well as this iced *poudre de riz* which makes the earth's brown face white. This virginal, immaculate whiteness, in which there are scintillating specks as in Parian marble, seems to me preferable to the richest tints; and when I tread a snow-covered road, I seem to myself to be walking the silver sands of the milky way. But this time it must be confessed my taste was over-satisfied, and my position upon the télega began to be no longer tenable. Even my friend, impassive as he was, and habituated to the rigors of hyperborean journeys, admitted that it would be more comfortable to be seated beside a stove in a very snug room, or even in a simple travelling-coach, if a coach could move in such weather.

The affair soon degenerated into a snow-blow. There is nothing more singular than this storm of plush. The wind blows low, brushing the earth, and sweeps the snow before it with irresistible violence. Puffs of white smoke whirl along the ground—icy smoke, escaping from some polar conflagration. When this water-spout of snow meets a wall, it heaps itself up against it, soon overpasses it, and falls, a miniature cascade, on the other side. In an instant, ditches and beds of brooks are filled up, roads disappear, and are only found again, thanks to the indicating posts. If you stood still you would be buried in five or six minutes. Under the power of the wind which carries these immense loads of snow, the trees sway, poles are bent over, animals lower their heads. It is the *khamsin* of the steppes.

This time the danger was not great; it was daylight, the amount of snow fallen was inconsiderable, and we had the show almost without the danger. But in the night this snow-blow may easily take you off your road and bury you alive.

Sometimes went by, through this whiteness, like shreds of black cloth, troops of crows or ravens blown before the wind, powerless and capsized upon their wings. Also we met two or three carts of mujiks fleeing from the storm, and trying hard to get to shelter.

It was with real satisfaction that we saw through these cross-lines of chalk, scratched in every direction, the post-house with its Grecian portico appear faintly on the side of the road. Never did architecture look to me more sublime! To leap from the téléga, to shake the snow from our pelisses, and to make our way into the travellers' room, was the affair of an instant. At the relay-houses the samovar is in a state of perpetual ebullition, and a few swallows of tea, as hot as my mouth could endure it, speedily re-established the circulation of my blood, which had been a little chilled by so many hours passed in the open air.

"I would undertake with you a voyage of discovery

to the north pole," my friend said to me; "I believe you would be a charming companion in winter-quarters. How happy we might be in a snow-hut, with a good store of pemmican and bears' hams!"

"Your approval touches me," I said, "for I know you are not disposed to be a flatterer; but now that I have proved my fortitude against jolts and cold weather, there would be no cowardice, I think, in seeking a more comfortable method of continuing our journey."

"Let us go and see if they have not some vehicle less exposed to elemental rigors, than this. Heroism uncalled-for is mere bragging."

The court-yard, half full of snow which they were vainly trying with brooms and shovels to throw up in corners, presented a grotesque appearance. Télégas, tarantasses, and droschkys were crowded together, raising their shafts in air like lateen-yards and masts of half-submerged vessels. Behind all this primitive collection of vehicles, I discovered,—through the whirlwind of white points sown broadcast by the breath of the tempest,—like the back of a whale stranded in the surf, the leather apron of an old calèche, which, notwithstanding its dilapidated condition, seemed to me a very ark of safety. They pushed away the vehicles, it was towed out into the middle of the yard, and we were able to satisfy ourselves that the wheels were in good condition, the springs sufficiently strong, and if the windows did not close exactly, at least there were none of them missing. To tell the truth, it was not a vehicle wherewith to shine in the Bois de Boulogne; but as I was not proposing to make the circuit of the lake, and bid for the admiration of the ladies, I was very glad that they were willing to let it, to go as far as the Russian frontier.

The installing of our persons and our trunks in this "wooden shoe" occupied but a few minutes, and we set off at the usual pace, slackened a little, however, by the violence of the wind, which drove whirlwinds of icy dust before it. Although we had all the windows shut, there was soon a line of snow upon the unoccupied seat. Nothing can keep out this impalpable white powder, brayed and triturated by the tempest; like the sand of Sahara, it enters through the smallest cranny, penetrates even to the inside of your watch. But we were no Sybarites, to complain of a crumpled rose-leaf, and we enjoyed with thorough gratification this comparative comfort. One at least could lean his back and his head against the old green-cloth lining; it was not very well-stuffed, it is true, but it was infinitely superior to the sides of the téléga. One might even sleep without danger of falling and fracturing his skull.

We profited by the situation to doze a little, each in his corner, but without abandoning ourselves too much to somnolence, which is sometimes dangerous at temperatures so low, for the mercury had now fallen to 6° or 8°, under the influence of the icy wind. By degrees, however, the storm abated, the particles of snow suspended in the air fell, and one could see the whole landscape white as far as the horizon. The weather moderated extremely, and the thermometer rose to 20° or 22°, a temperature quite spring-like for Russia at this season of the year. We crossed the Vilia, which falls into the Niemen near Kowno, by means of a ferry, and arrived at the city, which looked quite well, freshly powdered with the new-fallen snow. The post-house stood in a fine square, surrounded by regular buildings and adorned with trees which for the moment were all white like ramifications of quicksilver. Bell-towers shaped like onions and like pine-apples appeared here and there over the tops of the houses; but I had neither time nor the courage to go and visit the churches whose presence they betrayed.

After a light lunch of tea and sandwiches, we had the horses put in, in order to cross the Niemen by day, and the day is not very long in this latitude in the month of February. Many vehicles of different kinds, télégas, and carts were crossing the river at the same time with ourselves, and midway of the passage, the yellow, turbulent flood almost came up to the madriers bordering the boats which yielded under pressure and came up again as the teams drew near the farther shore. If any horse had been frightened, nothing would have been easier than to be overset, arms and baggage, into the stream; but Russian horses, fiery as they are, are very gentle, and not alarmed by such trifles.

A few minutes later, we were galloping towards the frontier of Prussia, which we hoped to reach in the night, despite the groanings and creakings emitted by our poor calèche, shaken up rudely enough, but holding firm for all that, and not leaving us basely in the road.

And, in fact, about eleven o'clock, we drew near the first Prussian outpost, whence we were to send back the carriage to the relay where we had hired it.

"Now," said my friend, "since our acrobatic performances are over, it would be well to take supper. tranquilly, and to apply some lotion to our faces, that we may not resemble spectres when we arrive in Paris."

It will readily be believed that I offered no objection to this discourse, brief but full of matter, and reproducing perfectly my own inner convictions.

When I was a small boy, I used to imagine that the frontiers of countries were marked upon the soil by a blue, red, or green line as they are on the maps. It was a childish fancy; but though it be not traced with a pencil, the line of demarcation is not less clear and well-marked. At the place indicated by a white post striped diagonally with black, Russia ended and Prussia began in a sudden and complete fashion. Neither country seemed to have affected its neighbor in the slightest degree.

We were conducted into a low hall furnished with a great porcelain stove, which roared harmoniously.

The floor was strewn with yellow sand; a few framed engravings adorned the walls; the tables and chairs were of German construction, and tall, stout servant-maids came to set the table. It had been long since I had seen women occupied with those domestic cares which seem the appanage of their sex; in Russia, as in the East, the house-work is done by men, or, at least, all that appears of it.

The *cuisine* was no longer the same. Instead of chtchi, caviare, salted cucumbers, *gélinottes*, and *soudacs*, there was beer-soup, veal with dried currants, hare with gooseberry jelly, and the sentimental German pastry. Everything was different: the shape of the glasses and the knives and forks, a thousand little details which it would be tedious to describe, reminded us at every instant that this was another country. We made a substantial repast, accompanied by Bordeaux wine—which proved to be good in spite of its showy label printed in colored inks—and a *quille* of Rudesheimer poured out into emerald-colored glasses.

All the while we were at dinner, I exhorted myself to keep my voracity within limits, that I might not die of indigestion like people rescued from a shipwreck, who, their slender store of biscuit being exhausted, have been forced to eat the leather of their shoes and the gutta-percha of their suspenders!

It would have been wise, no doubt, to content one's self with a plate of soup and a sop of bread dipped in Malaga wine, and so accustom one's self gradually to food again. But no matter! my supper is in my stomach, and there let it rest! Let us hope it will cause me no remorse.

Costumes are changed, too; at Kowno we saw the last touloupe; and types are as dissimilar as clothes. Instead of the undecided, pensive, gentle Russian,—here is the rigid, methodical, serious Prussian; an entirely different race. The little cap with a visor, crushed down over the forehead, the short frock-coat, and trousers tight at the knees and wide in the legs, between the lips a porcelain or meerschaum pipe, or a cigar-holder, with an odd elbow in it holding the cigar at a right angle:—such were the Prussians as they appeared to us at the first post; they did not surprise me, for I knew them before.

The vehicle in which we took our seats resembled the small omnibus that they send from French chateaux to the railway, for guests who are expected to dinner. It was suitably cushioned, very well closed from the air, and well hung; at least so it seemed after the trip in the télèga which we had first made, and which fairly represents that punishment of the *strappado* in use in the Middle Ages. But what a difference between the frantic speed of the little Russian horses and the phlegmatic trot of the great, heavy Mecklenburgs, who appeared to be falling asleep as they walked, and whom a caress from the whip, carelessly applied upon their fat backs, seems scarcely to awaken. The German horses doubtless understand the Italian proverb: *Chi va piano va sano.* They meditate upon it as they lift their big feet, and they leave off the second part: *Chi va sano va lontano;* for the Prussian posts are nearer together than the Russian.

However, one arrives at last, even if he does not move very quickly, and the morning overtook us not far from Königsberg, upon a road bordered by great trees as far as the eye could see, which looked like a veritable fairyland. The snow had frozen upon the branches, and outlined the most minute ramifications with a diamonded crystal of wondrous splendor. The avenue had the appearance of an immense arbor of silver filigree, leading to the enchanted chateau of some fairy of the North.

You see how it was—the snow, knowing my love for her, at the moment when she was about to leave me, lavished all her magic power, and regaled me with her finest display. Winter came as far as possible, and left us with the greatest reluctance.

There is nothing very gay in the aspect of Königsberg, at least at this season of the year. The winters are severe, and the windows still retained their double glass. I noticed many houses with stair-shaped gables, and façades painted apple-green, and sustained by highly wrought S's of iron work, as at Lubeck. It is the land of Kant, who, by his Essay upon Pure Reason, brought philosophy down to its essence. I imagined that I saw him, as we turned each corner, with his iron-gray coat, his three-cornered hat, and his buckled shoes; and I remembered the trouble that invaded his meditations from the absence of the slender poplar tree, which somebody had cut down, upon which, for more than twenty years, he had had the habit of fixing his eyes during his profound metaphysical reveries.

We went straight to the station, and we took, each of us, a corner of the railway-carriage. It is no part of my plan to describe a journey by rail through Prussia. There is nothing very interesting about it, especially when you do not stop at any of the cities, and we went through to Cologne, where, for the first time, the snow left us. There, as the trains did not connect, we were obliged to stop for a few hours, and profited by this delay to devote ourselves to the indispensable duties of the toilette, that we might resume in some degree the human aspect, for we looked like veritable Samoyeds come to show off our reindeer upon the Neva.

The rapidity of our télèga journey had produced an odd variety of damages in my trunks: the wax had fallen off my boots and showed the bare leather; a box of excellent cigars was no longer anything but *polvo sevillano*, reduced to fine yellow dust by the jolting it had endured; seals of letters entrusted to me were rubbed off or broken by excessive friction; neither armorial bearings, nor cipher, nor impression of any kind could be made out. Many of the envelopes were open. There was snow among my shirts! Order re-established, I went to bed, after an excellent supper, and the morrow, five days from the date of my departure from St. Petersburg, I arrived in Paris, at nine o'clock in the evening, according to my formal promise. I was not five minutes behind time. A coupé awaited me at the station, and, a quarter of an hour later, I found myself surrounded by old friends and pretty women, before a table brilliant with lights, whereon a fine supper was smoking; and my return was celebrated gayly until the morning.

THE END.